Lloyd Gutteridge

WITHDRAWN

Business Management

FOR THE IB DIPLOMA

2014 edition

OXFORD

UNIVERSITY PRESS

OXFORD
UNIVERSITY PRESS

Great Clarendon Street, Oxford, OX2 6DP, United Kingdom

Oxford University Press is a department of the University of Oxford. It furthers the University's objective of excellence in research, scholarship, and education by publishing worldwide. Oxford is a registered trade mark of Oxford University Press in the UK and in certain other countries

British Library Cataloguing in Publication Data
Data available

978-0-19-839282-8

10 9 8 7 6 5 4 3

Paper used in the production of this book is a natural, recyclable product made from wood grown in sustainable forests. The manufacturing process conforms to the environmental regulations of the country of origin.

Printed in Great Britain by Ashford Colour Press Ltd, Gosport

Acknowledgments

Cover image: c sa/Shutterstock.com **p41:** REX/London News Pictures; **p42:** © Bettmann/Corbis; **p79:** © Pulse/Corbis - Oleksiy Mark/Shutterstock – Wikipedia; **p83:** picture alliance / dpa; **p98:** © Richard Hickson/Demotix/Corbis; **p104:** www.sbgranadabooks.com; **p115:** REX/David Pearson; **p122:** Flickr Vision/Getty image; **p124:** © Andreas Gebert/dpa/Corbis; **p127:** © Steve Vidler/Corbis

This work has been developed independently from and is not endorsed by the International Baccalaureate (IB)

The author and the publisher are grateful to the following for permission to reprint the copyright material listed:

Boom San Agustin for extract from 'Entrepreneur or intrapreneur - what is the difference?' Our Knowledge - Asia, 15 May 2012.

C-Net via the YGS Group for 'Apple: Samsung made prejudicial and "false statements" during opening argument' by Shara Tibken, 4 April 2014.

The Co-operative Bank of New Zealand for statement: 'What is a Co-operative?' from www.co-operativebank.co.nz.

Fairfax Media Publications Pty Ltd for 'Coles shares personal flybuys and online data' by Phillip Thomson/Fairfax Syndication, The Sydney Morning Herald , 9 March 2014.

Guardian News & Media Ltd for 'Sports Direct: 90% of staff on zero-hour contracts' by Simon Neville, The Guardian, 28 July 2013, copyright © Guardian News and Media Ltd 2013.

Harvard Business Publishing for Table 'Differences between a red ocean strategy and a blue ocean strategy' from Blue Ocean Strategy: How to create uncontested market space and make the competition irrelevant by W Chan Kim and R Mauborgne (Harvard Business Publishing, 2005).

Independent Print Ltd (www.independent.co.uk) for extract from 'Filmmakers blame the critics as Disney reports a loss of $190 million on the Lone Ranger' by Nick Clark, The Independent, 7 Aug 2013, copyright © The independent 2013; extracts from 'Is life easy in the land of the 35-hour week, generous holidays and long lunches? Non! say burnt out French' by John Lichfield,The Independent, 28 Jan 2014, copyright © The independent 2014; extract from 'The iPad: what is it good for?' by David Phelan, The Independent, 26 May 2010, copyright © The independent 2010; 'Marmite, Irn-Bru and Bovril banned in Canada after they fall foul of food additive rules' by Adam Sherwin, The Independent, 23 Jan 2014, copyright © The independent 2014; and 'The moment it all went wrong for Kodak' by David Usborne, The Independent, 20 Jan 2012, copyright © The independent 2012.

Kiva Organization for 'Kiva microfunds statistics' table (February 2014).

MacRumours.com for extracts from 'Apple earnings' by Jordan Golson, 27 Jan 2014, and Gartner statistics table from 'US Mac sales grow...' by Jordan Golson, 9 Jan 2014.

McDonald's Corporation for 'Catering for local tastes' from www.aboutmcdonalds.com.

The New Zealand Herald for extract from 'ARC paid $2.9m for David Beckham' by Wayne Thompson, New Zealand Herald, 21 Feb 2009,

Quercus Books for extracts from 50 Management Ideas You Really Need to Know by E Russell-Walling (Quercus, 2007).

QSR Magazine via the YGS Group for extracts from an interview with Don Fertman, 'How Subway Went Global' by Blair Chancey, QSR Magazine.

Telegraph Media Group for 'What's it like to work at Pixar?' by Chris Bell, Daily Telegraph, 10 July 2013, copyright © Chris Bell/The Daily Telegraph 2013; 'David Cameron: Britain can bring jobs back from abroad' by James Quinn, Daily Telegraph, 21 Jan 2014, copyright © James Quinn/The Daily Telegraph 2014; extracts from 'Why are UK firms bringing manufacturing back home?' by Alan Tovey, Daily Telegraph, 3 March 2014, copyright © Alan Tovey/The Daily Telegraph 2014; and extracts from 'The British logistics firm that has out-competed China' by Anna White, Daily Telegraph, 12 March 2014, copyright © Anna White/The Daily Telegraph 2014.

Verve Management Inc for extracts from 'Will Santa Barbara's Granada Books be swept aside by the tide of Amazon?' by Sophia Rubenstein, 27 Oct 2013, from www.vervesocialmag.com.

John Wiley & Sons via Copyright Clearance Center for table from Big Brands, Big Trouble: Lessons Learned the Hard Way by Jack Trout (J Wiley, 2002), copyright © 2002 John Wiley & Sons; and for tables from Differentiate or Die: Survival in Our Era of Killer Competition (J Wiley, 2008), copyright © 2008 John Wiley & Sons.

Although we have made every effort to trace and contact all copyright holders before publication this has not been possible in all cases. If notified, the publisher will rectify any errors or omissions at the earliest opportunity.

Contents

Introduction

Thank you for purchasing this second edition of the *Business Management Study Guide*. In 2009, when the first edition was published, this IB subject was called Business and Management. This is only one of a number of changes, challenges and opportunities. The new IB Business Management syllabus will be examined in 2016 for the first time.

In keeping with the ethos of the first edition, the rationale for this second edition is to provide clarity, concise analysis and evaluation guidance. It should "sit alongside" both web-based and textbook resources to help students not only prepare for the final IB exams but also to provide a basis to develop an understanding of fundamental business-themed concepts.

In addition to the text – at a number of places in the guide – students are prompted to review YouTube Clips and additional ICT resources to assist in their learning. There are also a number of **"flipped learning"** activities where topics will be introduced before students have had a chance to read the accompanying notes. Students are encouraged to follow these prompts or view these videos to combine this resource with their own notes taken in class or through independent research. Business knowledge in 2014 is being created from a multitude of sources. The days of the teacher and the textbook as the only sources of information and knowledge are over.

This guide is written with both explicit and implicit intention to provide a basis for the student (and teacher) to apply the **IB learner profile** to the learning of IB Business Management, which underpins and drives the whole IB mission. In addition to the text provided, there are a number of inquiry-based activities and opportunities for students to be curious, creative, risk-taking, adaptive and, crucially, active researchers and knowledge gatherers with balance and reason to the fore. This guide should not be seen purely as a content revision crammer. It is designed to develop your competencies as a 21st-century learner of business management and your responsibilities as a global citizen. At the heart of inquiry-based learning is the hope that in addition to finding answers, students will be prepared to ask the right questions.

For 2016, six concepts that underpin the new IB Business Management course have been selected to allow students to make connections in their learning with other parts of their IB course and, importantly, deepen their understanding of today's complex, dynamic and uncertain business environment. These concepts appear at the beginning of the guide and will be embedded through the business content wherever possible.

These are some new features of the *Business Management Study Guide*:

- This guide has been written to satisfy the new IB Business Management course for the first exams in 2016. There have been a significant number of changes, including changes to external and internal assessment, which will need to be addressed.

- A "quick start" guide is provided to indicate learning tools, required skills, business concepts that need to be understood and the depth of study necessary. This guide assumes no previous study of business.

- Most of the units begin with a "Setting the scene" introduction to try to give an overview of the business content to follow. Some of these overviews are written as "flipped learning" activities.

- Wherever possible links between concepts and contexts have been provided but please note that these links are not the only ones possible.

- Thinking activities or research activities, which could be carried out individually or in small groups and aligned to the IB learner profile, have been updated. It is not the intention that these activities are completed on paper as part of homework or class exercise but they are to be discussed and points of view must be challenged. May the arguments begin!

Contexts

In order to provide what the author hopes are engaging case studies to develop understanding of concepts and content in business management, a number of recurring themes or contexts will be covered. This is justified for two reasons. In the author's experience of over 20 years of teaching business, provocative and thought-provoking case studies provide a very useful way to build discussion, create new learning opportunities and challenge current thinking. Case studies used in this guide include reference to Lego, Apple, Twitter, Sony, Kodak, Nokia, Pixar and Disney. (Students are of course encouraged to find their own case studies.)

Second, a major change in the summative assessment (or final exam) for both HL and SL is that the six concepts will be assessed in a separate section C of paper 2 and students are expected to provide knowledge, understanding and analysis of at least one real organization that they have studied. For many years, students and teachers have used case studies to reinforce the learning of business theory and knowledge in class. This learning will now have a direct impact on students' grades in the final exams. There is a separate unit on preparing for this paper with a sample answer provided by the author, who has many years of examining experience.

Before we begin, please read carefully the "quick start" guide and the six concepts to get a "feel" for what follows. The subsequent units (from 1.1 to 5.7) have been written in the expectation that students have these skills and concepts ready to apply.

Acknowledgments

I wish to acknowledge the IB in allowing permission to use some past paper questions in this guide. With over two years to go before the first exams in this new subject, please be advised that advice on the types of questions to be faced will be speculative.

I would also like to acknowledge the work of OUP in allowing me to develop a second edition of this study guide especially Mary-Luz Espiritusanto and the various unknown people who work to turn my shaky prose and handwritten diagrams into the finished, polished product you are holding in your hands.

Finally, it is said that it takes a village to raise a child. I would like to adapt this to "it takes a family to write a book". I have been very fortunate to have the support of my family in this writing process.

I would like to thank my wife Elaine for her unlimited and continuing support and encouragement to see this second edition come to light. I also thank my two sons, Sam and Joel, who continue to see "Dad at the computer".

Without resorting to too many Oscar ceremony platitudes, I would like to dedicate this book to my family members:

– Mrs Barbara Hollinworth: my big and kind-hearted sister

– my mother (Gerry) and mother-in-law (Pat), both of whom unfortunately will not be able to see their name in print as they have both moved on to a more peaceful place

– to Len (always).

I would also like to thank the following people for their support again:

– Nick Hindson from Marketshare

– my wonderful new colleagues at Albany Senior High School, especially Ross Martin, Sharon Kiely, Mike Nahu, Tim Tyrrel-Baxter and Trevor Sharp (legends, one and all).

And to all students, good luck on your new learning journey in business management.

Lloyd Gutteridge

1 July 2014

"Quick start" guide

How to use this book

Many consumer electronic companies (even Apple) include a "quick start" guide to help their customers enjoy their service as soon as possible. While it will not be possible to cover every detail of the new IB Business Management course in one chapter, students are **strongly advised to read** this section before they begin their study of IB Business Management. This "quick start" guide is provided to avoid undue repetition of text, to make explanations clearer and to make effective use of this book. To be forewarned is to be forearmed.

It may be a good idea for you to ask your teacher to give you a copy of the new *IB Business Management Guide* at the beginning of the course. We will be referring to this guide in this section and titles of content units will be taken directly from it.

What exactly is the study of business management and what am I going to be asked to do in this course?

This may seem like an odd question to start with (after all you have chosen to study this subject) but it is absolutely critical to have a sense or understanding of exactly what the study of business management entails given the IB mission. A mind map for HL and SL is given below.

Clearly the study of business management does not simply involve the study of business.

As outlined in the new *IB Business Management Guide*, the course that you are about to embark upon will encourage you to:

- study strategic decision-making in a contemporary context (i.e. business today in a rapidly changing uncertain world)

- explore how individuals and groups interact within an organization

- understand how these individuals and groups try to ethically optimize the use of resources in a world with increasing scarcity and concerns for sustainability

- appreciate ethical concerns at a local and global level.

Furthermore, as a student of business management you are going to exercise and develop your critical thinking skills, appreciate the pace, nature and significance of change, and plan for and create new strategic options for a range of small to global businesses.

It is important that you are aware of these demands, and the six concepts outlined below, before you begin.

The six concepts

You must ensure that you are aware of the six concepts which provide a framework around the IB Business Management course content. These will be briefly introduced after this "quick start" guide and be linked wherever possible to the syllabus content.

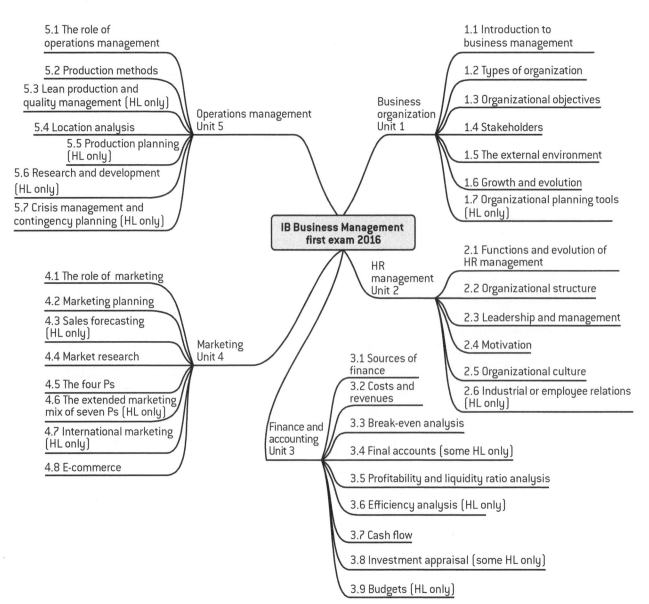

The Importance of understanding assessment objectives

Students will need to consider assessment objectives (referred to as AOs). For the IB Business Management course at both HL and SL these include AO1, AO2, AO3 and AO4. AOs are critical and they will be used extensively throughout this study guide as a form of shorthand or code to determine the depth of teaching and, by assumption, the depth of study required for a particular topic.

The following table is adapted from the *IB Business Management Guide* page 39 to provide some guidance. These command words will also be used in the exam question practice section, which follows the content units.

Assessment objective	Command term associated	Depth of study required with example and explanation with indicative marks awarded
AO1	Define Describe Outline State	*Define "price penetration".* (2 marks) Students are required to show that they understand what this business term means. Key skills are to show knowledge and understanding.
AO2	Analyse Apply Comment Demonstrate Distinguish Explain Interpret Suggest	*Analyse the appropriateness of the price penetration strategy of company X.* (2 marks) Students are required to consider both the benefits and costs to company X of using a price penetration strategy. *Explain two benefits to company X of introducing on-the-job training.* (4 marks) Students are required to show understanding of the benefits by first identifying a benefit, clearly explaining how this would benefit a company and then making their answer **directly** applicable to company X. Key skills are to show the application (linked to the company in question) and analysis (showing how business ideas can be broken into simpler parts and highlighting benefits and costs) to show knowledge and understanding.
AO3	Compare and contrast Discuss Evaluate Examine Justify Recommend To what extent...	*Evaluate the two options available to company X to increase its market share.* (10 marks) Students are expected to analyse both options highlighting positive and negative consequences of implementation. Ideas generated should be linked or to use the technical term "contextualized" to the company in the question and should not be generic (i.e. they should not be ideas that could be applied to any business). Students are also expected to provide a fully substantiated (or justified) conclusion based on the analysis which preceded this and not merely repeat earlier arguments. Key skills are the ability to provide convincing and justifiable analysis applied to the business in the question. Students will need to give a judgment or final solution to the question posed which includes and builds on the previous analysis – and, remember, does not merely repeat the same points.
AO4	Annotate Calculate Complete Construct Determine Draw Identify Label Plot	*Construct a break-even chart for company Z identifying the break-even point and the margin of safety.* (4–8 marks depending on the question being asked and whether any diagrams are requested) Key skills are the ability to use a range of quantitative and qualitative business tools, techniques and methods. Students may also have to redraw material such as a change to a financial statement, clarify financial information given using an accepted planning tool such as a Gantt chart or prepare a seasonally adjusted sales forecast.

Business vocabulary to be used throughout the guide

The IB Business Management course assumes no prior knowledge of business. However, at this early stage in the course as we build our understanding, it will be useful to have a working knowledge of the business ideas given in the table below before we meet them in the concept and syllabus sections.

Key idea	Condensed meaning
Sustainability	An increasingly important business idea which has begun to take on greater importance given increasing economic scarcity, population and social change. Sustainability can refer to: • environmental factors • economic factors • cultural factors • social factors. A number of business writers collect these terms into one – called the "quadruple bottom line". A business should try to limit the environmental impact of its activity and remain viable to provide income and job opportunities for future generations. In addition, the performance and role of business operations, especially for a business in a global context, should not damage cultural and social norms in countries other than the organization's country of origin.

Enterprise	Enterprise refers to the idea of responsible risk-taking by an entrepreneur, to create new business opportunities by bringing the three factors of production (capital, land and labour) together for productive ends. Enterprise has strong links to sustainability. Risk-taking should be carried out to add positive value to communities in terms of economic sustainability and not damage cultural and environmental sustainability. This is not easy to achieve.
External factors	These are factors that are outside the control of a business but which can act both negatively and positively on business decision-making giving rise to both threats and opportunities. They can be summarized by the acronym STEEPLE: • **s**ocial • **t**echnological • **e**conomic • **e**thical • **p**olitical • **l**egal • **e**nvironmental. (See unit 1.5 on the external environment for more detail.)
Transparency	Given the rise of social networking, email, instant messaging and Web 2.0 tools, which allow greater collaboration and feedback, business activity and decision-making now face greater scrutiny than ever before. This scrutiny has now forced many businesses to become much more **transparent**, ethical and open. Clear, consistent reporting and communication to stakeholders is now the norm for all businesses as part of the commitment to transparency. Of course, greater transparency brings significant opportunities and threats to an organization.
Stakeholders	Stakeholders are individuals or groups who have a direct or active interest in businesses' operations. They include external stakeholders such as customers, competitors, suppliers and the government and internal stakeholders such as employees, managers and shareholders. The degree of interest and impact of stakeholders will vary according to ownership stake, financial resources and influence.
Cultural intelligence (CQ)	Given globalization, the need for a businesss to undertake CQ activities becomes paramount: it needs to discover customs, values, and consumers' backgrounds and preferences about potential new markets it may wish to enter. CQ should not be considered as just more market research on consumer tastes but a more systematic attempt to build a consumer and social profile of existing and new customers across a range of global markets.
Uncertainty and complexity	Business decision-making and risk-taking have always **uncertain** and **complex** activities. Given the existence of external factors, an entrepreneur can never be confident that every business decision he or she has taken will be successful. In the new century, with globalization and change, uncertainty and complexity have taken on a whole new meaning. In 2007, Nokia effectively "owned" the mobile phone market with nearly a 50% global market share and a value of over $100 billion as a company. By 2013, Nokia had sold its mobile phone business to Microsoft to remain economically sustainable with the value of Nokia now 93% smaller at $7 billion. It is unlikely any stakeholder would have predicted such a fall from grace in 2007. For a future career in business, given the rapid social and technological changes occurring as these words are written, successful entrepreneurs will need to be able to incorporate uncertainty, complexity, greater transparency and CQ into their decision-making. For these reasons, the ability to be creative and forward-looking becomes critical.

Following a real-life business throughout the course

In addition to your notes taken in class, question and answer sessions or practising exam-style questions, your understanding of business management will be enhanced by a number of other learning strategies. One very good way to strengthen your knowledge of concepts and content is to follow a real-life business. To illustrate this point, this study guide will at various points reflect on real-life business examples in companies as diverse as:

• Lego
• Google
• Facebook and other social media
• Disney and Pixar
• Apple.

These examples reflect the author's own interest and are "contemporary contexts". You are advised to read through these case studies and are encouraged to seek out your own local and global business examples.

Not only is this a great learning opportunity but, as part of the new assessment for the IB Business Management course for HL and SL, students will have to apply their real-life knowledge of business to six concepts which form the backbone or framework of the whole course. HL/SL paper 2 requires this and a whole unit in this guide is devoted to this aspect of the final assessment.

The IB Learner Profile

In keeping with the IB mission statement, throughout this guide there will be a number of examples, activities and reflection points which will allow students to develop their understanding of business management through the IB learner profile. These activities will allow students to develop the qualities to be inquirers, knowledgeable, thinkers, communicators, principled, open-minded, caring, risk-takers, to be able to take a balanced view and to be reflective. (Icons alongside examples given and activities indicate these qualities.) The *IB Business Management Guide* states:

The IB learner profile represents 10 attributes valued by IB World School. We believe these attributes and others like them can help individuals and groups become responsible members of local, national and global communities.

Let's begin with a brief review of concepts.

Globalization can be defined as the growing integration, interdependence and general connectedness of the world through markets, labour mobility and capital transfer.

Why has globalization occurred?

There is considerable debate as to when globalization became a reality for business thinking. However, the following important "events" are considered vital in allowing globalization to flourish:

- A significant fall in air fares with an increase in the number of routes available led to greater competition in the airline industry.
- There was increased opportunity for large organizations to spread tax liabilities around the world, boosting profitability to shareholders.
- The increase of and availability of international schools helped with the relocation of families in response to the movement of labour and capital.
- There have been dramatic falls in the cost of communication and the simultaneous use of VOIP tools such as Skype and instant messaging with the increased use of video conferencing.

The impact of the Internet

The spread of the Internet and world wide web clearly has a defining role to play in explaining the pace of globalization. In his book *The World is Flat* Thomas Friedman identifies a number of factors where the Internet has flattened the competitive playing field (or world – hence the book's title) and driven the move towards globalization:

- The fall of the Berlin Wall on 9 November 1989 marked the world balance of power shifting towards more open economies and markets.
- The Netscape IPO on 9 August 1995 sparked interest in fibre-optic cables which allow much faster transfer of data.
- Power searching could be carried out on the Internet through Google and other search engines, allowing greater transparency about pricing, product availability and competition.
- Widespread adoption of wireless technology increased mobile and personal communication opportunities both locally and globally.
- Web 2.0 software facilitated a greater degree of online collaborative workspaces across a range of time zones and economic regions (Friedman, 2007).

Why is the study of globalization important?

Friedman's work clearly indicates that the competitive "playing field" for businesses has shifted. They now not only face competition from domestic and international markets but potentially from any region on earth. With delivery and transport costs falling and the increasing use of online retailing, as business management expert Gary Hamel indicates in a 2011 lecture (see page 6), businesses now really "have to earn their place in the market" and can take nothing for granted. Of course, a more balanced view is that globalization offers both opportunities **and** threats.

How does globalization link to the other five concepts?

Although all six concepts are treated equally in this course, it could be argued that globalization represents the key driving force for business management. Globalization has driven both economic and socio-political change that has forced businesses to become more innovative and retain their place in their own market. Greater transparency through the world wide web via communication and social media has promoted much greater awareness of ethical issues, leading to all businesses having to consider new strategic options. Moreover, greater transparency and "connectedness" through the Internet has heightened the need to be sensitive to different cultures.

Globalization: an example of taking opportunities

Subway is the largest supplier of fast food in the world. Its growth model of franchising (see unit 1.6, page 28) has led to rapid expansion resulting, in January 2014, in 41 217 outlets in 105 countries. Concept 1 Table 1 shows the rapid change in the growth of Subway in global markets.

Year	Event in Subway's growth
1965	The first Subway opened in Connecticut, USA and sold 312 sandwiches on the first day.
1981	The 200th Subway opened in Washington, USA.
1984	The first overseas Subway opened – in Bahrain, UAE.
1985	The 300th Subway opened in the United States and 100 stores opened in this one year alone.
1987	The 1 000th Subway opened. This figure doubled by the end of 1988.
1990	The 5 000th Subway opened.
2002	The 17 000th Subway opened.
2008	The 30 000th Subway opened.
January 2014	There are 41 217 Subway outlets operating in 105 countries.

Concept 1 Table 1 Rapid change in the growth of Subway outlets in global markets.

We will examine the globalization of Subway further in unit 1.6 on growth and evolution and in unit 4.7 on international marketing.

The world is changing economically, socially, environmentally and politically at a rate of speed, which, according to business management expert Gary Hamel, is "unprecedented" (Hamel lecture, YouTube, 2011 – see below for details).

Recommended resource

Watch the following YouTube clip to help explain the concept of change: search for "Gary Hamel on the future of management".

Now consider the following political and economic events that have all occurred since 2008 and had an impact on our lives:

- the global financial meltdown
- the Arab Spring uprising
- the economic rise of Brazil, Russia, India and China (the BRIC countries)
- the ongoing euro crisis
- the "Occupy" movement creation with its increased activism and social networking
- the Fukishima Tsunami in Japan
- the Wikileaks scandal and the rise of the "whistle blower".

We can also include the environmental and social changes suggested by Will McInnes (2012: 10), which are:

- global warming and the concern of being able to sustain the planet environmentally given competing pressure on dwindling natural resources
- creating a sense of social cohesion at a time of declining sense of local identify and poor turn-outs in general elections in the developed world
- providing care and finance for an increasingly elderly or "greying" population
- the social, mental and physical impacts on families where 24/7 living is becoming the norm, job security has all but disappeared and social media invasiveness has led to questions as to what kind of society we have become.

This is one quotation from the Hamel lecture video clip:

We are the first generation which is having to cope with an inflexion point (or accelerating rate) of change. Change is literally changing.

There has been "exponential" increase in the number of carbon dioxide emissions, Internet connections, the amount of data storage and mobile devices connected to the Internet.

We will be returning to some of Hamel's views on management and motivation in later sections.

Impact of change on business decision-making

Given the significant changes in external factors and the onset of globalization, businesses now have to constantly review their operations, as Hamel says, "to earn their place in the market".

Hyper-competition has forced many businesses to consider their role in the market and forced CEOs to develop new ways of being innovative. This leads to our next concept.

Innovation occurs when an invention (or new idea) becomes successful in the market-place. The product attracts customers and is economically sustainable.

Innovation is often referred to as either **fundamental** or **disruptive**, or as **incremental**. It is fundamental or disruptive when a product, such as the mobile smartphone or tablet, changes consumer behaviour indefinitely. Incremental innovation occurs where a business adds improvements or modifications to existing products resulting in added value to stakeholders and increased sales. The Apple iPad is an example of disruptive innovation while the iPad Mini is an example of incremental innovation.

Why is the study of innovation important?

Given the pace of globalization and rapid change, businesses now are being forced to consider how they can be innovative. As quoted in Robertson and Breen (2013) Gary Hamel notes:

With hyper competition, the only way for businesses to defend themselves is through innovation. Knowledge is now a commodity and knowledge advantages will disappear very quickly. A key question, which companies need to ask themselves, is how can I create new knowledge?

Hamel's point is worth stressing further. He argues that companies now not only need to be innovative through creating new products and services to retain their place in the market, but also companies need to be innovative in their leadership and management of workers, organizational structure and culture to ensure that creativity and innovation flourish.

This last point is very important. To encourage innovation, many business writers speak of the importance of creating an innovative culture at work where experimentation and enterprise is encouraged. However, there are number of competing views on how to achieve this.

Steve Jobs argued that:

Innovation is me saying no to a 1 000 things.

The CEO of Lego, Jorgen Vig Knudstrop (quoted in Robertson and Breen, 2013), argued that the innovation culture at Lego was such a part of the whole company ethos that:

I could leave and innovation would still flourish.

What is the impact of innovation?

95%
Competition
feel innovation can drive a more competitive economy

91%
Go green
feel innovation can create a greener economy

88%
Jobs
feel innovation is the best way to create jobs

86%
Partnership
feel partnership is more important than stand-alone success

87%
Society
feel we should bring value to society as a whole not only to individuals

Improve lives
can successfully change citizens' lives in the next 10 years in:

90% Communications **87%** Health quality **84%** Job market **84%** Environmental quality

 imagination at work

What drives innovation?

66%
Value of innovation
believe that innovation will happen when the general public is convinced of the value that innovation will bring to their lives

65%
Universities and schools
feel that innovation happens when local universities and schools provide a strong model for tomorrow's leaders

62%
Patent protection
agree that when the protection of the copyright and patent are effective then innovation can occur

58%
Private investors
believe that innovation will occur when private investors are supportive of companies that need funds to innovate

48%
Budget allocation
believe that when government and public officials set aside an adequate share of their budget to support innovative companies, innovation can brew

43%
Government support
think innovation can occur when governmental support for innovation is efficiently organized and coordinated

Data collected from an independent survey of 1,000 senior business executives across 12 countries on the state and perception on innovation

Concept 3 Figure 1 Impact and key drivers of the concept of innovation. Adapted from a Google image of data from an independent survey published online

Ethics in a business

Ethics in a business context refers to a code of behaviour that a business will adopt in order to guide how this organization will operate and how it will seek to influence the perception and view of internal and external stakeholders.

We can assume that businesses wish to be viewed positively by their stakeholders when the code of behaviour they adopt incorporates the idea of operating in a "morally correct" manner. Put simply, a business should be doing the "right thing".

Note that there is a theory of knowledge (TOK) implication here of what doing the "right thing" is.

Ethics and transparency

The increasing use of the Internet and pervasive social networking sites have forced companies to become more transparent and, by assumption, more ethically responsible and driven in their decision-making. The risk of receiving damaging negative publicity by failing to conform to society's expectations of what is morally "the right thing to do" is too great for businesses to bear.

The importance of ethical behaviour

The following two examples highlight the growing importance of ethical behaviour:

- Concern over media reports of unethical treatment by the manufacturer Foxconn towards its production line workers subcontracted to produce the iPhone and iPad forced Apple to improve working conditions and introduce a new health and safety policy.

- 3D printing has become an increasingly popular way to produce small, customized items. A number of business commentators have argued that 3D printing could easily become the next "disruptive technology" in the consumer goods market. One young entrepreneur – Cody Wilson – created some blueprints for the production of a 3D printed gun, which could fire real 3D printed bullets. Through social media he created the company Defense Distributed, offering the blueprints to "friends" for free.

Although the production of weapons is not illegal, ethical concerns created media frenzy and Wilson was forced to remove the blueprints. However, ethical issues over the future of 3D printing remain.

Here is a link to a story, which students may wish to view to deepen their understanding:

https://www.youtube.com/watch?v=6okfuCea7eY

IB Learner Profile

Balance with respect to ethical behaviour

The two examples from Apple and Defense Distributed show that it can be difficult to be objective about ethics and ethical behaviour.

Let's return to the example of Apple and Foxconn. The iPhone and iPad are global iconic products. Global consumers still queue up in some cases for days outside Apple stores in order to secure a new device. Apple sold 51million iPhones in the period between October and December 2013 – a 3% increase on the previous quarter.

Regardless of conditions for workers on the Foxconn production line, the company still has little trouble filling vacancies for new workers. The media attention (and thus free publicity) around the release of new Apple products enjoyed by the company easily outweighs the negative social media calls for Apple to act more responsibly towards the subcontractors who make the products.

Students of business need to apply a "balanced" approach to all of their analysis and evaluation of ethical decision-making and understanding of all concepts to become caring, compassionate but also rational global citizens – and not just to achieve high marks in exams.

Summary link to other concepts

Globalization, change and innovation

In the race to be competitive in a **global** market-place with rapid **change**, businesses will need to be **innovative** in order to retain their market share. Clearly, given increased transparency and social media scrutiny, applying ethical behaviour to business decision-making is becoming critical. The challenge is how to apply these issues into new successful strategies.

There are many different definitions of the terms "strategy" and "strategic management". At this early stage of the *Business Management Study Guide*, we can define strategy as a coordinated plan developed by senior managers involving all aspects of the business such as marketing, finance, operations and human resources (HR) to move a business towards a new goal or objective.

New goals set should be considered to be SMART:

* **s**pecific

* **m**easurable

* **a**chievable

* **r**ealistic

* **t**ime bound (to be accomplished within an agreed time frame).

IB Learner Profile

Knowledgeable and open-minded

The four previous concepts link clearly with strategy. For example, the rapid pace of **globalization** and accelerated **change** has meant that businesses have to be more innovative to compete with hyper-competition and, given increased transparency, have to be perceived as more **ethical** in their business operations than ever before. Consequently, new strategic decisions need to be made to allow businesses to ensure economic sustainability and growth.

However, it would be wrong to assume that strategic decision-making is wholly focused on delivering growth in sales revenue or the creation of new products. Businesses in the 21st century are now having to consider and implement new strategies affecting production, finance, marketing and HR management. Consequently, there is a much higher degree of business complexity in decision-making than ever before.

A new way of thinking about strategy

There are a number of strategic decision-making tools that businesses can use to develop a coordinated plan to achieve a new goal. These will be covered in the content section of this guide. However, we should look to the future given the enormous changes we have already said are taking place.

In their book *Blue Ocean Strategy* (2005) W Chan Kim and Renee Mauborgne argue that a successful strategic plan is not about competing in existing saturated markets (a plan they call a "red ocean" strategy). They believe that the key for businesses operating in a global market with hyper-competition is to develop a new "blue ocean" strategy: a plan that attempts to make the competition irrelevant.

They provide a compelling example of blue ocean strategy using the organization Cirque du Soleil (Chan Kim and Mauborgne, 2005). Guy Laliberte created Cirque du Soleil at a time when the external factors surrounding the opportunities for circus-style entertainment were very unfavourable.

External factors acting as a threat to Cirque du Soleil included the following:

* There were several competing entertainment options such as home video, DVD and games such as PlayStations. (Online gaming was not as big a threat as it would be now.)

* Decreasing revenue and profits were being earned by the existing firms, such as Ringling Brothers and Barnum & Bailey, who also had significant brand awareness.

* There had been a dramatic change in social attitudes and increased ethical concerns about animals being used in circuses for entertainment purposes.

* The circus market was aimed at children with parents, who found the cost of a family ticket compared to competing forms of entertainment too expensive.

Cirque du Soleil decided not to try to compete with the existing firms in what was clearly a very limited market space. Instead they made the competition irrelevant by creating a new experience featuring acrobats and human performers who catered specifically for adults, including the lucrative corporate client market. Their shows were offered at a price several times higher than that of traditional circuses.

Chan Kim and Mauborgne (2005) argue that the success of Cirque du Soleil and its founder, Guy Laliberte, was remarkable because it was achieved in a declining market with limited potential for growth and a set of unfavourable external factors. In 2014 Cirque du Soleil is the largest theatre production company in the world with its new production based on the music of Michael Jackson.

Concept 5 Table 1 shows how Chan Kim and Mauborgne identify the key ideas behind a blue ocean strategy compared to a red ocean strategy.

Red ocean	Blue ocean
Compete in an existing market-place	Create an uncontested market-place
Exploit existing demand	Create and capture new demand
Choose either differentiation or low cost	Use differentiation and low cost
Beat the competition	Make the competition irrelevant

Concept 5 Table 1 Differences between a red ocean strategy and a blue ocean strategy (Chan Kim and Mauborgne, 2005)

Interested students may wish to look at the case studies of Southwest Airlines (in the United States) and Yellowtail Wines (in Australia) as examples of other successful blue ocean strategies.

Culture is a difficult concept to define and is often overlooked.

Culture can be explained as either of the following:

- the way we do things in our business
- the beliefs, values and norms within a business that define communication, working relationships and motivation between internal stakeholders.

Professor Mike West from the University of Lancaster, UK has stressed the importance of organizational culture in achieving business success. In research quoted in Henderson, Thompson and Henderson (2006), he found the following in a study of 100 businesses over an eight-year period:

- Organizational strategy accounted for 2% of performance variability (i.e. how well the business performed when its actual performance was compared to what was expected).
- Organizational culture accounted for 17%.

His conclusion was that even with the best strategy in the world, a business would underperform **without** a supportive culture. Culture in a business drives performance.

Henderson, Thompson and Henderson argue that West's analysis shows that "the role of leaders today should be primarily focused on the effective alignment of the company culture to the organization's strategies and not the other way round" (2006). We will see the importance of this point when we look at organizational culture in more detail in unit 2.5.

IB Learner Profile

Critical thinker on a organization's culture

What would your opinion be of a company that has the following poster or noticeboard displayed in its reception area and stating its culture?

- Communication: to talk and listen. Information is meant to move people.
- Respect ourselves: no abusive or disrespectful treatment.
- Integrity: we work with customers openly, honestly and sincerely.
- Excellence: we will do the very best in what we do and have fun.

Your instant reaction would probably be favourable. You would think that this would be a valued, ethical place in which to work with a culture of listening and responding to stakeholders in a positive manner.

This culture statement appeared in the reception room of Enron. The company was responsible for one of the most infamous fraud and deception cases of modern times, the impact of which is still being felt.

Recommended learning

> Watch the film "Enron – the Smartest Guys in the Room" (available on YouTube) to learn more about the Enron scandal.

Marketing and cultural issues in a global context

The importance of cultural intelligence (CQ)

The definition of culture is broadened on the IB Business Management course to include external stakeholders, especially if businesses wish to locate their operations overseas. The "quick start" guide introduced the term of "cultural intelligence" (CQ) which requires that a business conducts a full investigation into the cultural norms and backgrounds of consumers, suppliers, government, etc. to allow it to operate more effectively in a new region. As we shall see, CQ can prevent some of the embarrassments in marketing that have occurred when businesses fail to investigate their new cultural market-place effectively.

Consider some the following cultural mistakes that were made by successful businesses operating in a global market-place:

- In the UK, the Vauxhall Nova was a successful small family car. When it was launched in Spain, the original name was used. The car was not successful because in Spanish "Nova" means "No go".
- Managers at one US company were startled when they discovered that the brand name of the cooking oil they were marketing in a Latin American country translated into Spanish as "Jackass Oil".
- A sales manager in Hong Kong tried to control employees' punctuality at work. He insisted they come to work on time instead of 15 minutes late as was their custom. They complied, but then left exactly on time instead of working into the evening as they previously had done. Much work was left unfinished until the manager relented and they returned to their usual time schedule.
- During business negotiations a US business person refused an offer of a cup of coffee from a Saudi businessman. Such a rejection is considered very rude and the negotiations were stalled.
- Kellogg had to rename its Bran Buds cereal in Sweden when it discovered that the name roughly translated to "burned farmer".
- One company printed the "OK" finger sign on each page of its catalogue. In many parts of Latin America this is considered an obscene gesture.
- Six months of work were lost when Pepsico advertised Pepsi in Taiwan with the advertisement "Come alive with Pepsi". The company had no idea that it would be translated into Chinese as "Pepsi brings your ancestors back from the dead". Such a statement would be very offensive.

As we stated above, culture should not be overlooked.

Before we begin our study an important question to ask is:

What is a business?

Given the significant impact of the Internet and world wide web and the subsequent growth of new business start-ups, defining a business can prove quite difficult. A traditional definition would look something like this:

A business is an entity that tries to combine human, physical and financial resources into processing goods or services to respond to and satisfy customer needs.

However, with the growth of the world wide web there are a number of examples of businesses (Facebook, Google and Twitter), which, apart from their head office, do not exist in the physical sense, but online instead.

It is also possible with a laptop and a secure Internet connection to create an online business with no additional human resources and at very little or no cost. We must also remember that despite the impact of large multinational and global brands, the majority of businesses in both the developed and developing world are classed as small.

The traditional idea that a business must contain a production or operations division with marketing, finance and human resources (HR) departments is also being challenged. The rise of **outsourcing** and **offshoring** has led to a number of companies now having their production or distribution facilities (loosely termed the "supply chain") located well away from head office.

IB Learner Profile

Inquirers and managing risk

A fundamental point, which is often missed by students, is that the creation of any business relies heavily on the ability of the entrepreneur to **calculate and manage risk.** We must not forget that the creation of a business involves considerable opportunity costs when combining human and financial resources.

As part of your study, research some successful global entrepreneurs from the developing and developed world and investigate their attitudes to risk-taking. You should consider the entrepreneurs' successes and their failures as both provide rich learning experiences.

Business departments (AO2)

Role and contribution to overall business activity (AO2)

Whatever the size of organization, we typically see four main departments:

- The production or operations management department is concerned with the manufacturing of the product in the case of goods, or with delivery and execution of a service.

- The marketing department will have responsibility for developing customer interest and awareness as the good or service is launched into the market-place and for monitoring its ongoing performance.

- The finance and accounts department is designed to manage and report on the **economic sustainability** of a business.

- The HR department is responsible for ensuring that employees are organized to allow a business to achieve its objects and determine the appropriate culture for an organization.

These areas and roles are inter-related, for example as described below.

Operations management, marketing and finance

- A new T-shirt manufacturing company has a very successful domestic product but no finance to promote or distribute this into an overseas market.

- The marketing staff of a fast-food company become very excited about the possibility of a zero saturated-fat French fry but the production department does not have the knowledge, technology or financial resources to create this.

HR and operations management

- A shortage of skilled labour forces a technology company to relocate its main production facility to another country.

- A successful start-up, which is growing quickly in its domestic market, is unable to recruit enough suitable sales staff to handle customer enquiries.

These examples highlight one key aspect facing all businesses. They must successfully manage and coordinate all departments in order to satisfy consumer wants and needs and be economically sustainable.

Business sectors (AO2)

Primary, secondary, tertiary and quaternary sectors (AO2)

We can classify business activity into four areas:

- The primary sector is concerned with extraction of natural resources such as agricultural products or fossil fuels.

- The secondary sector includes construction and manufacturing processes, for example by transforming raw materials extracted from the primary sector into finished products.

- The tertiary sector includes various providers of skills or services for business. For example, a provider of financial services, an electrician and a delivery company would be classified as being part of the tertiary sector.

- The quaternary sector is a recent classification used as a way to describe a knowledge-based part of the economy which typically includes services such as information generation and sharing, information technology (IT), consultation, education, research and development, financial planning, and other knowledge-based services.

It is expected, given the rate of technological change in the developed world, that the quaternary and knowledge sectors of the economy will become the most important in generating growth. This has a huge implication for stakeholders in these countries, as we shall see in this guide.

Impact of sectoral change on business activity (AO2)

In the developed world the share or percentage of both the primary and secondary sectors' activity towards an economy's total output has been decreasing. The tertiary and quaternary sectors' contribution has risen. For developing countries, the trend from data published by the Organisation for Economic Co-operation and Development (OECD) reveals that manufacturing remains the most important sector, especially in China and India. These changes in the economic structure of the economy have significant implications for business decision-making and activity.

For most of the developed world, this process is called de-industrialization. A full discussion of this is beyond the scope of this guide. However, the combination of de-industrialization and globalization has had profound effects on HR planning, production and marketing. It has also had an impact on organizational structure and culture and on decision-making, stakeholder activity and objectives.

Entrepreneurship and intrapreneurship (AO3)

Role of entrepreneurship and intrapreneurship (AO3)

The success of Facebook, Google, Apple and App developers such as WhatsApp and Flappy Birds has brought renewed media attention in 2014 on the importance of entrepreneurship in creating new needs and thereby new business start-ups.

Entrepreneurship should be viewed as a dynamic activity that centres around skills such as resilience, creativity and risk-taking. In short, entrepreneurship is having the courage to turn ideas into action leading to products and services which are economically sustainable.

MOVIE RESOURCE

Individuals who gave up stable incomes in larger organizations to pursue their passion and interests to, in the words of Steve Jobs, put a "ding in the universe" started all of the businesses mentioned above. The 2013 movie "Jobs" clearly illustrates the challenges new business start-ups face, especially in the first difficult years where finance is difficult to obtain.

Intrapreneurship

Organizations seeing the success of instant messaging Apps such as WhatsApp created by two young entrepreneurs (one of whom was rejected by Facebook as a potential employee) **are now looking inward** within their own organizations to see if they can create the conditions that allow creativity and innovation to thrive.

Given the need for innovation in companies that is driven by the rapid changes in technology and globalization reducing barriers to entry in global markets, the new business term "intrapreneurship" has been developed which looks at resilience, creativity and risk-taking **within an existing organization**.

IB Learner Profile

Knowledgeable

Link to concept 2: Change

As we saw with Gary Hamel's YouTube clip (details in concept 2: Change, page 6), companies such as HCL technologies in India and, more famously, Google allow their employees time (20% of their time in Google's case) and the autonomy to work on projects of interest as long as the results are shared with the senior management team. This autonomy is a key driver in Daniel Pink's theory of motivation, which we will see in unit 2.4 when we look at non-financial motivation.

Entrepreneurship and intrapreneurship: compare and contrast

An entrepreneur is someone who, through his or her skills and passion, creates a business and is willing to take full accountability for its success or failure. An intrapreneur, on the other hand, is someone who utilizes his or her skill, passion and innovation to manage or create something useful for someone else's business – with entrepreneurial enthusiasm.

Though both are visionary, it is the entrepreneur who spots an opportunity in the market-place and has the courage and desire to turn this opportunity into a business. In contrast, however, the intrapreneur uses his or her passion, drive and skills to manage the business or create something new and useful for the business.

The main difference between an entrepreneur and an intrapreneur is that an entrepreneur has the freedom to act on his or her whim, whereas an intrapreneur may need to ask for managers' approval to make changes in the company's processes, product design or just about any innovation he or she needs to implement. Since an intrapreneur acts on innovative impulses, this may result in conflict within the organization. It is important for organizations that are implementing intrapreneurship to create an atmosphere of mutual respect among employees.

When it comes to resources, the intrapreneur holds an advantage over the entrepreneur since the company's resources are readily available to him or her. Conversely, an entrepreneur has the difficult task of sourcing funding and resources on his or her own.

What makes entrepreneurs and intrapreneurs similar is their passion to see things through to the end and their courage to face failure.

Source: Adapted from www.ourknowledge.asia/1/post/2012/05/entrepreneur-or-intrapreneur-whats-the-difference.html

Reasons for setting up a business (AO2)

We can summarize and explain some of the key reasons why any individuals would want to set up their own business:

- They might want to become artistically and financially independent. This may be important for those who live in a rural rather than urban area.

- They might want to take the opportunity to pursue a passion or transform a hobby into an economically sustainable business.

- They can exercise a degree of control over their future, which they might particularly value if they have been made redundant by an organization.

- Having identified a market opportunity where customer needs have not been satisfied, an entrepreneur would wish to take a risk with a desire to fulfil those needs profitably.

- Another reason might be the ease with which it is possible to set up a new business in particular country.

The last point may seem slightly odd. However, a key factor in the decision-making process about starting a new business may be the bureaucratic hurdles one has to go through in order to register a new start-up; the idea being that the less time and paperwork required to set up a new business, the more an entrepreneur will be encouraged to do so. Consider Table 1.1.1 which shows data about procedures in some countries.

Country	Number of procedures to register a new company, 2004	Number of days taken for each procedure, 2004
New Zealand	2	12
United States	5	5
Singapore	7	8
United Kingdom	6	18
Kazakhstan	9	25
Nigeria	10	44
China	12	41
Paraguay	17	74
Indonesia	12	151

Country	Number of days to register a new company, 2014
Australia	1
New Zealand	1
Zimbabwe	90
Laos	92
Hong Kong	3
Brunei	101
Singapore	3
Canada	5
Brazil	119
Canada	5
Venezuela	144
Congo-Brazzaville	161
Iceland	5
Portugal	5
Suriname	694

Table 1.1.1 Data on procedures when setting up a business in selected countries

Source: Adapted from *The Economist: Business Miscellany, 2005* and *Pocket World in Figures 2014*

IB Learner Profile
Inquiry ❓

Research the number of days it takes to register a company in your country (your own country and your country of study if different) and reflect on what impact this has on the rate of entrepreneurship in the country. Is there a strong relationship?

Problems a start-up may face (AO2)

We can identify and explain a number of problems. The type of economy the business resides in and the state of the external environment may pose problems for start-ups. Both of these factors are of course outside the control of the individual firm.

We can also identify the following problems that a business start-up may face:

- Lack of initial finance is often a problem. A start-up is unlikely to be fully financed at the beginning of its life and will see cash outflows leaving the business many days or months before cash flows in.

- The owner of a start-up may have knowledge and entrepreneurial enthusiasm for the product or service but may lack the ability to prepare and monitor financial accounts, organize suitable promotional activities or delegate responsibilities. This multi-tasking aspect is difficult for a one-person sole trader.

- Incorrect pricing in the short run will lead to lower than forecasted sales with a further impact on the amount of cash the business receives.

- The need for clear, accurate and unbiased market research to guide pricing and promotion of a new product or service is overwhelming but new start-ups may not be able to afford independent objective market research provided by specialist agencies.

- The role of venture capital and technology start-ups has posed the following problems. During the dot.com boom of the late 1990s, venture capital poured into Internet start-ups at an unsustainably fast pace. This capital demanded a quick return or it would be removed and invested in "the next big thing". This external pressure, without allowing time for the business to build a customer base in an increasingly competitive market, led to many start-ups failing and becoming economically unsustainable. Reflecting on the news in February 2014, with Facebook having just paid US$23 billion for WhatsApp, some commentators are asking if we have reached another turning point in the growth of the new dot.com or technological boom. The successful initial public offerings (IPOs) of Twitter and Candy Crush do support the theory that once again we have entered a social media and gaming investment boom.

IB Learner Profile
Balanced ⚖️

We must remember that the issues facing all new start-ups depend on whether the business operates in the developed or developing world. Some of the issues will be identical but some will be completely different depending on the economy concerned. Check to make sure that you have the correct context for your answer.

Elements of a business plan (AO2)

Any business start-up will need a business plan. The type of plan presented will of course depend on satisfying a particular objective.

In the case of Coffee Republic, a new coffee start-up in the UK, the need for a business plan was to secure funding to launch the first coffee bar. The owners also had growth plans to open other coffee bars if the first one was successful.

In 1995, Sahar and Bobby Hashemi decided to set up a coffee and espresso bar in London. Without any previous business start-up experience, they described their "journey" in a best-selling book (2003). Their business plan, which was delivered to their bank and to prospective investors, ran to over 20 pages.

They identified a number of elements that a business plan should have:

- The aims of the business must be clearly stated.

- The business plan must include details of existing and potential competition.

- The amount of funding required must be stated, with a time line illustrating how the funding would be used to generate favourable trading options.

- Details must be given of finance needed under different scenarios if external factors move against the new start-up.

- Time lines for implementation and action to review aims if forecasts are not met must be outlined.

- A comprehensive marketing plan with sales forecasts must be included.

- A projected profit and loss account and cash flow forecast must be presented.

Source: Adapted from Hashemi and Hashemi, 2003.

Note that the above example was for a new business start-up. Other business plans drawn up by existing organizations may be driven by different objectives, for example to change an existing strategy or to restructure operations, and in fact a whole range of other possibilities. The elements contained in these plans will need to be adjusted accordingly.

Setting the scene

Significant government "bail-outs" or rescue packages accompanied the dramatic events of the credit crisis of 2008 and the deteriorating global economic situation. On 3 April 2009 the Heads of State of the leading 20 economies in the world announced a trillion US dollar stimulus package. A number of large private banks in the United States and the UK and companies such as General Motors received government assistance and have effectively become public sector companies. The term "re-nationalization" began to appear in the business pages.

This would have been unthinkable during the 1980s and 1990s when the private sector was being heralded as innovative, efficient and flexible. The public sector, on the other hand, was viewed as bureaucratic, complacent and wasteful.

In the new century, a new "third way" between the two sectors has been created, known as the **public-private partnership,** which attempts to combine the best characteristics of both sectors to help with the construction and finance of mostly social infrastructure projects involving irrigation, transport and other civil engineering needs. The final section of this unit tries to assess the effectiveness of this new partnership.

Distinction between the private and public sectors

If we were to identify one difference between the two sectors, as the IB asked students to in the May 2008 HL exam, a typical answer would contain a sentence very similar to the following:

The private sector focuses solely on profit maximization and the public sector tries to provide a service to consumers whatever the cost.

While this has some truth for many countries, increasingly many public sector corporations – which we define as being **principally** controlled, financed and operated by the government – are expected to operate as follows:

- They should provide greater levels of customer satisfaction and demonstrate characteristics found in the private sector such as rising levels of efficiency, managerial innovation and flexibility.

- They will be more "accountable" for public funding and, in some industries, will return a surplus to the government. Examples of changes in the education and health sectors relating to this accountability include the following:

    - Government-run academy schools in the UK are ranked in "league tables" according to students' performance.

    - The UK's National Health Service is now expected to deliver cost savings and productivity increases at the same time.

IB Learner Profile

Thinkers and knowledgeable

Many students assume that the public sector's only function is to provide goods or services to consumers at reasonable cost which private sector companies are either unwilling or unable to provide. Interested students may wish to look at the "free-rider" problem in economics and investigate merit and public goods to see this distinction between the two sectors clearly on a theoretical basis.

We will now look at the private sector in more detail.

Main features of some for-profit and not-for-profit organizations (AO3)

Table 1.2.1 highlights the key features of different types of for-profit and not-for-profit organizations. For study purposes it is assumed that a charity and a non-governmental organization (NGO) are the same entity.

Type of business	Ownership and transparency	Finance	Examples	Control/decision-making
Sole trader	One owner There is a limited need for published accounts except those for tax purposes	Past savings, government grants and loan schemes Retained profits after trading begins	Service-based firms such as home help Car and computer repairs	There is usually one person in overall control
Partnership	Up to 20 partners depending on the country of operation There is a limited need for published accountability	Savings Loans Capital from new partners Retained profits	Lawyers, medical practices	The partnership agreement specifies terms for control/decision-making Sleeping partners have limited liability
Private limited company	Depends on the country of operation In some countries businesses have to send financial statements to a registrar of companies	Contributing capital from partners New partners could be introduced through a partnership agreement	Family-run businesses with a desire to avoid unlimited liability Specific examples: Lego, Illy, Ferrari	Control/decision-making is according to the agreement signed Authority is usually handed down through family connections
Publicly traded company	This is unlimited if shares are advertised on local or global exchanges Period reporting with absolute transparency is required	Wide access to funds if shares are sold on various exchanges Success depends on the sentiment of the financial markets	Larger corporations with successful transparent financial histories Specific examples: Sony, Wal-Mart	Shareholders will vote at an annual general meeting (AGM) to decide on the board of directors and the dividend to be paid or retained
Volunteer organizations, NGOs and charities	Some NGOs are run in partnership with the government	Donations and funds from some government source A lot depends on the size and objectives of the NGO	Specific examples: Oxfam, World Vision	Control/decision-making is according to the terms of the individual agreement There is no one agreed accepted method to organize an NGO

Table 1.2.1 Key features of different types of business

Private sector for-profit organizations (AO3)

Discussion

Which type of organization is the most appropriate?

This is a difficult question to answer. Lego, for example, has remained a private company since its creation in 1932 with the Kristiansen family firmly in control. Richard Branson, founder of the Virgin Group, who "bought back" the organization in 1989 after a successful flotation in 1987 famously remarked that he felt that it was he the founder of the company rather than shareholders who knew best how to invest profits and make decisions. He has kept the Virgin Group private ever since this statement, although he has had to sell off parts of his company to fund his ambitious growth plans which we will see come to fruition in 2014 with the world's first commercially operated space flight – the Virgin Galactic.

There is an interesting cultural element to the question as to which type of organization is most appropriate. The "European business" model includes businesses such as Lego, Illy and Ferrari which have not become publicly traded companies and instead prefer private ownership. In contrast, in the United States there is a seemingly never-ending supply of business start-ups that wish to become publicly traded on the financial markets (or to use the current jargon they aim for an IPO – an initial public offering). Twitter is a recent example in a long line of Internet start-ups that despite low revenues and no profit have been valued highly by the financial markets as "sound investments". The Facebook IPO of 2013 was met with both excitement and with scepticism by many stakeholders who thought the company was overvalued.

Whatever the merits or demerits of a business being solely owned, operating as a partnership or remaining in private hands, we can briefly note some factors used to decide which type of organization is the most appropriate.

- The objectives of the firm in terms of growth, profit, vision and mission are of key importance.
- The degree to which the owner wishes to retain control is significant.
- The degree to which the business wishes to be transparent about its financial position is a factor. Publicly traded businesses have to very open and honest about their future profit and sales forecasts and their growth strategies. Privately owned organizations need only inform the tax department of their respective country of origin about the true state of their financial affairs.
- The extent to which the firm wishes to compete in international or global markets will be a factor, although with globalization and world broadband many smaller firms can trade outside their continent of origin.
- The owners will need to consider the speed and degree of flexibility in decision-making that they require. Clearly, the smaller the number of owners, the quicker decision-making can be organized.

Unit 2.2 on organizational structure will argue the proposition that the most appropriate structure for an organization is one that allows a firm to achieve its business objectives. There is a full discussion of organizational objectives in unit 1.3.

IB Learner Profile

Inquiry ❓

NGOs and charities

Although increasingly associated with charities and other not-for-profit organizations, over the last 10 years the number of NGOs with some significant governmental input has been rising. Research an NGO of your choice outside your country of birth or current residency and discover how the organization is financed and structured, and what is its mission and vision. Also consider that there is a very wide spectrum of debate as to what actually constitutes an NGO, and an NGO's effectiveness.

Main features of some for-profit social enterprises (AO3)

For the new IB Business Management course three additional types of for-profit organizations have been included for study:

- cooperatives
- micro-finance providers
- public-private partnerships.

Cooperatives

The best way to identify the main features of a cooperative is to let one tell its own story. The following excerpt is taken from the Co-operative Bank New Zealand's website (2014).

> ## WHAT IS A CO-OPERATIVE?
>
> A co-operative is an organization that's owned by the people who use it, and is managed for their best interests.
>
> That means that we're not owned by a big overseas company or the Government. We're owned by our customers – people from all over New Zealand – and our motivation is to do the right thing by our customers.
>
> Anyone who becomes a customer becomes an owner too. And anyone can become a customer – even kids.

IB Learner Profile

Caring and inquirers

The intentions expressed by the Co-operative Bank New Zealand would be repeated if we were to look at any other global organization. Cooperatives exist for their workers (a worker cooperative) or for their customers (as in the above example). Strongly driven by ethical intent, the cooperative movement has influenced a whole new generation of stakeholders in the 21st century concluding that the best way to ensure strong social and ethical outcomes for business is for workers and customers to be part of the ownership structure.

To find out more, research cooperatives such as REI – the largest cooperative in the United States.

TOK thought question

Given the social and ethical impact of cooperatives, how would the business community change if all businesses became cooperatives? What could be the impact on customers and workers?

Micro-finance providers

Kiva Microfunds

The Nobel Prize awarded to Muhammad Yunus in 2006 and the Grameen Bank in recognition of their work in trying to help struggling entrepreneurs in developing countries finance some of their start-up capital has led to the term "micro-finance". Table 1.2.2 gives a snapshot of the work undertaken by the micro-finance provider Kiva. The information was taken from Kiva's website in February, 2014.

Total amount lent through Kiva	$531 411 075
Kiva users	1 588 307
Kiva users who have funded a loan	1 050 337
Borrowers funded through Kiva	1 241 902
Number of loans made through Kiva	673 271
Kiva field partners	241
Countries where Kiva field partners are located	73
Repayment rate	98.97%
Average loan size	$415.42
Average loans made per Kiva lender	10.30

Table 1.2.2 Kiva Microfunds statistics (February, 2014)

The rapid pace of technological change and globalization has allowed Kiva and other micro-finance providers to widen their assistance. Kiva may appear as a charity and it does receive donations from organizations such as Google and other large corporations. However, as Table 1.2.2 shows, nearly 99% of loans are paid back to Kiva. This money is then returned to other entrepreneurs so that the financial system is sustainable.

Criticisms of micro-finance providers

Some commentators have argued that although the principle of micro-finance is ethical and laudable, entrepreneurs in developing countries who take out a micro-finance loan may put themselves and their community into a debt trap which they are unable to escape. There is also some evidence that while the number of business start-ups has grown, incomes in the community in which the start-ups operate have not, reducing the flow-on or multiplier effects claimed by the supporters of micro-finance. The debate continues.

"FLIPPED LEARNING" EXPLAINED

An increasingly popular way to discover new topics is to undertake a "flipped learning" exercise. The idea is that students watch a demonstration or video of an activity or topic they are unfamiliar with and make some notes or observations. They then take their notes and ideas back to the "flipped classroom" for a discussion. Where appropriate this study guide will make use of "flipped learning" activities. They will be introduced with the graphic shown at the top of this box.

PUBLIC-PRIVATE PARTNERSHIPS

For the first "flipped learning" activity watch the YouTube video clip "A quick introduction to public-private partnerships provided by UNECE" then consider the following discussion points:

- What is the justification for the combination of the public and private sector in projects such as power generation or water purification?

- Write down at least two advantages that:
  - the public sector will bring to the public-private partnership
  - the private sector will bring to the public-private partnership.

- Research public-private partnerships in different countries around the world. Consider two countries where public-private partnerships have been a success and two countries where they may have struggled to deliver stakeholder value.

- What can you conclude about your investigation into public-private partnerships?

Setting the scene

By attracting growing interest from the media, NGOs, pressure groups such as the Occupy movement and other stakeholders, the aims and objectives of business have come under renewed scrutiny. In addition, organizations now encourage feedback from their other stakeholders either directly via their websites or indirectly through the numerous social networking online communities. As unit 4.8 on e-commerce explores, there may be strong commercial reasons for doing this.

These factors have led to a greater degree of transparency between business and consumer and this has been reflected by the number of organizations that place ethical and social responsibilities at the top of their "objectives agenda". This aspect will form a significant part of the discussion in this unit.

Mission and vision statements (AO2)

There is some confusion about the difference between mission and vision statements. We will look at them in turn, giving examples.

A mission statement is a way of defining briefly and succinctly the reason for the existence of a business. Some examples may help to clarify this point:

- Lego's mission is to infuse children with the "joy of building, pride of creation" to stimulate children's imagination.
- Facebook states: "Our mission is to give people the power to share and make the world more open and connected."
- Google's mission is to organize the world's information and make it universally accessible and useful.

These mission statements are designed to give the impression that these businesses are entities greater than a toy brick company, a social media platform and a search engine.

A **vision statement** defines where the company sees itself moving to in the future. Some writers have called this a **strategic declaration** although it is clear from research that many vision statements are purposely vague.

It is clearly impossible to predict, given the existence of external factors and rapid change, how a business will be performing in five years' time. For this reason some companies only construct mission statements to avoid being accused of making bold and extravagant claims that they could be held accountable to by stakeholders.

Some examples of vision statements are:

- Heinz: "Our vision, quite simply, is to be the world's premier food company, offering nutritious, superior tasting foods to people everywhere."
- Ford: "Our vision is to become the world's leading company for automotive products and services."

We will now briefly analyse why companies create and use mission and vision statements.

Mission and vision statements can help clarify in the minds of stakeholders the **purpose motive** of the business. This will have important considerations for customers, investors and suppliers, both present and future. This is covered in more detail when we look at motivation in unit 2.4 and organizational culture in unit 2.5.

A vision statement can reassure shareholders that the business is forward-looking and willing to create and pursue new opportunities. A vision could be perceived as unobtainable in the short term, but stakeholders may feel that the company is striving to do the best that it can within its market. This "vision" idea was critical in the recovery of Lego, which we will discuss later in this unit.

However, the mission and vision must be credible and realistic in the minds of the stakeholders too. One chief criticism laid at the door of those companies who set them is that that mission and vision statements are too vague or imprecise.

Aims, objectives, strategies, tactics and their relationships (AO3)

There is also some confusion about the difference between an aim and an objective in a business context. An aim usually represents a vision or a future place where a business wishes to be (e.g. to become a market leader) and an objective is a step or milestone to help achieve the aim (e.g. increasing sales of the company's product by 42% in two years).

However, as we saw in concept 5: Strategy, there is broad agreement that aims and objectives should be SMART:

- **s**pecific
- **m**easurable
- **a**chievable
- **r**ealistic
- **t**ime-bound (within an agreed time limit).

We will look at this aspect in more detail later in this unit when we consider Lego's decision to change objectives in 2009 and innovate in response to changes in internal and external factors.

Typical business objectives

Business objectives will be influenced by the "age" of the firm and also the prevailing external factors. It should be noted that given the challenges faced by an entrepreneur in setting up a business (as outlined in unit 1.2) there is a key idea running through these objectives – business start-ups should aim in their first two years to be **economically sustainable** before they can consider making significant profits.

Typical business objectives include:

- survival or break-even
- cost minimization
- growth (usually in terms of increasing market share in the short term and actual physical size in the longer term)
- profit maximization.

IB Learner Profile

Open-minded

The importance of the profit motive – link to entrepreneurship

In economic terms, profit is considered as the reward for risk-taking. If the entrepreneur has decided to combine human and non-human resources including land to create a business, then earning profit should be seen as an incentive and finally as a reward. Without the profit motive, very few new businesses would be created and few would deny its importance.

Sometimes, however, the size and magnitude of company profits raise concerns.

Strategies and tactics and the link to aims and objectives (AO3)

It is useful to classify the above business objectives according to whether they can be perceived as strategic or tactical. Consider first an established organization:

- A strategy, as we saw in concept 5, can be defined as a longer-term plan with an aim for the business driven by the vision of the owner.
- A tactical or operational objective is much more short term in nature and is usually defined as an tool or mechanism designed to help achieve the overall strategic objective and support the overall vision. A tactical or operational objective is what a business will hope it can use as a stepping stone on the way to success.

From the perspective of a new start-up beginning its trading cycle, an aim or an objective will be slightly different. A tactical objective may be survival of the first year of trading in order to preserve and guarantee that a vision has a chance of being realized. Second, a tactical move to reduce costs and waste may allow a future goal of profit maximization or growth to take place.

Generally, tactical objectives are designed to be subordinate to but also try to affect the overall strategic direction.

Change and innovation (A03)

Response to changes in internal and external environments (A03)

Organizations will need to change their objectives and innovate in response to changes in their internal and external environments. An interesting example, which will attempt to link some of the ideas discussed above, is that of Lego.

Link to concept 5: Strategy

The Lego case study below also links to the points covered in concept 5: Strategy.

LEGO

In 2004 Lego found itself on the verge of bankruptcy just three years after the Lego brick had been recognized as the "Toy of the Century".

In 1998 Lego reported its first financial loss since its creation in 1932. A number of unsuccessful ventures to innovate its way out of its financial problems in 1999 led to huge cash outflows and with a weaker US dollar Lego found its revenues drying up so that, by 2004, the company was forced to lay off 1 000 of its workers. The company was very close to closing or being taken over by one of its major competitors.

The reason for the collapse in performance was not hard to find. Faced with a loss in 1998, Lego embarked on a radical programme of innovation which took the company into new markets such as software, children's clothing, lifestyle products and Lego dolls. Growing competition from online games and other electronic media compounded Lego's fear that children did not want to play with toy bricks any more. Lego felt that it needed to enter new markets. The organization decided to move away from its "core competency" of producing the famous brick **and** away from its mission. As we saw earlier, the mission was infusing children with "the joy of building" – encouraging children to play well and become creative builders – but this was quietly forgotten.

After a significant internal review, by late 2003 it was discovered that the company's new strategic move into rampant innovation had been supported by a management system that could not cope. There was a lack of coordination and communication and the culture of the organization was not appropriate. Lego departments were in sense competing against each other in the race for new product development and innovation. Lego had become fragmented and disconnected, much to the dismay of the original owners.

A quick management change saw an immediate refocus at Lego and the creation of a new **shared vision**, which took at least a year to create, agree upon and implement. This new strategic direction for Lego would need to be supported by new three tactical objectives: in the first instance **survival**, then **profit**, followed by **growth**.

Innovation was still retained but had to become more accountable inside the organization – unfocused innovation in the hope of making profits was banned. Closer control, budgets, targets and initiatives were set up to ensure that new focused innovations came to market quicker. Lego also decided to look outside itself and invited customer feedback on its product range.

One innovative idea was the creation of the Bionicle. This was a Lego piece that looked like "alien robot" – nothing like anything the company had produced before. Importantly, to use the industry term, it had to have "backward compatibility" with Lego bricks of the past – representing a true **continuity of innovation** that, according to Lego's CEO at the time, saved the iconic toy company.

As part of its new strategic aim Lego came up with incremental innovative ideas. These included Lego Mind Storm and Lego board games and the disruptive innovation idea of allowing Lego builders the opportunity to go online and post their own customized Lego sets which they could then order and build themselves.

As a result, Lego's profits between 2007 and 2011 rose by 400%. Between 2008 and 2010, Lego's profits had grown faster than Apple's, despite:

- few barriers to entry and aggressive global competition
- a production cost disadvantage by producing in high-wage Scandinavia
- no patent protection on its core product: the Lego brick.

CONCLUSION

Lego had responded to internal problems and perceived changes in external factors and, given its precarious financial position, had decided that a new strategic aim was required. This new plan was not without management changes and casualties but the creation of a shared vision and, importantly, culture allowed to company to return to the pre-eminence it enjoyed before that first loss in 1998. With the release of the Lego movie in 2014, the organization is now back to its very best. It has recently become the world's top toy maker.

The condensed idea from the Lego case study

The Lego case study has linked the concepts of innovation, change and culture to a business. The company had to respond to considerable internal and external factors and also had to refocus its aims and objectives to achieve the vision. This case study has also highlighted that change takes time and that we must also consider both internal and external factors when deciding on what new path to follow.

Ethical objectives and corporate social responsibility (A01)

Identifying an ethical objective

An ethical objective, reflecting corporate social responsibility (CSR), is a deliberate attempt on the part of the company to take a position that is viewed as morally correct and appropriate in the eyes of stakeholders. We can identify an ethical position by adopting an inquiry approach. Instead of looking for answers we can increase our knowledge by asking a number of questions:

- Should a multinational firm operate in a country that imposes harsh working conditions on its citizens and encourages the use of child labour?
- Should a pharmaceutical company that plans to produce an important vaccine in an area with a high prevalence of malaria charge high prices to those consumers who may be most affected and most in need?
- Should tobacco or alcohol producers be allowed to sponsor sporting events where young children may be in the crowd?

You should be able to come up with your own examples by questioning an action or decision made by a business known to you.

Definition of CSR

Russell-Walling (2007) argues that there is no single definition of CSR. The World Business Council defines CSR as:

the continuing commitment by business to behave ethically and contribute to economic development while improving the quality of life of the workforce and their families as well as of the local community at large.

The Global Reporting Initiative provides a framework for companies to report on their CSR commitments. It has 32 different performance indicators ranging from customer privacy and anti-competitive behaviour to the use of child labour.

Ethical objectives and the impact of implementing them (AO3)

There are several reasons why a company might wish to pursue ethical objectives.

There is considerable pressure from stakeholders to "do the right thing" in business after a number of high-profile and damaging corporate scandals such as the Enron and WorldCom scandals. The "fall-out" from the global financial crisis revealed that many financial institutions were guilty of mismanagement and fraud. Linked to this is the need for a company to differentiate itself from the competition by building a credible ethical stance (e.g. the Fair Trade Movement and the plight of coffee growers in the developing world). This could be the basis for a new mission and vision to develop a new strategic direction.

In addition, there is growing transparency through the world wide web and the rise of "citizen journalism" through blogging and by contributing to media forums. This has also increased the pressure on businesses "to do the right thing".

Discussion

Why should a company think carefully about adopting an ethical position?

If we consider opportunity costs, then an ethical position may conflict with the profit motive. Shareholders may not be happy to forgo future profits if the business is not allowed to compete in some markets or geographical regions because of ethical concerns raised by the company's managers (e.g. the prevalence of child labour).

If the ethical stance is leaning towards environmental concerns, the firm may have to spend vast sums of capital in the short term implementing environmental assurances about production processes. This will raise costs and have a negative impact on profitability.

The ethical stance will need to be credible and effective in the eyes of the market in order for the firm to build a competitive position. This again will take time and financial resources. There is also the fundamental point that if all firms in an industry follow an ethical strategic objective then the competitive advantage enjoyed by one firm will be dissipated and even lost.

Finally, in a deteriorating economic environment, an ethical stance may mean redundancy for some line workers if contracts are not won or projects are refused on ethical grounds. This could be an unpopular move affecting a range of stakeholders in the wider community.

The evolving role and nature of CSR (AO3)

In this section we look at how ethical business objectives and CSR are linked and explore the debate surrounding CSR.

IB Learner Profile

Open-minded and balanced

The topics of business ethics and CSR are closely linked. In his excellent review of CSR, Russell-Walling (2007) argues that in the United States the two topics are seen as one, while in the UK and Europe CSR is more idealistically associated with businesses wanting to leave the world a better place.

However, it may come as a surprise that not all business commentators are in favour of adopting a CSR strategy. Milton Friedman famously remarked that:

Businesses have no social responsibility other than to increase profits and refrain from deception and fraud. When businesses seek to maximise profits they always do what is good for society.

The Economist has added:

Businesses should not do the work of governments.

There is no space in this unit for a full investigation. However, we would ask you to consider some of the ideas presented and perhaps undertake some independent research on how the role and impact of CSR is evolving in your country or the country you are studying in.

Environmental audits and CSR

There is increasing use of environmental audits as part of establishing CSR. A number of governments have set up guidelines for firms that wish to carry out environmental audits, given the growing concerns of climate change and threats to sustainability. An environmental audit can form part of an organization's commitment to a **socially responsible objective.**

The Australian government, for example, has developed a series of guidelines for firms to follow if they wish to benchmark their environmental credentials against accepted government protocols.

The topics include how a firm can:

- readily change its influence on the environment
- prioritize actions to reduce impact
- demonstrate accountability to government, customers and shareholders.

This last point is important as clearly the value of an environmental impact or a decision to implement a CSR policy must have credibility and accountability in the minds of the stakeholders. Russell-Walling (2007) provides some interesting statistical work on this point in an international context.

Table 1.3.1 records some results from a survey to rank brands as ethical.

Rank	UK	US	France	Germany	Spain
1	Co-op	Coca-Cola	Danone	Adidas	Nestlé
2	Body Shop	Kraft	Adidas/ Nike	Nike/Puma	Body Shop
3	Marks & Spencer	Proctor & Gamble			Coca-Cola
4	Traidcraft	Johnson & Johnson Kellogg's Nike Sony	Nestlé	BMW	Danone
5	Café Direct		Renault	Demeter gepa	Corte Ingles

Table 1.3.1 Brands perceived as the most ethical

Below are two examples of benefits gained by a firm adopting a CSR approach.

Nike has adapted well to a UK-led campaign that accused it of employing child labour with very low wages and poor conditions in developing countries. It has responded proactively with a clear CSR strategy including the appointment of a director of sustainable development. However, perceptions take a long time to change and it is revealing that Nike does not appear in the UK rankings in Table 1.3.2. Warren Buffet, one of the world's most successful investors stated:

It takes 20 years to build a reputation and five minutes to ruin it.

Stung by criticism after the release of the film "Super Size Me", McDonald's has responded positively by taking certain sweet fizzy drinks off its menu and introducing low-fat and low-sugar options, including fruit, for its "Happy Meals" targeted at children.

Now we will turn to the drawbacks of pursuing a CSR approach. Russell-Walling (2007) notes some of the difficulties.

There are statistics that purport to show the beneficial impact of CSR on a company's profits but they are not yet overwhelmingly convincing. Some recent writers on this topic have argued that to provide greater clarity around a firm's CSR role, accounting and reporting requirements should include a reference to a firm's "quadruple bottom line" which includes environmental, economic, cultural and spiritual impacts of business activity. A number of businesses in New Zealand have adopted "quadruple bottom line" reporting in their end-of-year financial statements but this process is still in its early adoption phase.

Second, the costs of compliance with environmental audits or preparing CSR strategies may take up valuable time and resources, adding to the reporting and administrative burden of businesses, especially start-ups. This could force them to increase prices to the consumer as a way to recoup these expenses.

Conclusion

The role and nature of CSR is still a "work in progress" for many global businesses. A quick look at most company websites will indicate that CSR is taken very seriously and often given prominence with terms such as "global citizenship" and "sustainability" adorning organizations' mission and vision statements. However, the recent investigations concerning supplier chain responsibilities of successful technological companies such as Apple have shown that much is still needed to be done to ensure that mere words are backed up by action. The recent concerns raised by the Foxconn media investigation (a Chinese supplier for Apple and other computer companies – see concept 4: Ethics, page 8) are a very good illustration that this is a complex issue.

SWOT analysis (AO3 and AO4)

An important tool in planning and decision-making, the SWOT analysis has become a critical component for organizations looking to review current strategic aims and trying to ascertain where future opportunities may lie.

To increase objectivity, some organizations ask independent consultants to carry out the SWOT analysis for them and outsource the task of collecting and presenting the data. This can be an expensive process.

SWOT analysis: a guide for internal assessment

For HL students in the internal assessment or even in the extended essay for the IB Business Management course, a SWOT analysis (or other appropriate planning tool) should be included at the beginning of the assignment to determine how a new strategic path was identified.

As a moderator of internal assessments for a number of years, the author has noted three worrying trends. These form part of this discussion to evaluate the role of the SWOT in helping businesses to decide on a new strategic direction.

- Students are placing the SWOT analysis in the middle or end of their internal assessment report to recommend a certain course of action be taken. The SWOT is not designed to judge whether a course of action is appropriate. It should be placed at the beginning of a project to begin the process of decision-making and allow an organization to see its current position objectively.

- Once the SWOT has been created, it is often not analysed correctly. It is insufficient for a student just to write down the strengths, weaknesses, opportunities and threats of a business. Further analysis, investigation or research is required to try and measure the magnitude of each of the variables to determine whether a new opportunity is to be pursued or a threat eliminated.

- Too often a SWOT is created from only one source of data and for an HL internal assessment the source may be the owner of the business. How representative and objective can this be? If possible, a SWOT should be a conclusion of a number of lines of inquiry and if only one source of data is possible, the implications for bias in the final decision should be acknowledged.

Occasionally a SWOT analysis carried out by a student is followed by a PEST analysis. While there is some merit in this idea, students need to be careful of repetition. For example, some of the opportunities and threats raised by the SWOT could be part of the external factors suggested by the PEST analysis. This may lead to the internal assessment becoming too descriptive and this is not to be encouraged given the 2 000 word limit.

SWOT construction (AO4)

THE DISNEY COMPANY
THE DISNEY SWOT

After the death in 1966 of its founder, Walt Disney, the Disney Company found that its family films and animated cartoons had lost some of their appeal; audience numbers had matured. With revenues falling in the mid-1970s, the company launched a thorough overview of its operations and conducted a SWOT analysis. An interpretation of the findings is given below.

STRENGTHS (INTERNAL)

- Disney had very strong brand identity with family and children's movies and had been conveying a positive moral message since the 1930s.

- The company was the industry leader in animated cartoons and movies.

- Theme parks had created a total entertainment package and for some a once-in-a-lifetime opportunity.

WEAKNESSES (INTERNAL)

- The company had been run by the Disney family since creation.

- Disney was accused of a lack of fresh thinking in a changing industry.

- Labour-intensive methods of production had led to very high costs of production for animated movies and increased the time taken to produce them.

OPPORTUNITIES (EXTERNAL)

- Themes parks in other countries could provide opportunities for expansion.

- Moving into adult action movies, away from family-oriented films, should be considered.

- A once-in-a-lifetime visit to a theme park could be turned in regular visits, perhaps once a year.

THREATS (EXTERNAL)

- There was competition from new film companies such as Lucas Film (producers of "Star Wars") and established industry giants such as Universal, Paramount and MGM. Disney had mostly ignored the science fiction genre.
- Home video was a threat. The Disney family had long resisted the idea of releasing the company's valuable back catalogue of films onto video as this was viewed by some members of the board of directors as "cheapening the brand". Disney regarded itself as a movie production company and not in the home entertainment business. (See Levitt's thoughts on this in unit 4.1, page 78).

After a number of high-profile casualties on the board of directors, over the next 15–20 years the company designed and implemented a long-term strategy:

- It built Tokyo Disney in 1983 and Euro Disney in 1992.
- It bought an independent movie company – Miramax – to distribute more adult-only movies. The first production was Quentin Tarrantino's "Pulp Fiction" in 1993–94.
- Disney reduced the output of animated films but focused on quality with more subtle adult humour or special effects (e.g. seen in "Aladdin" and "Beauty and the Beast").
- It launched the back catalogue of classic movies on video from 1981 and created a division to produce its own "non-Disney" movies. This new sub-brand was called Touchstone Pictures.
- Animated sequels were launched direct to video without release in the movie theatres.
- A joint venture with Pixar was formed, leading to "Toy Story" in 1995 and a whole host of subsequent family-oriented animated movies which have been very successful.

With hindsight, it can be recorded that the strategy was successful. It guaranteed the survival of the company although there were significant cultural difficulties in bringing the Disney brand as a theme park to Europe, and changes in the senior management team.

Link to concept 1: Globalization, concept 2: Change and concept 5: Strategy

Key learning point

As part of the new assessment or final exams for the IB Business Management course, students will have to apply their knowledge of concepts, contexts and content under timed conditions. In paper 2 for both HL and SL, section C will explicitly ask students to demonstrate how concepts and content could be analysed and evaluated with respect to a business organization of their choice. Ideally, this business should operate in global context, as this would automatically allow students to apply knowledge of concept 1: Globalization.

Every IB World School will have its own way of organizing this process. One suggestion is that students keep a diary or blog of events involving their organization over the course of the two years of study and link these events to the six concepts introduced at the beginning of this guide.

A possible essay exemplar for HL and SL paper 2 section C follows. This essay should not be viewed as a model answer. However, it is an exemplar to see how concept 1: Globalization, concept 2: Change and concept 5: Strategy could be applied to an organization. Moreover, this essay neatly updates the Disney case study above.

DISNEY UPDATE

Since 2000, profits at Disney have increased by approximately 10% per year and the organization has grown significantly and branched out into a whole new range of media markets. An interesting development is that Disney is now "buying-in" creative talent and ideas rather than developing them on its own. The company's founder, Walt Disney, favoured this latter "in-house" approach. However, it was considered by subsequent CEOs of Disney to be too expensive and time-consuming to develop innovative ideas for movies and television productions.

In 2005, after a strained relationship, Disney began to negotiate the sale of Pixar to ensure that it could keep this innovative joint venture partner. In 2006 the sale of Pixar was completed and Steve Jobs (one of Apple's co-founders) became the largest Disney shareholder. Given that a member of the Disney family had been the largest shareholder in control of the company since 1923, this strategic move was significant. Disney has also purchased Marvel Entertainment – another media business with its own characters which were unlike Disney characters.

New theme parks opened in Hong Kong and in 2015 Disney Shanghai will open, reflecting continued growth opportunities outside the United States. "Frozen" (2013) was officially announced as Disney's most successful film ever in February 2014, overtaking "Finding Nemo" in box-office takings, and it may be the first animated film to earn $1billion. In total 66% of this revenue was earned outside of the United States. Disney is now fully aware of the benefits of operating in a global market-place and is looking to develop its product range to fit local markets such as China and India.

Disney is still looking to the future, and in 2013 the company purchased Lucas Film. This will allow Disney to produce three more sequels to the financially spectacularly successful "Stars Wars" franchise. "Star Wars Episode VII" is set to be released in December 2015 with two more movies to follow by 2020.

Interestingly, Disney turned down the chance to make the original "Star Wars" movie in 1976 as the company did not think that science fiction films would be popular. It would be reasonable to suggest that Disney has decided not to make the same mistake again.

Ansoff matrix for different growth strategies (AO3 and AO4)

We use the Ansoff matrix (Ansoff, 1965) to see how a business could identify a number of different strategies to pursue further growth, either within existing markets or, taking a riskier route, looking at potential future markets. You will be asked to explain and apply the matrix to a strategic decision, and to evaluate the situation.

Table 1.3.2 shows the cells of the Ansoff matrix.

	Existing products	**New products**
Existing markets	Market penetration	Product development
New markets	Market development	Diversification

Table 1.3.2 The cells of the Ansoff matrix

An important point to note when considering which cell of the matrix to allocate to a particular course of action is that there are no definitive rules by which a growth strategy could be labelled a product or market development. You are encouraged to argue your case for allocating a particular element of the Ansoff matrix and will be rewarded for the quality of your reasoning.

The four cells are briefly explained as follows:

- **Market penetration** – this is aiming to increase market share. It is the least risky of the four routes, but offers limited growth. Once the market reaches saturation another strategy is required.
- **Market development** – this involves targeting existing products to new market segments such as new geographical regions. It is more risky than market penetration.
- **Product development** – a firm develops new products targeted to existing market segments. This is a good strategy if the company enjoys strong brand loyalty from its customers. A good example would be Sony and its recent success with the Blu-Ray DVD format and, of course, the PlayStation.
- **Diversification** – this is the most risky strategy of the four – one writer has called it the "suicide cell". When it opts for diversification a company is stepping out of its comfort zone and perhaps moving away from its core competencies. Nokia has been a notable success story (although we have noted that circumstances can change very quickly). On the other hand, the Virgin Group has been criticized for having an unfocused portfolio: it includes air travel, music, soft drinks, mobile networks and in 2014 the company hopes to provide the world's first commercially available flight into space via Virgin Galactic.

In common with the SWOT analysis, you could be asked to construct an Ansoff matrix from a range of stimulus material.

From our survey of the Disney organization above we could apply the Ansoff matrix in the following manner:

- The decision to take over Marvel and Pixar could be an attempt to look at **product development** by using the new creative teams to generate new film and gaming ideas for existing Disney customers.
- The decision to open a new theme park in Shanghai represents a **market development** strategy to stretch the Disney brand even further in Asian markets.
- The purchase of Lucas Film may be viewed as **diversification** given that Disney does not have a strong tradition of producing successful science fiction films (although it did produce "Tron" and "Tron Legacy"). The merchandising opportunities to Disney given the strong brand identify of "Star Wars" may be a secondary strategy of **product development**.

Practice question on applying the matrix

This question is from the IB exam of November 2007.

Question: Using Ansoff's matrix, explain the growth strategies used by Toyota.

Suggested answer:

Market development is taking place through the export of cars to overseas markets. Toyota has also deliberately used foreign direct investment to develop a presence in many countries.

Product development or modification is demonstrated by the production of new models every two years. Toyota has produced 60 models in Japan and has adapted many to the US and European markets.

Market penetration is seen in the company's increasing market share in Japan and other countries after establishing a foothold as described above.

Ansoff matrix – a brief discussion
Link to concept 5: Strategy

To use a Twitter term, strategy is trending again. Given the rapid changes outlined already in this guide, and the need for innovation, strategic decision-making has become critical. Before Ansoff published his matrix (in 1965), the idea of strategy planning and management was under-developed.

Russell-Walling (2007) has argued that Ansoff said that strategy was "a rule for making decisions". Ansoff distinguished between objectives, which set the goals; and strategy, which set the path to the goals. He also highlighted that a key point to consider is that most decision-making is restricted by the existence of limited resources. This makes strategic decision-making difficult.

Ansoff's work led to a resurgence of strategic planning leading to SMART goals, forecasts and targets. However, even Ansoff recognized that his own framework could lead to the infamous "paralysis by analysis". A criticism of strategic thinking put forward by the "intuitive management" school of thought is that action is very much louder than mere words.

Finally, Ansoff's work was original and paradigm-breaking in the 1960s. However, given the significant changes in technology, society and globalization consistently outlined in this guide, how relevant is Ansoff's theory in 2014? To investigate further, refer back to the video clip of a lecture by Gary Hamel (details given in concept 2: Change, page 6).

Internal and external stakeholders (AO2)

A stakeholder can be a person, group or system that affects or can be affected by an organization's action.

Internal stakeholders include but are not limited to:

- employees
- shareholders
- managers and the CEO or head of the company.

External stakeholders include:

- suppliers
- customers
- special interest or pressure groups including NGOs
- competitors
- local and national government.

Stakeholder interests (AO2)

All of the stakeholders listed above could have an interest in a company's performance for a variety of reasons. Table 1.4.1 gives examples.

Stakeholder	Will have an interest in:
Owners/ shareholders	profit growth, vision, liquidity, efficiency
Government	taxation (direct and indirect), compliance with legislation such as health and safety
Senior management	financial performance, customer perception, profit and sales targets
Non-managerial staff	pay, conditions, job security
Customers	value, service, quality, ethical considerations
Creditors	liquidity, gearing
Local community	social responsibility, jobs, environment

Table 1.4.1 Different stakeholders' interests in a company

It can be very difficult for any company to be able to satisfy all these interests at the same time. Some stakeholders will be very happy with a company's performance while others could be disappointed.

The following example illustrates possible areas of mutual benefit and conflict between stakeholders.

Apple today announced financial results for the fourth calendar quarter of 2013 compared to the fourth quarter of 2012.

For the first quarter, Apple posted revenue of US$57.6 billion and net quarterly profit of US$13.1 billion, or US$14.50 per diluted share, compared to revenue of US$54.5 billion and net quarterly profit of US$13.1 billion, or US$13.87 per diluted share in the year-ago quarter.

Gross margin was 37.9% compared to 38.6% in the year-ago quarter, with international sales accounting for 63% of revenue. Apple also declared a dividend payment of US$3.05 per share, payable on February 13 to shareholders as of the close of trading on February 10. The company currently holds US$158.8 billion in cash and marketable securities.

Apple had previously issued guidance for the quarter of revenues between US$55–58 billion, with a gross margin of between 36.5 and 37.5%.

Apple sold a record 51 million iPhones in the quarter, up from 47.8 million in the same time period last year, and the company has now sold 472.3 million smartphones in total. It sold 26 million iPads, a new record, up from 22.86 million last year. Apple has now sold 195 million tablets. It sold 4.8 million Macs during the quarter, compared to 4.06 million in the year-ago period.

"We are really happy with our record iPhone and iPad sales, the strong performance of our Mac products and the continued growth of iTunes, Software and Services," said Tim Cook, Apple's CEO. "We love having the most satisfied, loyal and engaged customers, and are continuing to invest heavily in our future to make their experiences with our products and services even better."

Apple shareholders and market analysts reacted negatively to these financial releases and by the end of trading, Apple's shares had fallen by 8%. Apple is under increasing pressure to come up with new innovative products and market analysts are concerned that these results although in line with expectations cannot be maintained throughout the rest of 2014 without a significant disruptive technological change.

Source: Adapted from www.macrumors.com

A number of mutually beneficial aspects can be identified:

- The sales growth of its core products of iPhones, iPads and iMacs would have pleased some of Apple's investors and the board of directors.
- Apple customers clearly show brand loyalty and this can be very beneficial to the company given that it adopts a "high-price strategy" relative to the competition.
- The US government will enjoy the benefits of Apple's growth through higher employment, consumer confidence and of course through taxes paid on Apple's profits.

However, we can identify a number of conflicts:

- Shareholders and market analysts (who can influence share purchase decisions through their recommendations) are clearly expecting more from Apple given that share prices in the company fell even after this set of impressive results.
- Additionally, some shareholders may question why Apple has such a large cash balance sitting in its bank account. Could this not be used for research into new and innovative products?
- Finally, Apple's CEO Tim Cook does not give any detail of new products in development, instead simply mentioning funds to make customers' "experiences with [Apple] products and services even better".

The ability to analyse and evaluate possible areas of stakeholder conflict and mutual benefit is an important assessment skill for the IB Business Management course.

Setting the scene

In the external environment, we look at a whole range of external factors outside the individual control of the firm. These factors can have considerable impacts, both positive and negative, on business decision-making.

Many students will be familiar with PEST analysis, which is used to help a business examine which **p**olitical, **e**conomic, **s**ocial and **t**echnological external factors will have an impact on its decision-making.

PESTLE analysis is an enlarged version of the more traditional PEST analysis. In addition, some writers refer to an enlarged PEST as PEST-G where G represents **g**reen or environmental factors.

In PESTLE analysis, the additional E could refer to **e**nvironmental or **e**thical factors and the L to **l**egal influences on decision-making.

This unit looks at business analyses from PEST to SLEPT to PESTLE (or PEST-G) and then STEEPLE. First, consider the case study below.

THE INDIAN FILM INDUSTRY IN 2008

The Indian Hindi language movie industry – popularly known as Bollywood – is stepping up its fight against film piracy (illegal copying) both at home and overseas.

Infringement of copyright laws is rampant in India. A recent study estimated that India's entertainment industry loses $4 billion and 800 000 jobs because of piracy. The figures are higher if we include those Western countries such as the United States and the UK that are home to large Indian populations where Bollywood films provide an important link to their homeland.

Ever-increasing technology is making the copying of movies easier, home theatre systems are available and the impending economic recession is reducing discretionary spending on items such as visits to the cinema. For these reasons, the trend in buying pirated DVDs of new films is likely to continue unless government legislation, penalties and the legal process are tightened up.

For the Indian film industry a possible SLEPT analysis could be carried out – and extended to SLEPT-E – as follows:

Social	(S)	Societal needs include expatriates' needs to watch Indian movies.
Legal	(L)	The legal framework needs to support the film-makers against illegal copying.
Economic	(E)	The economic downturn has reduced spending on leisure.
Political	(P)	The government is trying to enforce a legal framework to protect film-makers.
Technological	(T)	The ability to copy and distribute movies is increasing.
Ethical	(E)	The ethical factor includes the attitudes of the "pirates" and the consumers who are purchasing these illegal copies.

It is important to note that not all the external factors in a SLEPT analysis are represented as threats. Firms or industries can look at opportunities such as supportive government assistance or favourable legal rulings, which can justify a certain course of action being taken.

The key point to remember is that these factors are outside the control of firms but they must be incorporated into their decision-making framework and be considered in developing any strategic aim.

From PESTLE to STEEPLE

The full external environment model has been now broadened to STEEPLE, which includes all the relevant external factors that can have an impact on business decision-making. Not all factors will be of equal magnitude or strength. However, failure to observe and react to any of them could be devastating, as the following two examples will illustrate.

Consequences of changes in STEEPLE factors (AO3)

Consequences for business objectives and strategy (AO3)

Links to concept 2: Change and concept 3: Innovation

THE MOMENT IT ALL WENT WRONG FOR KODAK

The world's biggest film company filed for bankruptcy yesterday, beaten by the digital revolution.

… this is a company we care about – at least if we were born before 1986 or so, when Kodak was at the peak of its commercial powers. A hundred years earlier George Eastman, the company's founder, had invented roll film, which replaced photographic plates and allowed photography to become a hobby of the masses. Kodak did not quite own the 20th century, but it did become the curator of our memories.

But 1986 was arguably also the year when Kodak, a company that for so long was the emblem of US industrial innovation, began to be eaten by others, notably from Japan. Japanese companies had learned to innovate too – and more quickly.

Kodak was the great inventor. In 1900, it unveiled the Box Brownie camera. "You push the button, we do the rest," ran the advertising campaign. Kodachrome film, the standard for movie-makers as well as generations of still photographers because of its incredible definition and archival longevity, was introduced in 1936 and only went out of production in 2009. Nor should we forget the Instamatic, the camera with the little cartridges of film that spared us the fumbling of trying to get film to spool properly. Between 1963 and 1970 the company sold 50 million Instamatic cameras.

The trouble began around 20 years ago, with the decline of film photography. In the 1990s, Kodak poured billions into developing technology for taking pictures using mobile phones and other digital devices. But it held back from developing digital cameras for the mass market for fear of killing its all-important film business. Others, such as the Japanese firm Canon, rushed in.

So who invented the digital camera? Ironically, Kodak did – or, rather, a company engineer called Steve Sasson, who put together a toaster-sized device that could save images using electronic circuits.

It was an astonishing achievement. And it happened in 1975, long before the digital age. Mr Sasson and his colleagues were met with blank faces when they unveiled their device to Kodak's bosses. Even the inventor didn't see its full potential.

"We were looking at it as a distant possibility. Maybe a line from the technical report written at the time sums it up best: 'The camera described in this report represents a first attempt demonstrating a photographic system which may, with improvements in technology, substantially impact the way pictures will be taken in the future.' But in reality, we had no idea."

For Kodak's leaders, going digital meant killing film, smashing the company's core competency to make way for the new. Mr Sasson saw in hindsight that he had not exactly won them over when he unveiled his toy.

Even before film began to fade, other manufacturers, notably Fuji, were nibbling at the company's dominance: at the 1984 Olympics it was Fuji that supplied the official film, after Kodak declined the opportunity. And Kodak's efforts in the last 10 years to shift its focus to consumer and industrial printers have faltered: at the time of writing, the company has posted losses in six of the last seven years.

In 1976, Kodak sold 90% of the photographic film in the United States and 85% of the cameras; 10 years later it still employed 145 000 people worldwide compared with a global payroll today of 18 000. Historians may one day conclude that most of the company's slow unravelling can be traced to the failure of its leaders to recognize the huge potential of Mr Sasson's invention.

Don Strickland, a former vice-president, who left the company in 1993 because even then he couldn't persuade it to manufacture and market a digital camera, put it this way: "We developed the world's first consumer digital camera but we could not get approval to launch or sell it because of fear of the effects on the film market."

Source: Adapted from the www.independent.co.uk, 20 January 2012.

SUMMARY

Senior managers failed to see the potential of the new digital camera as they were concerned that it would eat into their own company's dominant market share in the photographic film market. Kodak had a history of successful innovation so it is unclear why the digital camera was not fully accepted.

Perhaps the more critical factor was the company's systematic failure to respond to the changing technological and competitive environment it was operating in, even though the business was innovating disruptively. Two of the STEEPLE factors were changing before their eyes but senior managers seemed oblivious and wished for the status quo or current state to remain.

THE CASE OF NOKIA

Nokia's success began about 20 years ago with the rapid adoption of cellphones. The company recorded tremendous success among users because every cellphone the Finnish manufacturer launched was very easy to use: users learned instantly how to place phone calls and take advantage of the handset's features. But one day everything suddenly changed. The change was noticed by a journalist, who immediately wrote to Nokia as an individual to warn them about forthcoming failure.

Interestingly, his letter – sent on 18 August 2008 – triggered lots of phone calls from Nokia employees and executives, which finally ended with the journalist being offered a personal meeting with an executive. The journalist had the chance to explain in person what he thought of the company and to warn the executive that Nokia was heading in the wrong direction. A significant competitor was about to have a disruptive impact on Nokia's business model. What's interesting is that the executive himself agreed, but this didn't matter at the time, due to the company's cellphone strategy.

When the iPhone launched in 2008, the same executive had ordered some Apple handsets and took one home. He was amazed that that his four-year-old daughter learned to use it immediately. Finally, amazed by the cellphone's magic, the little girl asked her father before going to bed: "Can I take that magic telephone and put it under my pillow tonight?"

That was the moment when the Nokia executive understood that his company was in trouble.

Nokia has never recovered.

SUMMARY

- In 2007 Nokia had a global market share of over 40%, sales of 38 billion euros and profits of 7 billion.
- By 2012 Nokia's market share was 18%, sales were 20 billion euros and profits were negative 1 billion.
- By 2013, with the Nokia mobile devices and services division sold to Microsoft, market share had fallen to 5%.

Source: Adapted from an article by Istvan Fekete published on www.iphoneincanada.com, 10 October 2013.

The condensed idea of this unit

Businesses regularly have to review and update their knowledge of the external environment in which they operate. Given the existence of rapid technological and social change in an era of hyper-competition, businesses that fail to track market trends or changes in consumer behaviour will lose their place in the market.

Tracking these changes will require significant financial and human resources. An organization must try to be flexible and adaptable so that responding to change can be carried out as quickly as possible, without of course neglecting the original vision or mission, which may have established the business in the first instance. This is no easy task to achieve.

The following are opportunities for you to use a STEEPLE analysis in your preparation for both external and internal assessment:

- A STEEPLE analysis should be presented as a tool for decision-making for the IB Business Management internal assessment for HL.
- In order to guide preparation for paper 1 – the pre-issued case study for both HL and SL – it is also recommended that a STEEPLE analysis be undertaken.

Setting the scene

Business textbooks have assumed that all firms should try to grow and evolve. Given the rapid social and technological changes we have outlined already, there are a number of reasons why growth and evolution are important.

Growth allows organizations to become larger and gain greater financial muscle. A larger organization can withstand changes in the external environment much more easily than a smaller firm.

Greater risks yielding potentially much higher rewards can be taken if a firm grows. These risks may yield new innovations that will allow a business to **evolve** sustainably.

Increased growth and profitability can not only provide security but also entice additional investors and capital. This reinforces the upward spiral of success.

Or so it seems.

Currently, serious questions are being asked about the virtue of being a large organization. Issues of management control, communication and hubris (overconfidence) are now being voiced by some of the biggest and most successful industry leaders. We have already seen (in unit 1.3, page 18) the near disaster that threatened Lego when the company tried to expand too quickly and in an unfocused manner. This unit will try to provide a balanced assessment of the risks and returns.

Economies and diseconomies of scale (AO2)

The benefits of growth summarized above make a strong case for being a large organization. An important concept used to explain the advantages of being a large organization is the existence of economies of scale.

Economies of scale (AO2)

Economies of scale can be defined as follows. As the scale of operation changes, firms can benefit from reductions in long-run unit costs of production. These reductions can be obtained internally as the individual firm grows or externally if the whole industry expands.

A number of large firms such as telecommunication companies or, until recently, car manufacturers have been seemingly able to experience almost unlimited economies of scale. Small firms with their limited initial start-up capital and small market share cannot hope to match these cost advantages.

Table 1.6.1 gives examples of some economies of scale that can be found in various aspects of business.

Diseconomies of scale (AO2)

There are also arguments for remaining a small organization. Many larger firms have experienced periods where long-run unit costs actually increase, giving rise to the phenomenon known as diseconomies of scale. The arguments here can be technical and feature principally in economics textbooks but we can note that as a firm grows the following applies:

- It can become harder to control and manage the business effectively. Additional layers of management are required or spans of control may grow; mistakes and quality problems may arise. These will raise unit or average costs.

- Communication becomes more difficult with longer chains of command. This can lead to workers experiencing confusion and isolation, again perhaps leading to errors and quality control concerns. This can also raise unit costs.

- Large trans-national businesses may struggle to control and coordinate their supply chain process, which may stress across a number of regions and time zones. This process is a topic for HL only and will be explained in further detail in unit 5.5.

Type of economy of scale	Internal (I) or external (E)	Example
Financial	I	Finance costs are reduced because of increased collateral and lenders' confidence
Purchasing	I	Raw materials can be sourced more cheaply if bought in bulk
Risk-bearing	I	Large companies can risk entering new markets and finance prototypes of products which may or may not be successful
Marketing	I	Advertising using media with very large customer reach (e.g. satellite television) lowers unit costs dramatically
Research and development	E	As an industry grows, firms can share research facilities, reducing the costs of new product development
Training labour and pool of available labour growing as industry expands	E	As an industry grows, local labour migrates to other areas and people gain skills through work experience and/or attending training colleges

Table 1.6.1 Economies of scale

Key learning point

The application of economies and diseconomies of scale in a business will be directly influenced by a number of factors including the size of the market the firm operates in, its financial status and the vision of the owners.

The merits of small versus large organizations (AO3)

First we need to define what a business organization is. The legal definition of a "small" business varies by country and industry. In the United States a small business is one which employs fewer than 100 employees, in the European Union the figure is 50 employees, and in Australia, fewer than 20.

We will use the United States' measure as our definition but we must be aware that other indicators of size, such as market capitalization, could be used. Market capitalization is the number of shares a business owns multiplied by the current share (stock) price and sales revenue. Profit is rarely used as an indication of an organization's size.

Remaining small

The existence of diseconomies of scale is the most powerful argument for remaining small. Market size, the availability of finance and motivation remain key drivers to remain small.

Profit satisficing and forgoing additional growth

A number of small organizations, such as Scholastic and Lavazza, have decided to remain focused on a few key markets and have ignored potential growth opportunities. The reasons seem principally to stem from the need to keep control and retain the original vision of the company, free from outside (or non-family) interests and outside interference, which might occur if additional capital or shareholders were sought.

In these companies, profits are still an important driver for taking risks. Unaware of the potential profit to be earned, every publisher apart from Scholastic turned down J K Rowling's original "Harry Potter" story – it was seen as a risky proposition.

A key factor determining the size of the organization is the original vision of the founding members. It is hard to argue with the success of family-owned companies that have had this continuity of control, such as Lego, Ferrari and Disney, although there have been many recent challenges.

Profit satisficing for a small business is an objective that some readers may query. In essence, satisficing is a goal to achieve a maximum level of profit – just enough to keep the entrepreneur motivated (in economics this is termed as "normal profit") – but enough so that the business owner has time to pursue other interests or passions outside the day-to-day running of an organization. Remaining small allows for this option.

Remaining small: the link to globalization

We must also remember that some firms have decided to remain small because they can take advantage of the benefits of globalization and outsource elements of their operations. They could, for example, subcontract production to other suppliers in lower-cost countries, or outsource customer service functions while keeping control of their intellectual property and strategic direction. Improved global ICT opportunities have encouraged this process.

Conclusion

The size of an organization and, as we shall see, the structure is closely tied to the objectives and vision of the owner. We must remember that at one time all large businesses were small businesses and empirical studies show that small businesses are vital to develop entrepreneurial spirit in a country.

The role of economies of scale in determining the size of a business cannot be denied. For important considerations, such as economic sustainability in a highly competitive market environment, economies of scale allow consumers to enjoy a wide range of goods and services at lower cost.

How big is too big? This is an important question. Some pressure groups, such as the Occupy movement and the anti-globalization movements, have raised a number of concerns. As with most judgments in business management, the final answer may have to start with "It depends on…".

Internal and external growth (AO2)

Growth for an organization can be achieved in a number of different ways: chiefly organically (involving internal growth) and inorganically (through external growth). We will also consider the growth strategy of franchising, which could be classified as an external method of growth given that franchising requires external entrepreneurs (the franchisee) to invest in the business ideas and intellectual property of the original business owner (the franchisor.) However, strict franchise agreements exist which imply that franchisees have little room to improvise or create their own innovations; therefore, some have argued that franchising could be internal growth driven by external finance.

Internal growth – definition

A business can decide to grow organically – referred to as internal growth – by trying to capture a bigger slice of total market share by selling more of its existing products.

External growth – definition

A business can also try to grow inorganically – referred to as external growth – by becoming involved in:

- joint ventures
- strategic alliances
- mergers and acquisitions
- takeovers.

The following section requires students to undertake a great deal of evaluation. To avoid duplication of material in this section, we summarize some elements that can be used to help students discuss and evaluate a specific growth method in the form of a seven "C" model or framework.

The seven "C" framework for growth

This framework (for internal and external growth) can be applied to all discussion and evaluation questions. The content will need to be changed depending on the topic being evaluated.

When discussing a growth strategy a business will need to take the following factors into account:

- **Cost** – whether a firm decides to grow internally or externally, the financing of the new strategy will have to be considered. Will the firm have to borrow or can it use retained earnings?

- **Control** – clearly, the larger a firm grows the more difficult it will be to manage. Will the structure of the organization have to change? Will spans of control have to rise?

- **Conflict** – how will change be managed? Will there be any resistance from internal and external stakeholders to the new strategy? If two firms combine as in a merger and acquisition, will there need to be redundancies to avoid duplication of roles?

- **Compromise** – will the vision of the company be compromised by growth? Second, if the firm needs to attract more capital to finance this strategy, it may have to give up elements of ownership, perhaps with resulting impacts on objectives and vision.

- **Communication** – as the firm grows, can we ensure that communication channels will be effective to ensure that everyone is aware of the process of change?

- **Culture** clash – can a firm assume that, if it grows externally by either joint venture or merger, the combined organizations will be able to work together? As we shall see later when we consider Charles Handy's work on cultural imbalance in unit 2.5, it is important that the cultures of the two organizations fit. The disastrous merger of Time Warner and AOL is a good example of the problems that can occur if they do not. Evidence indicates that unless the culture of the new organization is appropriate, then strategic success is unlikely (see also concept 6: Culture).

- **Confusion** – in the case of joint ventures and mergers, clear lines of accountability and responsibility need to be drawn so that subordinates know to whom they are to report. This is especially true when the expansion involves moving into international markets and firms operate over a number of time zones.

Judging the success of a growth strategy

Below are possible lines of inquiry and some key questions that would help a business to decide whether a growth strategy would be successful:

- A key evaluative tool when reaching a judgment is time. How long will it be before the business can judge the success of the strategy? Does the firm need to consider the short and long run?

- Does the business need to focus on sales, profits or costs? Does it need to consult with stakeholders six months after the strategy has been put in place? What will be the nature of the external environment in six months' time?

- What can businesses compare the success of a merger to? (This question is impossible to answer precisely as we do not have any financial information about two merged companies if they have not merged.)

External growth methods

Joint ventures and strategic alliances

A joint venture or strategic alliance can be defined as an agreement for two or more firms to enter into a project to share risks, capital and expertise in order for both firms to benefit. Not surprisingly, joint ventures usually occur between firms in the same industry. Strategic alliances are effectively the same but a little less formal in structure. With joint ventures and strategic alliances there is no transfer of ownership.

If a firm wishes to enter a foreign market, it may well form a joint venture with a firm already situated in that country in order to take advantage of local knowledge of the market or labour expertise. Forming a joint venture with firms that are already established in their markets or regions could result in considerable savings in cost and time.

Mergers and acquisitions, and takeovers

Some business writers mean the same thing when using these terms. However, mergers and acquisitions normally imply some mutual agreement to join together whereas a takeover can occur involuntarily; it can take place even if one firm does not wish to be taken over by another.

There are usually three types of merger and acquisition. These are listed below, with the common reason for entering into them:

Horizontal merger

- Definition: the deliberate decision by a business to acquire the intellectual property (products or successful brands) of a rival company operating in the same market and industry.
- Justification: to acquire instant additional market share (subject to government approval), economies of scale and, it is hoped, the creation of "synergy". Synergy refers to the argument proposed that in the case of large mergers huge gains would be made. This has been simplified to the $1 + 1 = 3$ justification.

Vertical merger

- Definition: the merger of businesses operating at different levels in an industry's supply chain.
- Justification: the need to control the supply chain process either forwards (towards the customer – or "downstream" to use a business buzzword) or backwards (to monitor and secure raw material supplies "upstream").

Conglomerate

- Definition: the deliberate attempt by a business to acquire a new firm in an unfamiliar market or industry.
- Justification: to eliminate the need for costly research and development or spending vast sums of money on developing a new brand. Risk-bearing economies of scale could be earned quickly.

Mergers and acquisitions – discussion

If we take into account the seven "C" framework for evaluating mergers and acquisitions and then look at examples from the business world, it has to be said that in many cases mergers and acquisitions have not been as successful as CEOs would like to believe. Shareholder value has not necessarily increased. When senior managers from one or other of the merged companies have little experience in the industry or product markets they are now managing in the newly created, enlarged merger company, things can go badly wrong.

Hubris (overconfidence) on the part of the CEOs and senior managers has been observed in a number of high-profile mergers, with disastrous effects for internal and external stakeholders. This was particularly true in the case of the merger between Time Warner and AOL. Up to and including 2013, this merger produced the biggest loss in US corporate history.

Franchising

It might be tempting to focus purely on the most successful franchising company – McDonald's. We would see how the franchising strategy can prove to be rewarding for the company selling the idea (the franchisor) and the entrepreneur who wishes to put up capital in order to obtain the intellectual property rights in delivering the good or service (the franchisee).

IB Learner Profile
Inquiry ?

The McDonald's business model is not typical, and it would be wrong to assume that all franchises work in the same way. Investigating a franchise model that operates in your country or the country in which you study would be a fruitful exercise. You might wish to refer back to the example of the global growth of the Subway franchise (concept 1: Globalization, page 5). This could be an excellent place to start your inquiry.

Table 1.6.1 notes a few generic ideas about the effectiveness of the franchise model of external growth.

Benefits to the franchisor	Benefits to the franchisee
The franchisor is able to increase brand awareness of a successful product over larger geographical areas at minimal cost	The franchisee is able to run a new business with an established brand name, thus reducing the need for initial start-up costs such as advertising and market research
After initial payment to secure the franchise, the franchisor is able to receive royalties with no risk	The franchisee will receive training, equipment and expertise from the franchisor
The franchisee will be motivated to perform at a high standard to keep the franchise and because he or she has ownership. The franchisor gains a committed stakeholder to his or her business model	If the franchise agreement includes supplying the franchisee with raw materials and ingredients (as in the case of McDonald's), then significant economies of scale could be experienced
Ultimately, the franchise model will promote quicker growth for the company than by growing organically	The franchisee is able to use a potential global advantage in terms of large-scale advertising

Table 1.6.1 Selected characteristics of the franchise model

Of course there will be drawbacks to the franchise model, mostly dependent on the type of agreement that has been signed between the two parties. Some franchise agreements are relatively flexible while others allow for very little entrepreneurial initiative on the part of the franchisee.

Discussion of franchising

We can highlight a few drawbacks to this model apart from those relating to the agreement:

- Franchising encourages standardization of vision, service and product developments, which some entrepreneurs may, after time, come to regret as they may feel that their creativity is being "boxed in".

- A poorly performing franchise in one area can have an impact on the reputation of others locally. This point could also be extended to the problems of trying to establish a consistent reliable global brand.

- The Starbucks model of clustering franchises, for example, has actually led to competition between franchises, to the detriment of the franchisees. One franchisee cannibalizes the market share of others, with some franchisees ultimately being eliminated.

Judgment and other lines of inquiry

Look back at the seven "C" evaluation model on page 27 and apply this to the role of franchising.

The global franchise business was worth an estimated 1 trillion dollars in 2008. This domination of franchises and the ubiquity of franchise stores in high streets and malls around the world has been a symbol of globalization that a number of stakeholders have taken objection to. The steadily rising trend in franchising is a recent phenomenon with some franchise businesses such as Subway having enjoyed superlative growth.

Others franchisors have found this external growth method hard to control and are currently rethinking their use of this model. Starbucks is a good example of rampant growth in franchising but the company is now having doubts about the merits of this growth strategy.

For sole traders, the final assessment may boil down to a key dilemma. The risks associated with running a franchise (despite the initial high fees which have to be paid) are smaller than those for sole traders starting a business of their own, but entrepreneurial innovation will be limited.

Globalization – effect on business growth and evolution

The impacts of multinationals on host countries (AO3)

You are advised to read concept 1: Globalization in conjunction with this unit.

Globalization can be defined as the growing integration, interdependence and general connectedness of the world through markets, labour mobility and capital transfer.

IB Learner Profile

Inquirers and open-minded ?

You are advised to update your knowledge regularly in this area as the arguments surrounding the impact of globalization and the impact of multinational activity on stakeholders have been subject to considerable discussion and debate. With the recent financial crisis and "credit crunch" now behind us, the debate in globalization has shifted from the transfer of physical capital and resources towards concerns over the level and ease of human resource transfer. There have been recent calls for more "protection" of local economies and workforces with less openness – effectively calling for more regulation and restricted immigration. Surely these are the perceived enemies of continued integration and globalization?

Multinational or trans-national

A multinational company (MNC) or trans-national corporation is an organization that **operates, owns** and **controls** resources outside its country of origin. A company is not considered an MNC if it merely sells abroad.

What does a typical MNC look like? It may own research and development facilities to generate new intellectual property ideas in the host country as well as carrying out advertising, marketing and strategic direction but may allow customer service operations or manufacturing overseas (this is known as offshoring). Local managers may also be transferred frequently around the different international markets to increase knowledge and experience.

As we saw in concept 1: Globalization, Subway's growth as the most successful global franchise operation was fuelled by a desire to expand carefully into global markets. In the space of 24 years, the number of Subway outlets grew from 5 000 to over 41 000. Subway now operates in 105 countries. In 1983 it only operated in one country.

Apple's success as a global brand has been fuelled by its willingness to outsource the production of its portfolio of products to a number of countries in Asia. It has done this despite the inevitable language, cultural and other communication issues that may arise.

Students should not assume that the decision to outsource and have a global supply chain is purely based on lower costs, especially labour costs. Cost advantages are important but these have been present for a long time even dating back to the early 1950s and 1960s where even a 400% cost or wage saving was not enough for a large organization to globalize or use outsourcing in its supply chain.

It is clear from the comments in concept 1 that a range of factors has driven the move to globalization. The factors include:

- the increasing wealth in the developing world

- the need for businesses to be closer to the overseas market to service customer needs more closely

- the potential opportunity for businesses to take advantage of a host country's desires to see more MNCs operating in the country, for the reasons outlined in Table 1.6.2.

Benefit to the host country	Discussion
Creation of new jobs, employment opportunities	Jobs created may be lower down in the hierarchy with limited senior management positions for local workers
Revenue-raising opportunities for the host government	Some MNCs will be able to repatriate funds offshore due to the increasing ability of tax-free havens
Importation of new technology, skills and management techniques	This is a strong benefit especially in Asia which has become the largest outsourcing market. Examples include: • India and software • China and manufacturing
Increase in choice of goods and services available for host country citizens	Will local consumers be able to afford these goods and services bound for Western markets? Unfair competition for local producers may increase unemployment in some industries

Table 1.6.2 The impact of MNCs on the host country

IB Learner Profile

Inquiry **?**

The cases of Ireland and Singapore

Interested students are encouraged to investigate the following two cases.

First, carry out research into the experiences of the Irish economy, which went through a significant transformation by encouraging MNC activity. The consequences of embracing globalization have been both positive and negative for the Irish economy.

Second, look at Singapore's spectacular rise as an economic force, which was driven by a need to work with and learn from MNCs in areas where the country did not have any expertise. These areas included pharmaceuticals, banking and financial services, and niche innovative technology with a high requirement for research and development. The growth of the economy and the creation of related businesses by local Singaporeans have been impressive.

The activity of MNCs and globalization are credited by journals such as *The Economist* as being the most important driving forces in creating wealth in the economy. However, their impact and influence has been challenged by pressure groups such as the Occupy movement and it is left up to you to decide from your perspective which is the more persuasive view.

Setting the scene

This unit considers some of the planning tools available to help businesses put their aims and objectives into a practical format so that the decision-making process can begin. This topic is designated as HL only.

We will look at each of the planning tools in turn given that the depth of teaching required is **AO2**. Students should be prepared to use these tools not only in final exams but also in internal assessments and possibly extended essays. One could also argue that they could be used in everyday life.

When using these tools, it is important to remember that their value to an organization will depend on the quality of the quantitative and qualitative data being used and the management style and values or beliefs of the final decision-maker. The last section critiques these planning tools and argues that for some entrepreneurs intuition or "gut feeling" may play an important role in deciding a suitable course of action.

The fishbone or Ishikawa diagram

This planning technique is slightly different from other models we will consider, in that it does not offer quantifiable or qualitative solutions to decision-making problems. Instead its purpose is to identify causes of a problem that may exist in an organization; it is often referred to as a cause-and-effect diagram and can help with implementing solutions as well as identifying causes.

The diagram is constructed as follows:

- The basic problem of concern to be considered is entered at the right-hand end of the diagram of the main "bone". In Figure 1.7.1, it is a lost order from a customer.

- "Brainstorming" and discussions are carried out, usually to add possible causes to the other bones, and typically categories such as materials, machines, HR issues and operational methods are used to classify the possible causes of the problem.

- The causes can be subdivided to add greater detail and information. For example, on the "environment" branch details such as seasonal or heat factors are added. However, the aim is not to make the diagram too cluttered.

- When the fishbone is complete, the manager is left with a complete picture of all possible root causes of the identified problem.

- Further discussion takes place, usually in a group, to ascertain the most likely root causes of the issue. This can be a time-consuming process.

The fishbone diagram is a useful visual tool and if made available to a group it can provide a shared opportunity to help identify causes of a particular problem. Once a final root cause has been determined, it will be up to the manager to test a hypothesis using data to see whether it is a statistically significant cause.

Decision trees

Decision trees are regarded as a quantitative decision-making technique. They are constructed as follows:

- Squares (decision nodes) are points where a choice has to be made between different courses of action (e.g. develop a new product or advertise more widely).

- Circles (probability nodes) are points where there is a chance event which may lead to success or failure. P is the probability of success: if P is close to 1 there is a probability of success; if P is close to zero the probability is for failure.

- The next step is to calculate the expected monetary values at each of the probability nodes.

- Using Figure 1.7.2, for the first node this would be:

    $5 million $\times$ 0.75 + -$2 million $\times$ 0.25 = $3.25 million

- The second node would show:

    $3 million $\times$ 0.6 + $1 million $\times$ 0.4m = $2.2 million

- Then the costs of each new decision – either to develop a new product or modify a product – need to be taken into account and the higher of these two values will become the favoured outcome.

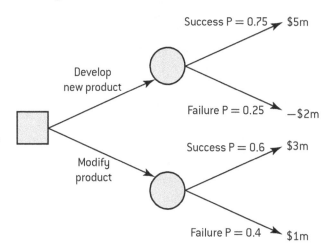

Figure 1.7.2 An example of a decision tree

A decision tree allows firms to:

- visually represent alternative courses of action (in Figure 1.7.2, new product development or modification of an existing product)

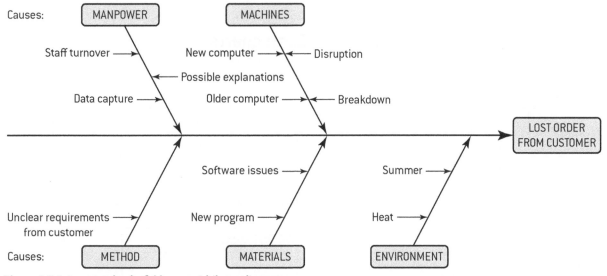

Figure 1.7.1 An example of a fishbone or Ishikawa diagram

- quantify the outcomes of each action in terms of revenue expected
- identify individual probabilities of success or failure
- view the costs of implementing each course of action
- decide on an appropriate course of action based on quantitative factors only.

Lewin's force field analysis

This planning tool is based on way in which an organization is regarded as comprising competing forces (see Figure 1.7.3). One type, called driving forces, can push it in one direction to achieve a goal and these are met with resistance by other forces not wishing to move, called restraining forces:

- Driving forces try to establish a new equilibrium or status quo.
- Restraining forces try to restrict a new equilibrium being achieved.

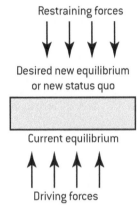

Figure 1.7.3 Lewin's force field analysis

In order to effect change the driving forces need to be able to move the organization to a new status quo and reduce the power or influence of the restraining forces. This is easier said than done. A number of operational tactics will be needed to achieve successful implementation.

Dearden and Foster (1992) argue:

- The team charged with implementing change must have authority to implement change, which is understood by those affected by that change.
- The board of directors through the CEO must indicate that change is necessary and extol clearly the virtues of this change for the whole organization.
- The change process, including contingencies, must be clearly communicated to all stakeholders early, including (as accurately as possible) time lines for implementation.
- Early successful outcomes of the change must be clearly communicated and celebrated.
- A constant reminder of the goals and objectives of the strategy change must be highlighted prominently around the workplace.

It would seem that clear effective communication plays a crucial part in the change and planning process.

We will now look at a typical example (adapted from www.mindtools.com) of a strategic change within an organization and use force field analysis to help us understand the competing forces.

The change

Our example features an organization looking to reduce unit costs of production to become more competitive, and reduce errors and defects. The organization's leaders decide to introduce new technology in the workplace to boost productivity and raise quality.

The process

The board of directors instruct a senior management team to investigate additional drivers to move the company to a new equilibrium while recognizing that restraining forces will exist. The senior management team is to rank the magnitude of the forces, with 1 being weak and 5 being strong.

Drivers

Customers looking to generate higher value at lower prices	4
Speed of production	2
Productivity increases	3
Control of maintenance costs	1

Restrainers

Loss of overtime for line staff	3
Fear of new technology	3
Disruption: time for implementation	1
Cost of transfer of technology	3
Environmental impact	1

Moving to a new equilibrium

A number of the restrainers affect the workers directly. Staff may become uncooperative if change is forced upon them so a key tactic in the change strategy is to try and weaken the restrainers rather than force the drivers. The following are examples of how this might be done:

- By training staff (involving an increase in costs) fear of technology could be reduced.
- The board of directors could convince staff that the changes are necessary to ensure survival and security for the majority of employees.
- Staff could be encouraged by the prospect of upskilling.
- An increase in productivity could lead to wage increases as long as the competitive objective in the new strategy is not undermined.
- The environmental impact of the change to new technology might satisfy local community concerns.

Gantt charts

There are a number of different types of Gantt chart. A simplified version is shown in Figure 1.7.4.

Source: Adapted from www.gantt.com

Task name	Q1 2014				Q2 2014			Q3 2014	
	Dec 13	Jan 14	Feb 14	Mar 14	Apr 14	May 14	Jun 14	Jul 14	Aug 14
Planning	▓	▓	▓						
Research			▓	▓					
Design				▓					
Implementation					▓	▓			
Follow up								▓	

Figure 1.7.4 An example of a Gantt chart

A Gantt chart, commonly used in project management to help with planning and the allocation of resources such as labour and materials, is one of the most popular and useful ways of showing activities (tasks or events) displayed against time. From the chart shown in Figure 1.7.4 the business can see that it will need to allocate resources to complete the planning stage from Dec 13 to the end of Feb 14. Research will begin at the start of Feb 14 and finish some time in mid-March. As there is some overlap between these activities the business will need to ensure that it has adequate resources to ensure that these activities finish on time. Otherwise completion of the whole project will be delayed and there could be substantial financial penalties.

As in Figure 1.7.4, on the left of a Gantt chart is a list of the activities and along the top is a suitable timescale. A bar represents each activity; the position and length of the bar reflects the start date, duration and end date of the activity. This allows you to see at a glance:

- what the various activities are
- when each activity begins and ends
- how long each activity is scheduled to last
- where activities overlap with other activities, and by how much
- the start and end date of the whole project.

To summarize, a Gantt chart shows you what has to be done (the activities) and when (the schedule).

The Gantt chart is often drawn to accompany a network or critical path analysis to assist with planning but, from 2016, network analysis has been removed from the *IB Business Management Guide*.

As part of the research proposal for the HL internal assessment, students are expected to produce an action plan to show they are going to plan and tackle the research process, the analytical frameworks to be used and the final conclusion and recommendations. A Gantt chart mapping out students' activities is a very useful tool to employ.

The value of planning tools (AO3)

This section considers the value to an organization of the different planning tools described above. First, we will consider the decision tree. In doing this we will be able to see some of the issues involved when trying to ascertain the value to business decision-making of any of the planning tools described in this unit.

Decision trees: the problems

The probabilities used in a decision tree, which are integral in calculating the expected values, can sometimes seem to have come out of thin air. How were they calculated and on what basis? Some managers use experience or perhaps secondary data to calculate these probabilities but how can we objectively measure the probability of success or failure?

External and non-financial factors, which could influence the final decision, are not included in the actual analysis when calculating the expected monetary values.

Finally, the decision tree does not take into account the attitude to risk of the entrepreneur and by assumption the level of intuitive management present in the organization. For example, Richard Branson was warned repeatedly that setting up an airline to compete with British Airways on the popular transatlantic route between the UK and the United States was futile, especially given the low prices Virgin was charging and small predicted revenue streams.

The decision-tree approach would most likely have suggested that Branson should not enter this difficult market. He did and was successful.

Summary

Link to TOK thought question – is business an art or a science?

All of the planning tools' success in assisting organizations relies heavily on the accuracy and quality of the data provided. For Lewin's force field analysis, the magnitude of the drivers and restrainers will depend on the values assigned. For the fishbone or Ishikawa diagram, detailed discussions on causes will need to be collected, analysed and then reviewed in order to come to a final judgment as to which cause of the problem is worth investigating further.

This scientific approach to decision-making has been challenged not only on the problems of collecting accurate and unbiased data. A number of entrepreneurs and decision-makers in the same mould as Sir Richard Branson argue that intuition, past experience and simple "gut feeling" are equally important in deciding an appropriate course of action. Branson is clearly a supporter of Ansoff's assertion that one can have "paralysis by analysis". Steve Jobs famously never looked at balance sheets or other financial documents as CEO of Apple (a fact that was behind his removal as CEO before being rehired and turning the computer company into the world's most valuable brand before his early death).

Planning tools can provide clarity and purpose and if used correctly can allow managers to understand highly complex problems and possible solutions in an easy-to-read form. Managers will hope that this leads to more accurate decision-making. However, it must be said that all business decision-making is a risk. A firm can run into difficulties even if market research data tells it that its new business idea is a sure-fire success. There are no guarantees.

Setting the scene

Go back to the Gary Hamel clip on the future of management (introduced in concept 2: Change, page 6). Watch the clip again before starting units 2.2, 2.3 and 2.4 to see some ideas about the evolving role of management and change within an organization. We will make reference to this rich learning resource as we proceed.

QUESTION FOR REFLECTION

Why does Gary Hamel feel that organizations have to **change** in order to be "fit for human beings" in the 21st century?

Introduction to workforce planning (AO1)

In previous units we have highlighted the fact that businesses face an increasing number of pressures forced on them by changes in the external environment, the growing onset of globalization and the impact of sectoral change. An area of the organization directly affected by these developments is the recruitment planning and management of HR. Firms have had to rethink their workforce planning requirements because of:

- slowing birth rates in the developed world
- the increased ageing of the working population
- the trend towards migration of workers
- the trend towards the new "24/7 economy" (especially in the retail and service sectors).

In this context, **workforce planning** is defined as follows:

the business process for ensuring that an organization has suitable access to talent (potential candidates that have the ability to undertake required activities including decision making) to ensure future business success.

This unit will discuss these external factors and the implications for recruitment, training and appraisal. We will also need to look at internal factors driving workforce planning and the increasing trend towards outsourcing the HR function as part of an overall strategic move.

Demographic changes in the developed world (AO3)

Influence on workforce planning (AO3)

Demographic changes in the developed world influence workforce planning in various ways:

- The tertiary sector represents the biggest employer and the biggest contribution to overall output and will soon be rivalled by the quaternary sector.
- Male participation in full-time work has decreased relative to female participation.
- According to OECD figures, the number of hours worked by full-time employees has fallen by one third but the number of workers participating in the workforce has risen by one third. This is a good indicator of the growing importance of part-time work.
- There has been a fall in domestic birth rates leading to an ageing or "greying" population.
- Immigration is increasingly important to provide workers to cover both short-term and long-term gaps in human resources outlined above.
- Some businesses are simply unable to recruit workers in some primary or secondary sector roles due to de-industrialization.

Conclusion

The impact of these changes has required the development of a number of new strategies designed to prepare for future shortages of human resources:

- Online recruitment of workers from other countries has increased.
- The use of overseas employment agencies and recruitment consultants to find key highly skilled workers has increased.
- With the lower cost of operating in overseas countries, a number of firms have taken the decision to outsource some or all of their operations.

Impact on recruitment

One effect of these changes is that many businesses now recruit or search for new workers almost constantly.

The traditional model of recruitment demanded that an employer carried out a job analysis to see what new work was required. A job description was then devised and the job was advertised in job centres or in the local media to encourage people to apply.

Many employers now encourage potential applicants to apply or send in their curriculum vitae (CV) or résumé with a covering letter, even if a job does not exist. These potential applicants can then be added to the organization's database or if recruitment managers are suitably impressed by an applicant's skills they may consider creating a role for the individual. The Internet, social media and other communication technologies have made this process easier with the result that many large businesses recruit globally rather than locally especially for highly technical job opportunities.

Impact of changes in work patterns and practices (AO2)

In response to changing external demographic factors, social factors and new communication technologies, we can note that traditional working practices are also changing. There are various impacts on employers and employees, for example as follows:

- Extended opening hours in the retail sector including weekend shopping has led to job-sharing and the creation of additional part-time opportunities.
- A culture of the 24/7-service sector has been established, with online retailing growing in importance.
- The 9am to 5pm convention of the "normal working day" has ended.
- The growth of childcare services allows both parents of young children to participate in the workplace. Some governments, such as in the UK and New Zealand, are actively promoting early childhood education and offering "vouchers" to people who are keen to return to the workplace after having children.

Internal factors affecting workforce planning

Faced with rising overhead costs, seasonal and fluctuating demand for goods and services and the increasing use of remote Internet connections, employers have also contributed to the paradigm shift in working patterns by:

- allowing employees to undertake flexi-time arrangements outside the normal 9am to 5pm regime
- enabling employees to work from home via technology such as remote Internet access
- replacing permanent positions with contract workers to release temporary workers if there is insufficient demand at certain periods in the financial year.

Conclusion

There has been a fundamental shift in perception as to what constitutes the trading and working day. Employers are trying to make more effective use of human resources, given the enormous changes in demographic and social factors outlined above, signalled by the term "flexible working" which has created opportunities and threats for all employees. HR planning has never been so important. Within this area of business organization we will look at recruitment, training, appraisal, dismissal and redundancy.

Labour turnover (AO2)

In most organizations the pool of available human resources should be regarded as a flow concept, ever changing and responding to the aims and objectives of the organization. It is a dynamic part of a business. The days when employees could expect to have a job for life with one company are now effectively over. Some commentators are arguing that young workers may have 4 or 5 changes in career by the time they are 40 years old.

Labour turnover can be defined as the rate at which employees leave an organization and is usually expressed as a percentage per annum. For example, a labour turnover of 10% per annum would infer that 10% of an organization's employees will leave each year.

Employees leave organizations for a number of personal and professional reasons. Economists would argue that employees moving into more productive jobs or seeking new opportunities is a positive move for the economy. Labour turnover is inevitable and necessary.

However, if too many employees leave an organization then stakeholders such as customers, investors and employees in other rival organizations will start to take greater interest. If the labour turnover in a business is higher than the industry's average it may be a symptom of difficult working conditions, a poorly managed organizational culture or outright management failure. Moreover, a CEO of a large organization should be concerned if key managers or recently trained employees are leaving for other opportunities elsewhere.

At the other extreme, a low rate of labour turnover could signal a stable labour force. A lower than average industry rate has certain merit. Consistency and certainty in an ever-changing business landscape could be considered a positive aspect by some stakeholders such as suppliers or current and potential investors.

However, if we look from the perspective of younger newly recruited workers into an organization, a low rate of labour turnover may act as a signal that the opportunities for advancement and growth in terms of increased responsibility are few. Unfortunately, newly recruited workers may only discover this aspect of an organization after they have joined. (It is unlikely that a business would reveal its labour turnover rates during the course of an interview.) As we shall see in unit 2.4 on motivation, "generation Y" workers (or "gen Y" to give them their media name) can quickly sense frustration if their enthusiasm and abilities are not recognized and quickly by the organization which is clearly lucky to have employed them.

IB Learner Profile

Inquirers and knowledgeable

A visual and thought-provoking way to see some of the demographic changes outlined above (and perhaps some of future challenges for students as well as organizations) is to view the latest version of "SHIFT-HAPPENS" on YouTube.

Again, the Gary Hamel YouTube clip "The Future of Management" is an excellent source of information. Of course, as it was made in 2011, it could conceivably be considered out of date by the time you read this.

Recruitment, training, dismissal and redundancy (AO2)

Common steps in the recruitment process

The process of recruitment of human resources has become increasingly important in the new competitive global environment. Mistakes made in the recruitment of line managers or senior managers, for example, can create significant opportunity costs for a firm; as time passes these "inappropriate appointments" can turn into significant financial and HR problems. The objective of recruitment is to employ the right employee at the right time for the right job and allow him or her to be productive. This is not an easy task.

IB Learner Profile

Knowledgeable

Recruitment methods are changing. The traditional job advertisement and interview are now often supported by the innovations outlined below. It is also critical to consider that in recruitment processes the legal obligations of the employer and the responses by the employee vary significantly between countries. You are encouraged to check the recruitment processes operating in the country in which you are studying.

Jobs are advertised on the Internet or through social media once a job analysis has been carried out and a job description drawn up. If there are labour shortages locally, specialized global recruitment agencies are able to locate highly skilled workers who are in short supply; however, this service can be expensive and time-consuming.

Psychological profiling and psychometric testing of potential candidates who have been identified from the job search may be undertaken. Employers are also increasingly checking social media sites as a way of judging a potential employee's character. (This action of course has significant ethical considerations.)

Interview processes are now being developed which may stretch over a number of days rather than hours. Some of these interviews may be carried out over the Internet via Skype in the case of overseas appointments.

IB Learner Profile

Risk-taking

Suggested book and movie resource

In his excellent book *Are You Smart Enough to Work at Google?*, William Poundstone (2012) recounts some difficult questions that Google has asked to test the innovative and creative abilities of potential recruits. Google receives over 1 million applications yearly. Consequently, the organization has had to come up with some additional methods of recruitment to see whether, in addition to their academic qualifications and skills, potential employees have the right fit for the Google culture.

Here are two famous interview questions asked by Google to potential employees. The second was featured in the recent movie starring Vince Vaughn and Owen Wilson called "The Internship" which although it is a fairly average Hollywood comedy does provide some interesting insights into the Google recruitment process and organizational culture.

1 What number comes next in the series?

10, 9, 60, 90, 70, 66

2 You are shrunk to the height of a penny and thrown into a blender. Your mass is reduced so that your density is the same as usual. The blades will start moving in 60 seconds. What do you do?

The "answers" are given on page 130. Note that Google is not looking for the right answer in each case, just the answer that fits best with the evidence presented. All IB students would be wise to follow this type of thinking as demanded by the IB learner profile.

Training (AO2)

Traditionally, training has been categorized in one of three areas:

- induction
- on the job
- off the job.

There are benefits and drawbacks to all three, as summarized in Table 2.1.1. The disadvantages of off-the-job training will look very similar to the advantages of on-the-job training.

In addition to these more traditional forms of training, two other types have been developed to reflect the growing demands made on employees in the 21st century.

Cognitive training (AO2)

Increasingly, employers are looking to develop both the physical skill base of their workers through on-the-job training and their mental capabilities through the use of cognitive exercises as part of **cognitive training.** We saw earlier that the recruitment and selection processes of some organizations are now being driven by psychological testing or the ability to think creatively and quickly (see the Google example.) Research in neurology has found that mental and problem-solving capabilities in employees can be enhanced by a form of "brain training" or cognitive training.

> Lumosity is an example of one type of online training system designed to boost "brain power" and improve important skills such as speed and flexibility of thought, attention and problem-solving.
>
> For more information on the science behind the Lumosity training programme and a free sample exercise, visit www.lumosity.com

Behavioural training

Ultimately, the purpose of training is to develop and allow employees to grow their skill base so that they can be more productive for an organization. As we shall see in the unit 2.4, Herzberg's theory of motivation relies heavily on the role of training undertaken. Herzberg believes that "the more somebody

can do, the more they can be motivated to do" and that training is the best weapon in a manager's armoury.

Behavioural training is really the summary or final outcome of all the types of training so far explained. The objective behind behavioural training is to initiate training to change employees' behaviour at work. Whether the training is carried out by external providers, internally or through cognitive approaches, the intention is the development and nurturing of current and future employees so that they are ready for the challenges that await them. Many of these challenges are of course unknown so behavioural training needs to be flexible in nature.

Appraisal (AO2)

Many workers fear appraisal as they assume that it is merely a way of judging performance at work – and assume the views expressed will be negative. This is a narrow view. If appraisal is carried out effectively, it can become a very motivating process for both the employee **and** the employer and can improve work relations.

When appraisal is carried out efficiently it will have the following positive consequences:

- The employer has the opportunity to restate objectives and vision for the company. (This is especially important for senior managers.)
- The employer can praise high-performing workers and reaffirm their role in the future of the organization, thus aiding the retention of key workers.
- The employee may get a chance to voice concerns about the organization's direction, giving him or her an opportunity to channel frustration. Managers will then hear about "grass-roots" problems quickly and will be able to pre-empt future conflict. Frustration can be turned into a productive experience.

Many companies leave the appraisal process to the end of the financial year. Some companies take a more flexible view and encourage employees to discuss issues with managers more regularly. How appraisal is carried out will depend a great deal on the **culture** of the organization.

Types of appraisal
Formative

Formative appraisal occurs when employees are being monitored to see whether they have acquired a particular skill as their job is proceeding. You could argue that a formative appraisal

Type of training	Benefits to employer	Benefits to employee	Issues or problems
Induction	This allows the employer to set expectations of the new employee right at the beginning of the employment period	There are clear guidelines as to culture, role and expectations. This method allows the employee time to settle	This can be costly and it diverts senior managers away from important tasks
On the job	The cost of this is lower than the cost of off-the-job training. The training is specific to the needs of the firm	There is minimal disruption to the working day. Skills learned can be readily put into practice	Lack of outside training may narrow the experiences of the employee (it is too inward-looking). This is not a good way to train in fast-moving technological industries
Off the job	This is an expensive method and cover may be needed for staff who are absent	Being away from the workplace for training may allow perspective and sharing of best practice. The firm creates external outside networks	Skills learned may take time to be put into practice in the firm. Too much off-the-job training may lead to resentment by other employees who have to cover absences

Table 2.1.1 Advantages and disadvantages of three types of training

is like a weekly check-up involving your manager just to see how operations are working. In a classroom environment, your teacher may check your understanding of a topic such as recruitment by asking you some questions or by presenting a case study. Formative appraisal should occur throughout the working cycle at regular intervals and will form part of the summative process explained below.

Summative

Summative appraisal normally occurs at the end of a trading period or year. For newly recruited workers, summative assessment could occur in the first six weeks. For an experienced worker, a summative appraisal could take place at the end of the working year. As an IB student your summative assessment will occur at the end of your two-year course.

In summative appraisal a formal interview is usually held with an opportunity for both employee and employer to put forward their views and present evidence to justify a particular point. This evidence could include formative reviews. It is the intention that the summative appraisal process will lead to an agreed new goal being set for the employee so that performance and personal growth at work can be enhanced.

360-degree feedback and self-appraisal

Some of the evidence referred to in the previous point to help with the summative appraisal process may include 360-degree feedback surveys and self-appraisal questionnaires. At HCL Technologies – one of the new business models referred to by Gary Hamel in the YouTube clip on the future of management – 360-degree feedback surveys are taken to mean that individuals receive feedback from all those workers including managers who are "near" to them. Effectively at HCL, **any** employee can give feedback about **any** other employee or manager. This process is so transparent that all workers can see the feedback given by them and the feedback they have received. All comments are posted online. Culturally speaking some stakeholders may have issues or may feel uncomfortable with this type of feedback and appraisal.

Self-appraisal is a powerful method of appraisal but again we should note that there are significant cultural implications of introducing such a scheme. Of course, there are also practical issues: how objective can people be about their own performance?

Self-appraisal is usually carried out by an employee via a series of questions. The results are viewed by a manager before the final summative review takes place.

Dismissal and redundancy (AO1)

Dismissal is defined as the process when an employee fails in his or her obligation to an employer and is dismissed (or to use the colloquial terms, "sacked" or "fired").

Possible reasons for dismissal

- An employee has been advised that his or her performance is below expectations (perhaps during an appraisal meeting) and continues to perform below expectations despite written and verbal warnings.

- An employee may not have followed company rules and regulations on issues such as working hours, rest breaks or sick leave.

- An employee may have a pattern of poorly explained absenteeism.

- Other issues may have occurred which contravened the employee's work contract.

In order to satisfy the requirements of employment legislation laid down by the government in a particular country, the employer would normally issue both verbal and written warnings if any of the above incidents occurred. Failure to do so may lead to disputes and possible legal proceedings in the case of an unfair dismissal.

Redundancy

Redundancy occurs through no fault of the employee. A worker's position in an organization may simply disappear, for example for one of the following reasons:

- There has been a sustained decrease in demand for the company's products. The organization's production levels cannot support the current workforce level and cuts are required to keep the organization sustainable.

- There is a need to restructure due to other changes in the external environment (a change in one of the SLEPT factors such as new technological innovations).

- The organization's leaders have made strategic decisions to move some parts of the operation overseas or to outsource a particular job to reduce costs and remain competitive (see below).

When redundancy occurs an employee will normally be entitled to a redundancy payment based on the number of years' service to the company. However, redundancy payment arrangements differ widely between companies and countries. Organizations that have made large numbers of workers redundant may offer counselling and training to affected workers to help them find new jobs. These out-placement services are expensive, however, and therefore not universally offered.

Outsourcing, offshoring and reshoring (AO3)

Definitions

- Offshoring: moving part of a company's operations to another country

- Outsourcing: a business function or operation performed by a third party either onshore or offshore

- Reshoring: a deliberate attempt to move functions back to the country of origin.

We shall be looking at these issues in greater detail in unit 5.1 on operations management. Here we offer a brief discussion on the strategic decisions to move the HR function offshore before considering why some large organizations that have done this are now thinking that they should bring this function back.

Offshoring or outsourcing the HR function

The growing use of the Internet, ICT applications on a global scale and the creation of the 24/7 business model have made the use of offshoring almost a given now for many firms in HR areas such as customer service and software development. According to figures from *The Economist Business Miscellany* in 2007, 80% of the offshore market was located in India.

Supporters of offshoring argue that the associated problems have been quickly minimized. Staff training, cultural awareness and intelligence (CQ) programmes have enabled workers in India to offer the same level of service as offered in the host country.

The dilemma is that offshoring may become the victim of its own success. As demand for workers in India rises, local wages will grow and, if sustained over a long enough period, then the competitive position of the firm offshoring could be undermined.

However, possibly for political and economic reasons given the growing recovery in the world economy, a number of organizations have now begun to rethink this HR strategy. They are starting to repatriate or **reshore** some management positions.

Reshoring

Read the following article and discuss some of its implications for UK and overseas organizations.

David Cameron: Britain can bring jobs back from abroad

David Cameron – the British Prime Minister – has said Britain has the potential to become the "reshore nation" as he announced the creation of a new government body to encourage companies to locate jobs in the UK that would once have gone to the Far East.

The Prime Minister said that although the practice of offshoring – which involves jobs being moved to countries such as China or India to cut costs – is well known, "reshoring" is a growing phenomenon that can help to drive economic growth.

"There is an opportunity for some of those jobs to come back."

"I want to give dedicated help," he said, "a one-stop-shop to help business capitalize on the opportunities that reshoring brings".

The new body – Reshore UK – is to be set up, bringing together the expertise of UKTI and the Manufacturing Advertising Service, and sit with the Department for Business, Innovation and Skills (BIS).

Mr. Cameron, speaking at the World Economic Forum in Davos, said that a recent survey showed that one in ten small businesses in the UK is considering bringing production back from overseas to the UK, more than double the number heading east.

Examples cited in his speech included train set maker Hornby, which is bringing some production back from India to the UK, and fashion brand Jaeger, which 15 years ago stopped making clothes in the UK but now is bringing home an initial 10% of its output.

Mr. Cameron said this was a trend from which not just the UK could benefit from but other parts of Europe and the USA.

He also said it was important to appreciate why this is happening – noting that costs are rising in Asia, with senior management salaries in China now at or above those in the USA and Europe, and that Western companies want to benefit from being nearer to the consumer markets they serve to aid customization and privatization.

The Prime Minister emphasized that reshoring would not bring back all the jobs that have been lost offshore, nor would it stop offshoring, but he added that UK businesses are ready to look closer to home and tap into the expertise and innovation in manufacturing which existed in the UK and Europe.

Source: Taken from the UK newspaper *The Daily Telegraph*, 24 January 2014

IB Learner Profile

Inquirers and knowledgeable

Questions for reflection

- Based on comments in the newspaper article, analyse two reasons for the move to reshore.

- In his speech Cameron made the assertion that Western companies will "benefit from being nearer to the consumer markets they serve". Discuss whether he is correct, given:
  - the rapid changes in technology such as social media
  - communication tools such as Skype
  - the pace of globalization.

- If a UK business reshores, what are the implications for other UK businesses looking to outsource parts of their operations, including HR management?

We will consider in further depth the arguments around outsourcing, offshoring and reshoring in unit 5.1 on operations management.

Setting the scene

This unit and subsequent units rely heavily on an understanding of a large number of terms and definitions. It is "jargon heavy". You are advised to check carefully your understanding of each term used, as the assessment objectives in this unit are predominantly AO1 and AO2. You will need to define, explain and possibly even analyse the terms used.

Organizational structure terminology (AO1)

Delegation

Delegation is the process of entrusting a subordinate to perform a task for which the manager or superior retains overall responsibility. A subordinate is an employee who has to report to and is answerable to a manager.

Span of control

Span of control refers to the number of subordinates under the control of a supervisor. In your class the span of control is the number of students directly supervised by the teacher. Large spans of control require strong inclusive leadership and clear communication.

Levels of hierarchy

Levels of hierarchy refer to the number of levels of formal authority from the top to the bottom of an organization. To a large extent, the choice of a particular span of control will dictate the number of levels. This interaction of span of control and levels of hierarchy gives the two hierarchical structures:

- tall – small span of control and many levels of hierarchy
- flat – larger span of control and fewer levels of hierarchy.

Chain of command

The chain of command is usually depicted on an organizational chart as a vertical line of authority enabling decision-making or responsibility to be passed down through the layers of hierarchy. The chain of command also establishes the formal communication channels between managers and subordinates.

Bureaucracy in a business context

Bureaucracy can be defined as:

the administrative system of a business, which relies on a set of rules and procedures, separation of functions and a hierarchical structure in implementing controls over an organization.

Source: Adapted from investopia.

A bureaucratic system is one which will thrive in a culture of set procedures and regulations with clear lines of responsibility.

Centralization

Centralization is a method of organizational process where the formal power (authority) and responsibility of those higher up in the hierarchy influences both **tactical** and **strategic** decision-making. Centralized organizations allow for little if any discussion or involvement with subordinates and/or managers. Centralization has been termed as "top–down" management and is popular in government-run (public sector) organizations.

Decentralization

Not surprisingly, decentralization is defined as the opposite of centralization. Lower-level decision-making and the empowering of staff to bring new ideas to management has led to the business term "bottom–up" management. This can define a decentralized organizational decision-making process.

Centralization can be perceived as being part of an autocratic, paternalistic leadership. Decentralization is linked to an approach focused on tasks and problem-solving and tends to be existential

or based on individualism. We will return to this in unit 2.5 when we will look at Charles Handy's (1978) four categories of organizational culture (page 51).

Delayering

As the term would suggest, "delayering" is a process designed to remove the number of layers in the hierarchy in an organization. Through delayering, an organization will hope to streamline chains of command and improve and increase communication. The objective of delayering could be to shift an organization from a tall to a flat hierarchy (see Figures 2.2.1 and 2.2.2). A second reason could be that an organization wishes to "downsize" and reduce the number of layers in a cost-reduction exercise as part of a new strategic plan.

IB Learner Profile

Inquiry ?

Organizational charts (AO4)

Before you embark on the analysis of organizational charts and structures, you should try to draw an organizational chart of your school or college. Avoid names and personalities and focus on roles. Ask a classmate to do the same thing and if possible ask another stakeholder with a strong association with the school to do the same. Then compare your results.

Questions for discussion

- How easy or difficult was it for you as a stakeholder in your school or college to draw the organizational chart?

- Are the organizational charts you, your classmate and another stakeholder produced similar in terms of levels of hierarchy and span of control?

- If you show your diagram to a stakeholder who was at the school a few years ago (such as a teacher), do you think he or she will find that there have been significant changes in structure? Has the hierarchy become flatter or taller?

- If, as expected, the school has grown in size, have spans of control become wider?

- Should an IB World School be centralized or decentralized in its decision-making? What would be the consequences of making the IB World School more decentralized?

The theoretical approach to organizational charts (AO2)

We now present a number of standard diagrams, with a brief explanation, to illustrate how organizational charts can be drawn.

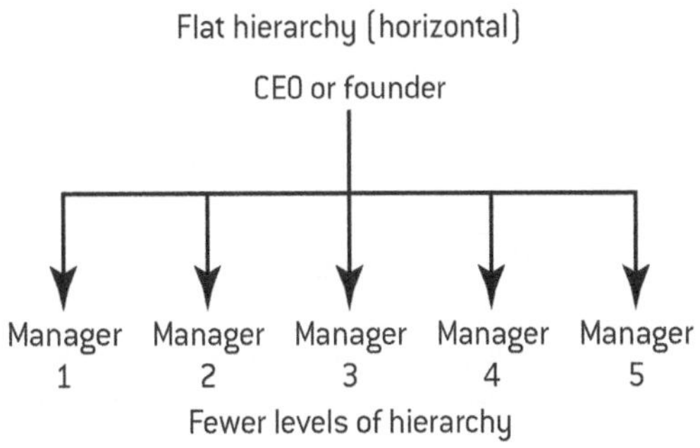

Flat hierarchy (horizontal)

CEO or founder

Manager 1   Manager 2   Manager 3   Manager 4   Manager 5

Fewer levels of hierarchy

Figure 2.2.1 Flat or horizontally hierarchical structure

By delayering, the organization is attempting to reduce the "gap" between the senior management at the "top" of the organization and the subordinates at the "bottom" in Figure 2.2.1. Flat hierarchies tend to widen spans of control and have their most effective use in small- to medium-sized enterprises (SMEs).

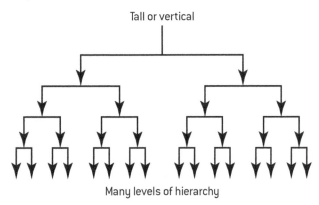

Figure 2.2.2 Tall or vertical hierarchical structure

Figure 2.2.2 shows the opposite structure to the flat or horizontal organizational chart in Figure 2.2.1. Levels of hierarchy increase and chains of command lengthen. Large or multinational corporations may feel that a tall structure provides clarity and clear lines of responsibility. They will hope that this can reduce the possibilities of diseconomies of scale. Typical structures for businesses organized by function, geography and product are shown in Figures 2.2.3, 2.2.4 and 2.2.5.

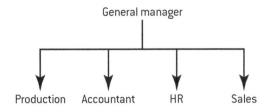

Figure 2.2.3 Typical structure for a business organized by function

Figure 2.2.4 Typical structure for a business organized by geography

Figure 2.2.5 Typical structure for a business organized by product centre

Table 2.2.1 can be used to analyse the different methods of structuring an organization.

Changes in organizational structures (AO2)

Here we look at changes in organizational structures using the examples of Handy's shamrock organization and project-based organizations. In its description of cell production, unit 5.1 also covers project-based organizations.

Project teams

The idea behind the project team (or matrix) structure is that traditional functional and department boundaries are ignored. A project team is selected to work on one "problem" for which the members' individual qualities are ideally suited. Dearden and Foster (1992) argue that IBM used this technique when developing the original personal computer. The argument follows that specialist project teams are best suited to solve problems across departments and avoid one department dominating or influencing the final outcome.

In unit 1.7 we looked at the fishbone or Ishikawa diagram as a business tool used to identify causes of a problem. This could be used with project teams, which could be assigned to look into causes across a range of departments. This is more likely to lead to a more representative set of decisions being made and ensure that all possible causes are highlighted.

Of course, project teams are by their nature temporary. Once the problem under discussion has been solved the team is usually broken up and individuals return to their functional roles or departments. Organizing and monitoring a project team's work will also take additional time and scarce resources.

Structure	Benefits	Issues or problems
By function	Clear lines of communication and responsibility are established. This structure is good for new stakeholders, especially employees, to see how the organization is structured. It encourages specialization leading to economies of scale	This type of structure may encourage departments to view themselves as isolated and set their own goals and objectives. It relies heavily on the success of the general manager to communicate and manage effectively
By geography	This structure gives autonomy to local managers to allow more accurate local decision-making. Being closer to local markets means a firm can gain updated research such as customer feedback	Given geographical location or time differences, there is potential loss of control of overall objectives. (With the onset of communication technologies this may not be such a big issue). The organization may have to set local goals and aims
By product	Expertise in specific products and markets is gained. There is rapid decision-making and objective ways of measuring the performance of individual centres. Greater flexibility exists for growth and expansion. Additional centres can be added without affecting the operations of the other centres. This is good if a takeover or acquisition has been made	There is conflict and competition between individual centres. There is some duplication of functions such as accounting, marketing and HR management. The allocation of overhead is crucial in influencing the pricing strategies of individual centres.

Table 2.2.1 Methods of structuring an organization

Zero-hour contracts for 90% of staff

Sports Direct's entire part-time workforce of over 20 000 staff is employed on zero-hour contracts at a time when 2 000 full-time staff are about to cash in bonuses of up to £100 000.

The contracts, handed to 90% of the company's 23 000 employees, leave staff not knowing how many hours they will work from one week to the next, with no sick pay or holiday pay, and no guarantee of regular work.

Bosses at Sports Direct, the UK's biggest sports retailer, were this month hailing their bonus policy for full-time staff as that of a model employer.

The four biggest supermarkets in Britain – Tesco, Asda, Sainsbury's and Morrisons – said they do not use zero-hour contracts. Other UK retailers to confirm that they do not employ staff on these terms include Argos, B&Q, Homebase, John Lewis and Marks & Spencer.

Politicians have been campaigning to ban the contracts and have called on Mike Ashley, the billionaire owner of Sports Direct, to consider introducing part-time contracts with guaranteed hours.

Former and current part-time staff have also spoken out against zero hours, stressing the uncertainty created by the contracts, under which work can be cut with less than a day's notice. Others said regional managers may reduce staff hours if targets are not met.

Source: Adapted from an article in the UK newspaper, *The Guardian*, 28 July 2013

In their creation of **quality circles** and **kaizen** (see unit 5.3) the Japanese have used project teams (the matrix structure) enthusiastically. However, in Japanese management this structure is viewed as being very much a long-term commitment and not just for one-off projects. Japanese managers regard project terms as being a very powerful motivating force in terms of teamwork and breaking down barriers that may exist between departments working in the more traditional structures.

However, it is worth noting an important aspect of the project team or matrix structure. With individuals joining from different departments, clear lines of authority need to be established at the start of the project to indicate who is in charge overall.

Handy's shamrock organization

Charles Handy has become well regarded in the business world for his work on organizational culture and management. He is particularly well known for his vivid use of engaging metaphors and examples (see his books *Gods of Management* and *The Empty Raincoat*).

One of Handy's contributions to workforce planning was his insight into the roles of workers required in the new demographic and social changes outlined in unit 2.1. Handy identified the need to have a flexible workforce to allow firms to adjust faster to changing external environments.

He identified core, contract and peripheral workers and developed the idea of the shamrock organization. His three categories are as follows:

- **Core** workers are full-time employees with trusted experience and are small in number.
- **Contract** workers are employed on a short-term basis for a specific task. Examples of these tasks are the recruitment of senior managers or the installation of a new data management system.

- **Peripheral** workers are flexible workers employed on a part-time basis for reasons such as seasonal shifts in operations.

The implications of Handy's work should be clear. Given the significant changes in working patterns and external social and demographic changes outlined earlier, fewer full-time workers are necessary. Organizations need to be "nimble and flexible" in the 21st century to cope with "an inflexion point of change" (Gary Hamel) but of course this has also led to job insecurity and in some cases, some commentators have argued, exploitation of workers.

IB Learner Profile

Balanced ⚖️

Application of shamrock theory to a real-life organization

Consider the Sports Direct case study, which may amplify the concerns mentioned above.

QUESTIONS FOR REFLECTION

- Is the introduction of a zero-hours contract by Sports Direct innovation or exploitation?
- What are the ethical implications for an organization that decides to pay a bonus through a share scheme to full-time staff (core workers) but award zero-hours contracts to part-time staff (contract or peripheral workers)?
- What are the advantages to a retail business, such as Sports Direct which is operating 24/7, of utilizing more part-time staff?
- What are the disadvantages?

We will return to use this case study in unit 2.4 on motivation and financial rewards.

Traditional inflexible 20th-century organization with core full-time staff

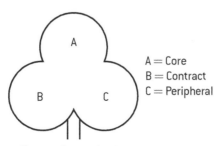

Shamrock organization

A = Core
B = Contract
C = Peripheral

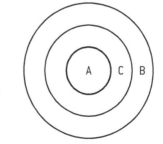

New flexible 21st-century shamrock organization

Figure 2.2.6 Traditional organization and the shamrock organization

IB Learner Profile

Knowledgeable

Handy has become well regarded in the business world for his work on organizational culture and management. He is particularly well known for his vivid use of engaging metaphors and examples. Students are encouraged to read excerpts from *Gods of Management* and *The Empty Raincoat*.

IB Learner Profile

Balanced and reflective ⚖️ ЯǀR

Communication technologies (AO3)

Cultural differences and innovation in communication technologies (AO3)

Now we will look at how cultural differences and innovation in communication technologies may have an impact on communication in an organization.

Search for the quote and Google image from Einstein online: 'The day that Albert Einstein feared has arrived.' Reflect on your own experiences of using mobile communications. Do you think that Einstein was right?

Figure 2.2.7 Albert Einstein

We must balance this point of view with further analysis that organizations with new and dynamic cultures, such as Google and Pixar, would clearly approve of the use of communication technologies fit for use for the new "generation Y" worker (see unit 2.4) which allow creativity and innovation to thrive.

IB Learner Profile

Inquiry ?

To consider the issue of how innovation in communication technologies has had an impact on communication in an organization from an individual point of view, consider your own school. Ask the following probing questions.

Questions for discussion

- Given the increased use of mobile devices and social media platforms, has communication in your school improved?

- On the other hand, rather than an improvement in communication, do you see evidence of more "noise" in schools – communication overload with the result that messages or advice are lost?

- Has email improved the efficiency of communication in your school? (Efficiency in this context is hard to define but we could say that it includes messages being understood or answers to questions being received promptly.)

- Given that IB World Schools are made up of a number of non-English native speakers (ESOL students), has innovation in communication technologies allowed for improved communication where the dominant language of instruction is English?

The discussion points raised by these questions could easily be applied to a business. They become especially significant the larger the organization that is attempting to develop a presence in global markets. As any organization moves into new overseas markets, cultural differences and communication technology innovations become much more important.

Management versus leadership (AO2)

There is some confusion as to the difference between leadership and management. Russell-Walling (2007) puts it succinctly:

Leaders do the right thing; managers do things right.

Linking back to our previous discussions on aims, objectives and strategic decision-making in unit 1.3, we could argue the difference as follows. Effective leadership requires the setting of clear aims and strategic goals while the role of an effective manager is to ensure that objectives are met in pursuit of the overall aim.

Successful leadership within organizations is often applauded and revered. Steve Jobs, Mark Zuckerberg, Sir Richard Branson and Larry Page are often quoted as being inspirational and successful entrepreneurs and leaders, but how much do we really know about their management skills? (We have already seen that Steve Jobs was often described as brilliant but demanding and autocratic.)

Students studying for the IB Diploma often overlook effective management yet it will have an impact on them every single school day. Your principal (leadership) may have a very critical role in your IB World School as the public face to a whole range of external stakeholders. However, your academic success as a student may well be determined by your year head (or dean of students) or the head of the department in which your subject sits and, of course, your teacher. Effective management in schools will often start and end with these very important internal stakeholders.

IB Learner Profile

Reflection ЯR

- Do you see yourself as a future leader or manager?
- What evidence from your life so far would you include in order to make this judgment?
- Do you think that leaders are born or can they be made?

Key functions of management in a business context (AO2)

Some writers separate management into **administrative** and **operational** roles for an organization. The **administrative** **function** of the manager coordinates the functions of finance, marketing and production by planning and defining procedures, the procedures and objectives of the organization having been decided by the board of directors and the senior executives. The **operational role** for management refers to the implementation of these plans, aims and objectives.

Gabriel (1998) identifies five key functions for a manager. They are:

- planning a suitable course of action given the overall vision of the CEO
- organizing the human and material resources to achieve this vision
- manpower planning including recruitment and selection of key workers for specific tasks to achieve tactical objectives
- motivation to achieve goals once a plan of action has been put in place
- controlling, monitoring and maintaining performance to ensure that the vision is SMART (see page 17).

Leadership styles (AO3)

You may accept that students often overlook the importance of effective management in their student lives. Perhaps you believe that effective leadership should be clearer cut and easier to understand. It may come as a surprise that, even in 2014, there is still a good deal of confusion as to what effective leadership actually looks like.

In this unit we discuss the five leadership styles on offer from the new *IB Business Management Guide*.

Definition of effective leadership

Peter Drucker's 1966 definition of effective leadership (quoted in Trout, 2001) has stood the test of time:

The foundation of effective leadership is thinking through the organization's mission, defining it and establishing it, clearly and visibly.

We can use Drucker's definition as a hypothesis to test the effectiveness of some of the leadership models, as shown in Table 2.3.1.

Leadership style	Description	Discussion
Autocratic	The decision-making process is determined solely by the leader or chief authority figure. There is little or no consultation. Examples are the armed forces or other organizations with tall hierarchies	It can be demotivating for some workers not to have an input into the process. Autocratic leaders can be effective in crisis situations
Democratic	The decision on what is to be done and how it is to be carried out is taken after group discussion and consultation. Examples can be found in media industries especially advertising and public relations	Increased motivation and productivity may result from some key skilled workers. Decision by committee can be time-consuming and expensive. It may not be an effective way of decision-making in a crisis situation
Laissez-faire	Effectively there is no leadership. Groups are unsupported and left to decide for themselves. Handy has argued that many universities operate under laissez-faire conditions	Given no formal leadership, new employees may find the workplace environment confusing as they will lack knowledge of workplace conventions. Setting overall organization objectives may be difficult without formal leadership
Paternalistic	The leader of the organization acts in a "fatherly manner" towards employees in the same manner as if he were a parent or mentor. This is typical of family businesses (see also club culture in unit 2.5 and note that, although this style is called "paternalistic", the role of parent or mentor may also be taken by female leaders)	The leader will demand loyalty in return for his influence. This could lead to resentment from some employees especially if they see themselves as "outsiders" from the family. These cultures may be too inward-looking and paternalism may be seen as rewarding bloodlines rather than ability

Table 2.3.1 Different leadership models

If we apply Drucker's definition to each of the four leadership styles, we can make the following points:

- Paternalism if present in small family businesses may lead to jealousy and favouritism among some key managers. (It is unlikely that the leader would appeal directly in the same manner to all). These inward-looking cultures may lack a leadership style which responds to external changes as quickly as other leadership styles.

- Laissez-faire leadership needs to ensure that the mission is clearly articulated and understood by all workers. Clear communication is vital.

- Many business students assume that democratic leadership is always best, and the fairest method of decision-making. However, too many people in the decision-making process may lead to delays in defining roles and the implementation of a new strategic direction.

- Although unpopular and unfashionable in today's business environment, an autocratic leadership style may actually be closest to Drucker's intention. Successful CEOs such as Jeff Bezos from Amazon, Jack Welch of GEC or Steve Jobs of Apple have successfully adopted this.

IB Learner Profile

Risk-taking and inquirers

We must go back to the Gary Hamel clip on the future of management (introduced in concept 2: Change, page 6) and take a brief moment to reflect on one aspect. Hamel makes a very compelling argument that current management models were created for a very different era. He calls this "management 1.0".

Hamel firmly believes that we need new models of management to make organizations of the future "fit for purpose". These new models must embrace the enormous social and technological changes which have taken place. In his presentation he focuses on one organization – HCL technologies – that has used a process of "reverse accountability" in its management structure in particular.

As future business leaders and managers, students of the IB Business Management course who are now termed "generation y" or "gen Y" workers need to ask themselves whether the leadership models suggested above really apply to them. Increasingly, organizations are finding that "generation Y"

workers need to be led and motivated by a completely different mind set than their parents. As we will see in unit 2.4, Daniel Pink touches on some of these themes in his theory of motivation but this question remains: can today's "generation Y" be led and managed according to theories which are nearly 100 years old?

IB Learner Profile

Inquiry ?

Gore-Tex and Namaste Solar

Research the US organizations Gore Tex and Namaste Solar to investigate whether they present new models of leadership and management for the 21st century.

Perhaps Gary Hamel had Gore-tex and Namaste Solar in mind when he referred to "learning from the fringe". These organizations are run in a unique way, which is both paternalistic and laissez-faire.

Questions for discussion

- If Gore-Tex's leadership style and approach to organizational structure (job titles, communication channels, etc.) is so effective, then why do other similar businesses not use some of its features?

- Can an organization such as Namaste Solar truly be 100% democratic?

The situational approach: Frederick Fiedler

The basis of situational leadership is that it takes the view that it is the situation in which the leader is trying to lead that is important, rather than any character attributes the leader may have, or any dominant leadership style that may be used. Fielder stated that the situation in which the leader is trying to lead may be a function of the characteristics of the organization, the nature of the task itself and the "group atmosphere" that exists. Fiedler attached a great deal of importance to this last point. The leader is followed and obeyed not because of rank or power but due to positive group emotions such as loyalty, liking, trust and respect.

Think of examples, both past and present, of leaders who have demonstrated a leadership style based on the above situational analysis. Famous sports captains may provide a rich source of research.

We begin this unit by including a flipped learning exercise on motivation theory.

Motivation theory

This activity is based on two YouTube clips.

Clip 1: Frederick Herzberg "Jumping for the Jelly Beans"

In the early 1970s, Frederick Herzberg gave a presentation called "Jumping for the Jelly Beans" to a group of British businessmen, which can be watched in two segments on YouTube. Below is a selection of quotations from the presentation.

Motivation is when you want to do a good job rather than having to.

The more someone can do, the more they can be motivated to do.

The key motivators, which will motivate someone to play the piano, are:

- *Can I play the piano? (Ability)*
- *Is there a piano for me to play? (Opportunity)*
- *Do you want to do something for me? That is motivation.*
- *Do you need a bribe or a threat? That is hygiene.*

Clip 2: Daniel Pink "The Surprising Thing about Motivation"

According to Daniel Pink, three key motivators for an activity that requires some degree of complexity are:

- mastery – getting better at the activity
- purpose – the reason for doing the activity
- autonomy – being left alone to get on with doing the activity.

Watch this excellent YouTube clip, which has been animated by RSA Animate. The presentation in itself is highly innovative.

IB Learner Profile

Reflection Я|R

Questions for reflection

- What are the key similarities – if any – between the ideas on motivation of Herzberg and Pink?
- According to the two clips presented, how important is financial reward as a motivator?
- When considering motivation theory are there significant cultural influences on the types of motivation reward needed?

Motivation theories (AO3)

We will look at the following five motivation theories:

- Taylor – scientific management or "economic man" approach
- Maslow – hierarchy of needs
- Herzberg – two-factor theory of motivation
- Adams – equity theory
- Pink – mastery, purpose, autonomy.

A diagrammatic approach is used for two of the theories, as they are well established (see Figures 2.4.1 and 2.4.2). A brief summary of the remaining theories is then given.

Maslow – hierarchy of needs

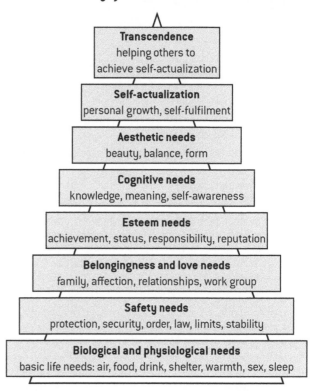

Figure 2.4.1 Maslow's hierarchy of needs (updated eight-stage model)

Herzberg – two-factor theory of motivation

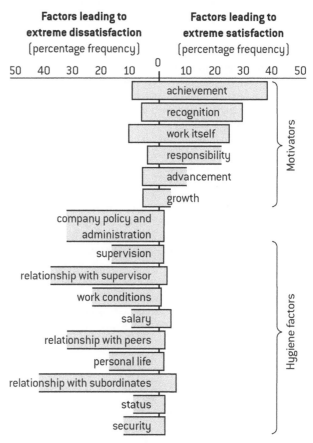

Figure 2.4.2 Herzberg's motivators and hygiene factors

IB Learner Profile

Inquiry ?

Your family

Construct a Maslow pyramid based on yourself, your parents or carers and, if possible, your grandparents.

- Are there any differences between the three diagrams?
- Do you think that you, your parents or your grandparents have reached self-actualization?
- Do you think that Maslow's pyramid is a relevant model of motivation given the thoughts of Herzberg and Pink?

Frederick Winslow Taylor

Students often overlook the work of Taylor and assume that his contribution to business motivation theory was simply that "money motivates". Taylor's work in business management was new and revolutionary. Drucker has argued that Taylor deserves a place alongside Darwin and Freud in the making of the modern world.

Taylor's motivational theory is based on the idea that a unit of work carried out by a factor of production should be measured and a performance standard be created which was "fair and acceptable". To set the standard, a performance measurement should be carried out once the worker has been shown the demands of the unit of work and trained in how to complete it.

Taylor then argues that workers who achieved the performance standard would be paid a living wage; those who exceeded the standard would be paid more. Exceeding the standard would guarantee a bonus if this performance were sustained but the overall intention from Taylor was that his motivational theory would generate "a bigger cake for all". Workers would be supervised in order to achieve a target rate of production.

Taylor's scientific management principles were put quickly into practice in the early part of the 20th century. A number of industrialists began to make huge profits, especially Henry Ford, whose Model T Ford soon became the symbol of this new management style. Many students have viewed Taylor as the enemy of the worker and the theorist who said that people will only work for money. Few realize that his underlying philosophy was that he wanted scientific management to produce **greater outcomes for all employees**.

Equity theory

The key element in equity theory credited to John Adams is that motivation is a function of workers perceiving that the reward they are receiving for their efforts fully reflects their contribution to the organization. If workers feel that their contribution is being recognized then motivation to stay will be high, and vice versa.

Workers' contribution cannot always be measured objectively. However, firms who use equity theory have discovered that, for example, giving a worker time off for compassionate reasons or allowing flexible working for part-time workers can create an environment of "fairness", which can be very motivating.

IB Learner Profile

Thinkers and balanced 💡

Discuss the implications for equity theory of the "fairness" of awarding senior managers large bonuses in loss-making organizations which have recently been the recipients of government assistance. Moreover, consider that in some large organizations the CEO may earn up to 200 times the average salary of a subordinate who is employed at a lower level of the hierarchy.

Questions for discussion

- Can equity theory support the payment of such high compensation packages in this case?
- Can high compensation packages be justified under any circumstances?

Daniel Pink

Of all the above theories, Pink's research into motivation theory is the most recent attempt to find out the key drivers of motivation in the 21st century. Interestingly, the two surveys featured in video clip 2 (Daniel Pink, "The Surprising Thing about Motivation") which are used to explain motivational behaviour are from very different ends of the cultural and social spectrum, yet they yield very similar results.

Pink cites the creation of Wikipedia as typical of this newly found "**purpose motive**" in motivation. It illustrates how individuals in well-paid highly skilled occupations will give up large amounts of their free "discretionary" time in order to develop a service or information source to help others.

Autonomy – the ability to be self-directed at work – also seems to have a very strong influence in the new century. Modern technologies and communication possibilities have allowed this to happen (as noted in unit 2.2). Pink also highlights the organizational culture at Atlasian, which runs similar to the Google 20% free time we noted earlier. This allows for a degree of **intrapreneurship** within an organization, which could lead to the creation of new product ideas and services and that all-important innovative edge in global markets.

Motivation theory – a brief discussion for AO3

Is Taylorism misunderstood?

Given the above arguments put forward by Pink and Herzberg surrounding motivation, one is tempted to suggest that Taylor's approach to scientific management has no place in the new millennium. Supervision, control and payment by results seem inconsistent with the purpose motive and autonomy advocated by new thinking on motivation.

However, there is nothing "wrong" in adopting Taylorism. In some situations it may be totally appropriate to adopt more autocratic and bureaucratic forms of leadership to enhance workers' motivation and to improve productivity (see crisis management and contingency planning in unit 5.7).

Moreover, as we shall see when looking at supply chain management and in our discussion of outsourcing, Chinese suppliers working for Apple and other hi-tech corporations adopt very Tayloristic-style management processes. There are no shortages of workers who wish to take advantage of these companies' job opportunities and earn a living wage.

The importance of hygiene factors

Herzberg's hygiene factors are not motivators themselves but it would be wrong of employers to neglect them. If appropriate, when hygiene factors such as a "living wage" or supportive working conditions are not in place, then the worker may become dissatisfied. Hygiene's presence allows the motivators to work.

One commentator critiquing hygiene factors remarked that Herzberg did not care for money. In sheer desperation, Herzberg had to raise his fees to speak at business presentations. As Herzberg himself says in the video clip, "I wallow in hygiene".

Conclusion

We should not forget that the above theorists, apart from Pink, focused most of their research on US or other Western companies, and the samples used in the investigation were small.

Maslow's sample consisted only of managers. We must also remember that there may be specific cultural factors that may have an impact on workers' motivation.

Finally, not all motivation theories can be applied to all forms of employment. Struggling artists or musicians (or teachers) may sacrifice lower-order Maslow needs such as physiological needs or security (by refusing to take a higher-paying job) in order to have the time and space to attempt to achieve self-actualization through their passion. To illustrate this with Pink's model, an individual may seek mastery and purpose but be unable to afford autonomy.

Application of motivation theory

We shall now try to apply these theories to given motivational situations. Below are examples of workers' actions analysed in the light of the theories.

- **A worker wishes to learn new skills in order to gain promotion.**

The self-esteem needs in Maslow's hierarchy are to be satisfied with a desire to grow professionally, as advocated by Herzberg.

- **A manager is requested by the board of directors to achieve higher sales targets. Higher bonuses will be paid if the targets are met.**

The board of directors is using scientific management to encourage middle managers to be more profitable.

- **Workers in a call centre are threatening to walk out over poor conditions and long hours.**

Hygiene factors may be absent, which will not allow the motivators to function. In addition, the security needs in Maslow's hierarchy are not being met.

Types of financial reward (AO2)

It is expected that business textbooks will cover the financial rewards shown in Figure 2.4.3, so a full treatment is not given here.

IB Learner Profile

Open-minded and principled

Sports Direct

To try and analyse some of the reward systems shown in Figure 2.4.3, we briefly return to the newspaper article about Sports Direct in unit 2.3, page 41). The article reported the introduction of zero-hours contracts for part-time staff at this major sports retail outlet in the UK, accompanied by a bonus share scheme to 2 000 full-time employees.

(Continued from page 41):

Sports Direct's chief executive, Dave Forsey, told the *Guardian*:

"The share scheme glues this company together. These schemes are typically only for the executives, but this goes deep into the company. I'm surprised more businesses haven't adopted something like this sooner."

The *Guardian* has seen a copy of the share scheme rules, stating it is "intended to drive group performance and to motivate and retain permanent employees at all levels of the group, and to align the interests of those employees with those of shareholders".

However, the document adds that employees can be excluded from the scheme.

It says that any "participant who is determined to be an unsatisfactory performer" will not get the shares. Unsatisfactory performance will normally be accompanied by a written warning and continued poor performance may lead to suspension.

Employment lawyers have said the wording of the share scheme is too vague and could be abused. David Cohen, consultant solicitor at Keystone Law, said: "It is unusual under an all-employee share scheme for the directors to have the power to deprive continuing employees, as opposed to 'bad leavers', of their share awards."

"If workers generally became aware that the scheme was being operated in an unfair and arbitrary way, the company would risk losing the reputational and motivational advantages of putting in place such a generous scheme."

By comparison, John Lewis, a retail competitor which runs one of the best-known employee bonus schemes in the country as part of its partnership structure, pays all employees a bonus regardless of disciplinary warnings against them.

Sports Direct declined to comment.

QUESTIONS FOR REFLECTION

- Using Adams' equity theory of motivation, do you think that it is fair for some full-time managers to receive a bonus and that part-time workers should receive nothing?

- Bonuses have been paid in other organizations – most notably financial institutions – to senior managers who received government bailouts after the global financial crisis of 2008. Can these bonuses be justified? If not, then why are financial institutions still paying substantial bonuses in 2014?

- TOK question: Can bonuses given out by a business ever be regarded as fair unless everyone receives an equal amount?

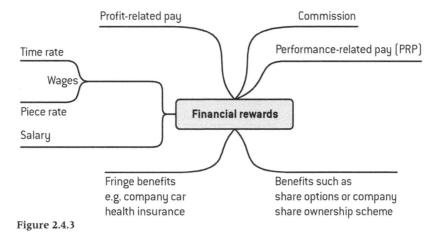

Figure 2.4.3

Types of non-financial reward (AO2)

There are a number of non-financial methods of motivation. They are shown in Table 2.4.1 to explain the link between job satisfaction and productivity that will help our final discussion.

Further analysis of non-financial rewards

Job enrichment

McGregor and Herzberg have been two key figures in the development of this school of thought on motivation. The YouTube clip we referred to earlier has a number of examples from Herzberg himself as to the virtues of job enrichment. We can group these into two areas:

- Job enrichment allows "personal growth" or "psychological growth" of the individual. ("The more someone can do the more they can be motivated to do.")
- Meaningful work and self-checking of this work via the job enrichment programme provides the opportunity for the individual to be responsible and have a degree of autonomy, which will lead to motivation. Herzberg argues that you must not make somebody a "responsible idiot". Employees must perceive that they are contributing "meaningful work" to the organization's overall effort.

Problems with job enrichment

Herzberg notes that training is a key element in the process. This will cost money and take time to bear fruit in an organization.

Managers will need to ensure that "meaningful work" is available and possible for each worker to complete. Herzberg argues that the two key functions of motivation are ability (enhanced through training) and the opportunity for individuals to put into practice what they have learned. Otherwise demotivation will occur.

Criticisms of job enlargement and empowerment

Some writers have argued that job enlargement is really just offering workers "more of the same" and is not really an opportunity to develop talents. Others have gone further to suggest that job enlargement is merely a ploy by the organization to boost productivity by asking fewer employees to do more.

For empowerment, the argument is extended. Empowerment is viewed as a simple way to cut costs and remove management layers (by delayering) as part of a strategic cost-cutting exercise.

Without sufficient training, some workers may be unable or unwilling to be responsible for their daily routine, preferring instead to work in areas with clear lines of communication and responsibility. Empowerment may not be appropriate in some cultures internally such as an autocratic or bureaucratic culture. It may not be appropriate externally given the cultural intelligence (CQ) found in some parts of the developing world.

Teamwork

The motivational impact of employees working in teams has very strong support from a number of motivational theorists. One of the most powerful is **the Hawthorne effect** observed in the 1930s by Elton Mayo. This led to the creation of the human relations school of motivation. Motivation here is driven by the need for acceptance and consideration for other individuals and the economies of scale by sharing workloads, ideas and responsibilities.

Strong evidence from companies such as Nissan, Volvo and Toyota and other Japanese manufacturers is that teamwork should be introduced wherever possible into the workplace.

However, in one of his last interviews before his death, Drucker was sceptical about the benefits of teamwork. He states:

It is generally assumed today that there is only one kind of team – call it the jazz combo – where each participant does his or her own thing but together they make great music. Actually, there are perhaps a dozen types. Different teams each with its own area of application and its own limitations and difficulties and each requiring different management.

Unless we work out, and fast, what a given team is suited for, and what a given team is not suited for, teams will become discredited as just another fad.

Source: Peter Drucker quoted in *Forbes Magazine*, 10 May 1998, in an article entitled "How to prosper in the new economy".

Method of non-financial motivation	Explanation
Job rotation	This is a system used in organizations where a production process is broken down into smaller parts and workers are trained to complete all tasks but are rotated to reduce boredom (especially if the tasks are repetitive in nature) and increase productivity. This also provides automatic cover for absent workers through illness but training must be extensive
Purpose/the opportunity to make a difference	See the YouTube clip of Daniel Pink "The Surprising Thing about Motivation" and analysis above
Job enrichment	This is sometimes referred to as "vertical loading" where an employee is offered more challenging work with increased levels of responsibility to motivate him or her
Job enlargement	This is sometimes referred to as "horizontal loading" where an employee is challenged by performing more tasks at the same level of responsibility. The argument is that the variety of tasks stops boredom and creates improved satisfaction as the employee is able to participate in the whole production process
Empowerment	The individual is given more control over his or her daily work routine with minimal supervision. This creates a sense of trust in the organization which can be motivating for some and can lead to productivity increases
Teamwork	This motivating factor can take many forms depending on the nature of the team, the task and the reward offered. Motivational research has found strong increases in productivity for those who work consistently in teams rather than individually

Table 2.4.1 Non-financial rewards

How financial and non-financial rewards may affect job satisfaction, motivation and productivity in different cultures (AO2)

Now we will look at possible effects of financial and non-financial rewards on satisfaction, motivation and productivity in different cultures. **It can be quite difficult to generalize about these issues**. Without conducting a full investigation of CQ we are left with anecdotal or personal experiences which inform our views.

For example, we saw in the Daniel Pink YouTube clip "The Surprising Thing about Motivation" that for "rudimentary tasks" productivity and motivation can be influenced by small monetary reward. However, to motivate employers to carry out cognitive or thinking tasks, **monetary rewards are ineffective**. Instead the purpose and autonomy motives are more influential. Pink's research included surveys from the United States and India.

As we shall see in units 5.4 and 5.5 (HL only) on the supply chain, Taylorism is alive and thriving in Chinese manufacturing despite the long working days and repetitive work. New Zealand and Australia have some of the highest average hours worked in the developed world. Recent research from New Zealand shows that people in employment there work nearly 2 500 hours per year, the fourth highest total, yet productivity still remains lower than in many countries where people work fewer hours.

And what about Europe? There is the perception that Europeans' work patterns and practices are out of touch with the rest of the world. However, consider the following article.

Is life easy in the land of the 35-hour week, generous holidays and long lunches? 'Non', say burnt-out French.

French workers may have a reputation for having things a little easy, but according to a new study millions work so hard that they are close to burn-out.

In the land of the 35-hour week, generous holidays and long lunches, a study found that 3.2 million people – about one in eight of the workforce – were working so hard that they risked mental or physical breakdown.

According to Technologia, a company which studies work-related illness or stress, almost one in four French farmers and one in five French company bosses are overworking and could face burn-out. One in five executives and one in seven blue-collar employees are also working too hard.

Technologia says that the economic crisis is placing pressure on employees at all levels to work excessively hard and take on more overtime. New technologies mean that many white-collar employees are taking their work, or work worries, home with them, making a mockery of the 35-hour week.

Official statistics suggest the French (who work 41.2 hours a week) work slightly less on average than the Germans (41.9 hours) or the British (42.8 hours). They have an even higher productivity per worker than Germany's but also greater stress.

Source: Adapted from www.independent.co.uk, 28 January 2014

IB Learner Profile

Inquiry ?

Carry out a survey in your own business management class to see whether there are any trends or data which could support or defeat the following hypotheses:

- Financial rewards motivate students from all cultures in the class.
- There are students from some cultures who are motivated by non-financial rewards and others by financial rewards.

More questions you might ask include the following:

- What does the term "job satisfaction" mean in your class?
- Discuss whether your class values job satisfaction above financial rewards or whether the reverse is the case.

Setting the scene

As we have seen from concept 6, culture is one of the six concepts that underpin our learning of business management and therefore should be at the forefront of any analysis and discussion of the issues facing HR management.

Although organizational culture is a designated HL-only topic, SL students are **strongly advised to read through this material**, as it will assist in their conceptual understanding of organizational culture.

ORGANIZATIONAL CULTURE (AO1)   HL

The culture of an organization is defined as the attitudes, beliefs, experiences, norms and values which determine working relationships between internal stakeholders and ways of interacting with external stakeholders.

In this unit we are going to focus more on culture that exists inside an organization. External cultural influences referred to in concept 4: Culture will be examined in later units, such as when we look at international marketing.

Let's start with an inquiry example of organizational culture before looking at a specific theoretical framework.

IB Learner Profile
Inquiry ?

In this "flipped learning" exercise you are provided with a context that you will be familiar with, but you may not be familiar with some of the terms used. We will refer to this context throughout the remaining parts of unit 2.

The example below is adapted from an article published in a UK newspaper. Read the adapted article and ask yourself what would it be like to work at this organization.

Moving onto a theoretical approach

It would appear difficult to categorize Pixar's organizational culture accurately. Some business management textbooks use terms such as "open", "free" "contemporary" or "inclusive". These terms, while well intentioned, are too vague to be useful.

In the absence of any recognized classification of different cultures, for the rest of this study guide we will use Handy's suggested framework from his highly influential book *Gods of Management* (1978).

What is it like to work at Pixar?

Deep, deep inside the vast buildings that house Pixar Animation Studios lies a dark secret. It's heavily disguised – a small room hidden among the furry life-size statues of Sulley from Monsters, Inc. But inside is something that runs so contrary to the Pixar philosophy that employees will only talk about it off the record, and with a furtive glance over their shoulder.

It's a bar. A real, alcoholic bar.

This, sadly, does not form part of the official tour of Pixar's headquarters – a series of low-rise, modern hangars in Emeryville, California, across the bay from San Francisco. Which is a shame, as it's a rare example of a human vice in an otherwise eerily perfect working environment. One that, at times, feels either like a youth club or a well-funded cult.

For example, we've already enjoyed the free, 24-hour staff Cereal Bar, boasting 14 kinds of breakfast cereal from Frosties to Lucky Charms, and an endless supply of milk. There is a Pizza Room, offering free slices for those working late. There is even a "Breathing Room" – although we're assured this is actually for yogic meditation, rather than being the only location where basic respiration is permitted.

Somehow it seems like the best and, simultaneously, the worst place to work on Earth.

However, Pixar must be doing something right. Because at the other end of the atrium, in a glass cabinet, sits the proof. Twenty-six Academy Awards, five Golden Globes and three Grammys. Not bad considering that, in 1991, Pixar was a high-end computer hardware company with just 42 employees, teetering on the brink of bankruptcy.

Everyone loves Pixar and the films the company makes. The riotous, clever, benchmark-setting "Toy Story" made its name, of course – and "Toy Story 3" is now the second highest-grossing animated film of all time after "Frozen".

Maintaining its unprecedented 15-year rise, bookended by "Toy Story" and "Toy Story 3", has not been easy for Pixar. The company is no longer the maverick outsider, nimbly taunting the big studios with its indie credibility; since being bought by Disney for $7.4 billion in 2006, Pixar is now most definitely the mainstream.

What is this magical formula that keeps enthusiasm and inspiration bubbling throughout the four years it takes to make a Pixar movie? Why does almost nobody from the 1 200 staff ever leave?

Certainly, the headquarters itself has to be responsible for much of the attraction. Indeed, it's a mark of Pixar's status that even cynical film hacks are moved to childish wonder at the prospect of a visit to the site (with one comparing it to winning Willy Wonka's golden ticket). And for films fans, it's like a theme park. Pixar characters are everywhere.

When Steve Jobs took over the company in the late 1980s, during his hiatus from Apple, the design of the building itself became a personal fascination. Working with architects Jobs gave them a simple brief: to design headquarters that "promoted encounters and unplanned collaborations".

Thus, the atrium of what's now posthumously called the Steve Jobs Building is the centre of all things Pixar – housing focal points like the café, football tables and a fitness centre. Rather cruelly, Jobs also insisted at the time that it would also contain the only toilets on the entire 22-acre site – to ensure that introverts would be forced into conversations, even if they took place while washing their hands.

This kind of design was revolutionary. In the late 1990s, film studios were still housing their employees in drab office blocks. But here, on the banks of the San Francisco bay, was a workplace offering its staff use of an Olympic-sized swimming pool, volleyball court, jogging trail, football field and basketball court – as well as an organic vegetable garden used by Pixar's chefs, flower-cutting gardens and even a wildflower meadow.

Inside, too, there was freedom. There are no set working times – instead, the offices are open 24 hours a day for those who prefer to work in the small hours.

It was a model that Apple, Google and hundreds of Silicon Valley start-ups would later copy – one where a job became a lifestyle in itself. Keep employees happy with free sustenance and diversions in a youth club atmosphere, the theory goes, and they'll never feel any need to leave. It is this free atmosphere that many employees attribute to Pixar's success.

It's perhaps no wonder, then, that the interview process to become part of this Pixar family is harsh. With an estimated 45 000 applications received for each new position, only a chosen few make it. One successful employee remarks about the recruitment process. "They want to get as many people to see you as possible – just to make sure everyone is comfortable with your personality, how you hold yourself, if you fit in."

Once through that process, however, employees are given almost total free rein. The Pixar in-house theory is simple: mistakes are an inevitable part of the creative process, so it's far better if you pile in and start making them quickly. John Lasseter, chief creative officer at Pixar, confirms this: "Every Pixar film was, at one time or another, the worst motion picture ever made," he once said. "People don't believe that, but it's true. But we don't give up on the films."

Another senior executive agrees "It's a mentality," he says. "You're responsible for your mistakes, but there's no blame culture. As a freelancer in London, I knew that if I'd made a critical error, I'd be out of a job. Here, they'd say you have to learn from it, and strive to do better. It's the most grown up place I've ever worked in that regard. It's all about ownership."

And it looks like this culture is about to bear fruit again. As if determined to silence its critics once and for all, Pixar's release slate over the next few years looks purposefully innovative. "The Good Dinosaur", set for release next May, asks what the world would be like if dinosaurs had never become extinct. The year after sees "Inside Out", entirely based inside the mind of a little girl. And after "Finding Dory", a sequel to 2003's "Finding Nemo", Pixar is set for even odder themes with "Día de los Muertos", based on the Mexican Day of the Dead celebrations.

Source: Adapted from an article in the UK newspaper *The Daily Telegraph*, 10 July 2013

QUESTIONS FOR REFLECTION

- How would you describe the organizational culture at Pixar?
- Question for discussion: If Pixar's organizational culture is so successful then why do more organizations not adopt it?
- How does Pixar's culture lead to motivation of its workforce?
- How would you judge success at Pixar? Would you focus on innovation and happiness at work, or attribute its success to product development or in terms of revenue generated or awards won?
- Can you think of any disadvantages or problems that a business might experience in trying to move from a "traditional" culture to a more "contemporary" one such as the culture present at Pixar?

Classification of cultures (AO2)
Elements of organizational culture (AO2)

Table 2.5.1 is adapted from Handy (1978) where he assigned a classical figure to each of four possible cultures present in an organization.

First we must note the following:

- There is no "cultural purity" within an individual or organization. For example (using the categories in Table 2.5.1), we cannot really say that a culture is all "Zeus" or all "Athenian". Handy argues that businesses and stakeholders are combinations of all four cultures. What is important is the dominant or most prevalent culture.

	Zeus	Apollo	Athenian	Dionysus
Culture	Club	Role	Task or problem-solving	Existential or based on individualism
Example of an organization	Family business	State services, local government	Media company	University
Example of an individual in this culture	Richard Branson – seems to be the epitome of Zeus	Accountant or immigration officer	Advertising executive. Prefers to work in matrix structures	Groundsman in a school, ICT specialist, teacher, nurse
Leadership style appropriate to culture	Paternalistic	Autocratic, bureaucratic	Laissez-faire or flexible	Anti-management. Does not wish to be managed
Ways of describing a typical individual in this culture	Charismatic, impulsive, hardworking, aggressive, optimistic	Gets on with the job, thoughtful, reliable, rational	Sociable, responsive, extrovert, anxious to solve problems	Rigid, introverted, reserved but loyal
Ways of motivating	Power and influence. Money acts as an enabler to take more risks. Values networks and connections. Likes to be able to influence others	Clear career path offered. Promotion based on work ethic. Visible signs of recognition, e.g. corner office and company car	Training giving new skills with the opportunity to use these new skills in a dynamic problem-solving environment	Allowed to get on with the job with minimal interference. Earns professional respect from colleagues because of talent
Issues or problems	Hates to be constrained by rules and regulations	Can be too inflexible. Hates change. Perceived as rather dull but can be excellent in a crisis	Expensive form of decision-making and can be indecisive in crises. Irritated by certainty and stability	Can be viewed as selfish. The organization is viewed as helping the individual and not the other way around

Table 2.5.1 Handy's four categories of organizational culture (1978)

- All cultures have strengths and weaknesses. No culture or mixture of cultures is "bad" or "wrong" in itself, but it may be simply inappropriate given the situation or issue facing the organization at a precise moment in time.

IB Learner Profile

Risk-taking and open-minded

A questionnaire designed by Dr Harrison is given in Handy (1978). Handy credits Harrison with the original analysis on differences in culture. Interested students may wish to answer this questionnaire to determine their own cultural viewpoints and those of their organization. In addition, there are a number of cultural and personality profile exercises which can be downloaded from the Internet and used to determine your dominant culture.

Culture clashes (AO3)

Reasons for and consequences of culture clashes (AO3)

Culture clashes often occur when organizations grow, merge and when leadership styles change. Referring to Table 2.5.1, we can predict the following cultural clashes between individuals within an organization:

- Zeus characters may be become irritated with Apollo colleagues' insistence on sticking to rules. Individuals in Zeus cultures would dislike to be constrained in this manner.

- Athenians need to be challenged or they may become bored. Can the organization provide enough challenges to motivate Athenians to stay?

- Dionysians may be perceived as impossible to manage but can be absolutely vital to the smooth running of an organization. Some have argued that the best way to manage Dionysians is to leave them alone.

- Apollos appear to be dull and inflexible but may curb the excesses of the Zeus and Athenian cultures. This pragmatism can be essential as an organization grows.

Now think of other potential clashes and discuss how these might be resolved. Research carried out by Professor West on 1 000 businesses is relevant here. West's study indicated that without cultural alignment (i.e. reducing possible culture clashes) a strategic direction undertaken by a business will be difficult to achieve.

Discussion

In any organization the key is to manage these differences so that some equilibrium can be achieved. (See also force field analysis in unit 1.7, and leadership and management in unit 2.3.)

This issue is particularly relevant when we consider culture clashes when organizations merge. The Time Warner (Apollo) merger with AOL (Dionysus) mentioned in unit 1.6 seems to have been jeopardized from the start as there was no significant review of how two such opposing cultures were to remain in balance.

Another issue is that when an organization grows it can be difficult to control or maintain the original culture, which may have been the inspiration or driving force in the beginning. A good example of this is the growth and development of Apple which started as a "passion" project for Steve Jobs and Steve Wozniak, employing three people. Both Jobs and Wozniak wished to challenge the prevailing business models of IBM and other computer companies and create a new way of thinking. Apple wanted to be different and innovative and create new, attractive computer products designed from the inside out.

By the time Apple had grown into a larger more sustainable business, additional managers and investors were required. Some of these stakeholders were enthused by Jobs' vision but others (possibly Apollos) were sceptical. They believed that Jobs was spending funds erratically on trying to create new products and wasting management resources on developing ideas which were characterized by too much "out of the box" thinking.

By 1985, Jobs was fired by Apple. He later returned to grow the company into the world's largest – this time with his vision in tact.

The example of Apple reveals that as an organization grows or merges with another business it can be very difficult to keep the original culture or purpose in place. This inevitably leads to clashes between stakeholders.

Organizational culture and individuals (AO3)

This section looks at how individuals influence organizational culture and how organizational culture influences individuals. Again, Apple provides a good example.

The tributes paid to Steve Jobs after his death in 2011 reflected the admiration and adulation of his leadership style as he lifted Apple to become the biggest company in the world. When we think of Apple and the successes the company has achieved (such as the iPhone, iPad and iPod), Jobs' role in the creation of Apple products is always highlighted. An interesting question though is how much influence Steve Jobs had in the creation of the Apple culture.

We have already noted (in concept 3) that Jobs' view on innovation was "saying no to 1 000 things". Biographers and media commentators have written that Jobs could be ruthless and autocratic and very demanding. Yet in common with Pixar (featured at the beginning of this unit) Apple has a history of successful innovation and creativity. The issue is compounded by the fact that Jobs worked for both companies although in a much more withdrawn role at Pixar.

We must also note that the members of the Kristiansen family, who own Lego, have strongly influenced the culture at this organization. Similarly, for a long time the Disney family held a very strong influence on the direction and culture of the Disney Corporation. Both companies have enjoyed success and failure and tried as much as possible to remain true to the original vision of their founders.

Pixar's organizational culture clearly influences animators and designers. The Google culture has played a very strong role in allowing individuals the opportunities to be creative and risk-taking. Famously, Google allows its employees 20% of allocated company time to work on any idea or innovation that motivates them. The only requirement is that these ideas must be fed back to and shared with senior managers. This is also happening in a number of other companies, as we saw in unit 2.4 on motivation.

We can conclude from this small survey that an individual can exert a significance influence on organizational culture. We have evidence that once the culture is established it can be very pervasive and influential over other individuals, whether they are internal stakeholders or external.

Setting the scene

Unemployment, especially youth unemployment, is increasing in the developed and developing world, despite the global recovery. The nature of the relationships between the employer and the employee therefore remains critical.

Social and technological change is having an impact on the working day. We have already noted the significant changes in work patterns and practices, such as the zero-hours contracts introduced by a number of employers in the UK. De-industrialization (as mentioned in unit 1.1, page 11) is also having an impact on employment patterns with many low-skilled or semi-skilled workers automated out of the employment market and now having to consider that career changes will become the norm rather than the exception.

During uncertainty, employees especially need to be realistic as to the extent that they can bargain for wage increases. A job with a modest pay rise for all workers may be preferable to some workers receiving a higher rate and the firm having to make compulsory redundancies. Consequently, the new language of employee and employer relationships is being revised. In many cases, instead of conflict and confrontation we now are now witnessing conciliation and cooperation.

IB Learner Profile

Knowledgeable and inquirers ?

The current *Business Miscellany*, published by *The Economist*, reports an interesting finding about the number of strikes recorded in various countries (many strikes go unrecorded as they last only a few hours). According to the *Business Miscellany* research, as a function of working days lost in a whole range of countries from Canada to the United States, the number of strikes recorded is at an all-time historical low.

This unit investigates the nature of the dynamic relationship between employees and employers and their representatives. This relationship will be different in every country depending on the cultural environment and the prevailing legal framework that governs industrial relations law. In this guide we cannot cover every country's situation and thus our analysis will be presented in generic terms. You are encouraged to research the current legislation that exists in the country in which you are studying.

Employee and employer representatives (AO2)

Roles and responsibilities (AO2)

Traditionally, the role of an employee representative such as a trade union has been focused on achieving fair pay, safe conditions at work, the protection of workers' rights and ensuring that employers meet their responsibilities. An underlying responsibility or philosophy, which drives most if not all trade unions, is to improve the lives of working people and their families, in whichever country they are located.

In comparison to trade unions, employer representatives are more loosely organized and membership will depend on a number of factors, for example:

- the size of the industry and the number of eligible members
- the current political and economic environment, especially any new government policy initiatives which may affect whole groups of employers.

As an example we consider the mission statement of the Employers and Manufacturers Association (EMA) based in New Zealand. The EMA has a key role in supporting its member organizations in growing and developing their business. This is achieved by offering services such as:

- employment relations advice
- occupational workplace and safety advice and training
- skills training and education courses
- publications, media statements and occasional campaigns such as "Fix Auckland" to improve the environment in which to do business.

It could be argued that both organizations have the same intentions for their members. Yet the degree to which these intentions are easily satisfied remains the potential source of conflict.

How employee representatives pursue objectives (AO3)

We can identify a number of methods a trade union or similar organization, which has been elected to act as a representative on behalf of the employees, may use to promote collective objectives. These include maintaining the current level of employment in an organization or improving pay and conditions for its members. These are achieved through a process called "**collective bargaining**".

However, we can note other methods used to pursue key objectives:

- **Negotiation** – the trade union or employee representative begins a period of negotiation or bargaining with the employee, usually face to face. At this stage, the production process continues.
- **Go-slow** – employees are instructed by their representatives to work at reduced speeds without jeopardizing the production process.
- **Work-to-rule** – employees are instructed to work deliberately to the letter of their contract and withdraw "goodwill". Goodwill in this context refers to the unpaid additional duties workers gladly take on although they are not normally included in their formal job description. Examples include ambulance drivers who could reluctantly withdraw goodwill by refusing to drive an emergency patient to hospital at a certain time if their contract stated that they should have finished work before that time.
- **Overtime ban** – a number of public sector organizations rely on workers working overtime during weekends and unsocial hours. This could include nurses, teachers and doctors. The introduction of an overtime ban could have an impact on these sectors and services considerably.
- **Strike action** – employee representatives usually treat this "weapon" as a last resort. If negotiations have broken down and there is a clearly an impasse or in the extreme an unbridgeable gap between the two sides, a strike or prolonged stoppage may be called by the employees' representatives. The production process stops.

In many countries a strike can only be sanctioned after a ballot of members has taken place. Otherwise the strike may be deemed unlawful. This is important for two reasons:

- If the strike is unlawful, workers may not be entitled to receive "strike pay" (if any has been agreed) which is intended to support them while they are not working.
- An unlawful strike may generate a lack of stakeholder support for the strike action and lead to a loss of public sympathy or goodwill for the cause. This may weaken the position of the employee representatives once the negotiations resume.

IB Learner Profile

Inquiry ?

You are encouraged to watch a DVD resource outlining the role of trade unions and employer representatives, and the relationship and tensions that exist between them. "I'm Alright Jack" is an outstanding movie made in 1960 about the whole issue of strike action, union democracy and the sometimes fractious relationship with employers. It is a comedy but lurking beneath the humour is a not-so-subtle satirical look at working practices, scientific management (time and motion in the spirit of Taylorism) and the "them and us" approach to industrial management that dominated during this time.

How employers exert pressure on employees (AO2)

During industrial disputes, employers are also not limited to negotiation. There are also a number of methods or "weapons" open to them through collective bargaining in order to achieve their own objectives. We must note, however, that these methods could be considered aggressive and likely to inflame employees and their representatives, especially if there is no end to negotiations in sight. In some countries, some of the following practices may be unlawful:

- **Threat of redundancies** – some firms may announce that redundancies are inevitable if the trade union presses ahead with its industrial action. This may attempt to blunt the union's industrial action even if the threat is not as large as the company claims.

- **Changes of contract** – given a downturn in an economy an employer may announce that changes of contract are required to keep the organization in business. We have already noted the introduction of zero-hours contracts in the retail industry.

- **Lockout** – faced with mounting tension a firm may lock workers out of the workplace. This is a difficult and dangerous tactic. The publicity surrounding a lockout may create poor public relations and sympathy may shift from the employer to the employees, especially if some workers not covered by the union action wish to work (and earn a wage).

- **Closure of the workplace** – this is the last resort as clearly closure would not only have an impact on the employees but on the employers as well. Effectively, the organization could cease to exist, affecting the livelihoods of a number of stakeholders. Given increasing unemployment, this course of action would only be taken if all other means of settling the dispute had been exhausted.

Sources of conflict and resolution (AO3)

Conflict within a dynamic large organization is inevitable. We have noted that some new organizations have tried to introduce greater democracy and empowerment into the workplace in order to reduce tensions but disagreements over pay levels, job responsibilities, working conditions and appraisal will lead to an uneasy working environment.

Even at Google, some disaffected employees have taken to social media to voice their concerns. An article in the UK newspaper *The Independent* (4 November 2012) printed a "thread" concerning some issues for those working for one of the most innovative companies in the world. According to the same article Google has the fourth highest **labour turnover** of the Fortune 500 top companies. Amazon is at number two in this list.

Possible solutions

Given the inherent tensions that may exist between employee and employer during an industrial dispute, a number of conflicts have been decided instead by a third or outside party in a process of **conciliation** and then **arbitration**. Once the conciliation process has taken place, the decision of the third party (the arbiter) is final. Both sides that decide to enter into conciliation must abide by the outcome. However, the process of deciding the outcome can take time and is costly.

Other employers have tried to use other tactics such as **no-strike** or **single-union agreements**:

- Employers may offer a union a deal where, in return for not striking, an employer may automatically allow a dispute to go to the conciliation process and then arbitration by a third party. This could lead to a much quicker resolution than if the strike had taken place.

- Single-union agreements allow the employer to avoid negotiating with three or four unions, which could delay final resolution and lead to competition between the unions for the best deal. Time, lost production and goodwill could all be saved through bargaining with only one union.

In extreme cases a firm may offer a no-union deal.

There are also other ways in which employers encourage the resolution of conflicts. Workers at Wal-Mart are treated as "associates" and through employee participation programmes are encouraged to participate in a form of industrial democracy giving workers rights collectively over the resolution of key issues. This model has been employed with enthusiasm in Japan, which has the lowest recorded number of strikes measured by working days lost (where reliable statistics exist). The system of participation has led to significant improvements in morale and productivity.

IB Learner Profile

Inquiry ?

Watch the 2005 documentary about Wal-Mart "The High Cost of Low Price" on DVD (available in long and short versions on YouTube).

Unfortunately, the Wal-Mart model has its critics with Wal-Mart being the most famous example of a company that did not allow union activity within the company or its supply chain. Recent criticism by pressure groups has softened Wal-Mart's perceived hard-line stance.

Conclusion

With changes in legislation making strikes more difficult and the need for employees and employers to work together a new era of workplace relations may be upon us. Clearly, the recent social, economic and technological changes noted earlier have aided this process.

Resistance to change (AO2)

We have already considered Lewin's model of force field analysis (in unit 1.7) and used an example of how this model could be used to help an organization change and adopt a new strategy. In this section we must go back and analyse possible reasons for resistance to change and how an organization may act to reduce but not eliminate the impact of change.

Reasons for resistance

With any new strategic decision to change there will always be resistance. This resistance will mostly stem from fear caused by misinformation and misinterpretation so that the various stakeholders involved do not know exactly what the changes may mean for them. We can anticipate a number of stakeholder responses to planned change:

- When will the changes take place?
- Who will be affected and why?
- My job is important to the success of this organization (self-interest response).
- Why do we need to change? We seem to be doing fine as it is (low-tolerance response).
- It is other departments' fault (self-interest response).

We can summarize and broaden this resistance to change by considering the viewpoints of a selection of stakeholders (see Table 2.6.1).

Stakeholder	Resistance due to:
Line workers	fear of new working practices, threat to Maslow lower-order needs such as security, love and belonging
Customers	fear of losing a product that they were loyal to
Suppliers	fear of losing a place in the supply chain; fear of job losses and lost revenue
Managers	fear of having to implement change and dealing with adverse reaction by line workers

Table 2.6.1 Reasons for various stakeholders' resistance to change

Reducing the impact of change

In unit 1.7 we looked at the process of reducing the impact of change using Lewin's model of force field analysis. According to this model, in order to effect change the drivers (the reasons for change to occur) need to be able to move the organization to a new status quo and reduce the power or influence of the restrainers (the resistors to change).

This is easier said than done. To achieve successful implementation, a number of operational tactics will need to be used.

As we saw in unit 1.7, Dearden and Foster (1992) argue:

- The team charged with implementing change must have authority to implement change, which is understood by those affected by that change.
- The board of directors through the CEO must indicate that change is necessary and extol clearly the virtues of this change for the whole organization.
- The change process, including contingencies, must be clearly communicated to all stakeholders early, including (as accurately as possible) time lines for implementation.
- Early successful outcomes of the change must be clearly communicated and celebrated.
- A constant reminder of the goals and objectives of the strategy change must be highlighted prominently around the workplace.

It would seem that clear effective communication and management play a crucial part in the change process.

Conclusion

Again we must consider the thoughts of Gary Hamel, who has indicated on a number of occasions that change is pervasive and inevitable. Organizations that do not adapt their management systems, their ability to innovate given that knowledge is now a commodity and their ability to recruit and attract the best "generation Y" workers will lose their place in the market-place.

HR strategies, given the significant changes in working patterns and practices, the onset of globalization and rapid social and technological change, have to adapt given that most of the management theory now being discussed in business textbooks was created nearly 100 years ago. This is a major challenge for all organizations.

Setting the scene

Link to concept 1: Globalization and concept 3: Innovation

First, with the 2008 global financial crisis and subsequent recovery, the importance of finance to the global business community has been brought into sharp focus.

Second, given the globalization and interdependence of the world's financial systems and new technology, new models of sourcing finance have been created. It is now possible for even very small business start-ups in the developing world to obtain finance through organizations such as the Grameen Bank and the Acumen Fund. Such was the impact and success of the Grameen Bank and its founder Muhammad Yunus that the organization was awarded the Nobel Prize for Peace in 2006.

Third, after the financial horrors that accompanied the dot.com boom and the collapse of Enron in 2002, there has been greater attention from media commentators and governments on the role of accounting and finance. Financial "transparency" is now a new buzzword. The mood is such that stakeholders should focus attention not just on the figures but seek greater clarification and understanding of the "stories" behind the numbers.

Finally, the Internet has also given rise to innovation through a new finance source termed "crowdfunding". Aspiring entrepreneurs can now seek an additional source of funds through programmes such as Kickstarter to finance new product ideas (e.g. Pebble Watches) or even media such as movies and documentaries and receive finance from investors they may never meet in person.

The role of finance (AO2)

Capital expenditure

Capital expenditure involves the purchase of resources that an organization intends to keep for longer than one year and that help with the productive capacity now and in the future. Capital items include buildings, machinery, equipment and vehicles. An accounting definition of capital expenditure is the purchase of fixed assets. Capital expenditure can also include one-off costs, which will benefit the business over a number of time periods. These include legal and delivery costs.

Revenue expenditure

In contrast to capital expenditure, revenue expenditure is much more short term. Fixed assets will need maintaining and repairing and these costs are counted as revenue expenditure items. Second, fixed assets themselves are unproductive without resources such as labour, material, electrical power, etc. These items fall under the broad category of working capital, which we will consider in more detail in unit 3.7.

Clearly, a balance between capital and revenue expenditure needs to be struck. Too much capital expenditure and the firm will not be able to produce products and services for sale. Too much revenue expenditure and the firm may find that resources are wasted, especially if the firm reaches over-capacity. In addition, too little capital relative to revenue expenditure could lead in the longer term to diseconomies of scale.

Internal and external sources of finance (AO2)

Source of finance	Description	Analysis
Internal		
Personal funds (sometimes referred to as owner's equity for sole traders)	The initial contribution to capital to a business from the entrepreneur. These funds can be sourced from past savings, inheritances or even redundancy payments	These funds will be critical to start a business and provide finance for initial revenue expenditure and some capital items. There is no interest to pay on using these funds but of course there is an opportunity cost
Grants and subsidies	Governments or local community bodies may provide grants and subsidies to encourage new business start-ups. A grant may be a lump sum and subsidies may allow discounts on renting premises or other capital items	Depending on the nature of the grant or subsidy, these are not normally repaid. However, they may only be small sums and not sufficient to finance a start-up. Other sources of finance will still be required
Profits	A firm uses retained earnings to finance projects	There will be no interest to pay and no dilution of ownership (see below). The action may be viewed positively or negatively by stakeholders depending on their objectives
Sale of fixed assets	A firm disposes of "old assets" for cash	Selling assets reduces productive capacity and weakens balance sheets and shareholder value, so it may be unpopular
Improve the working capital cycle Debt factoring Trade credit	(See unit 3.7 for a full explanation of the working capital cycle.) Debt factoring is allowing a third party or debt factor to collect an unpaid debt owed to a business. The debt factor charges a fee for this service. Offering trade credit means allowing customers to receive goods and services without full upfront payment, or allowing discounts for early payment	The advantages for a business in using a debt factor are that it does not have the difficult task of recovering the debt and, once the factor succeeds, the business receives the cash required to trade
Sale and lease back	A new method where firms may sell an asset but then lease or hire it back to use without the responsibility of ownership. An initial lump sump is received to finance other projects	There are a number of complex sale and lease-back schemes. They are used mostly for large fixed assets or, increasingly, ICT systems. In lease schemes only, firms may be able to update assets periodically to avoid obsolescence. This has become a feature of new outsourced ICT schemes

External		
Sale of shares	A publicly traded company may issue further shares to existing shareholders (a rights issue) or to new shareholders to raise funds	Significant sums can be raised in the capital markets but there may be dilution of ownership issues (see "The debt versus equity dilemma" below).
		In order for the share issue to be successful, a clear growth objective or strategic plan will need to be given to encourage shareholders. Shares might not be purchased if the perception is that the funds are only going to be used to pay off existing debts
Overdrafts Loans	A firm borrows additional funds from a multitude of different financial institutions. Overdrafts are very short term while loans vary in duration from 1 to 30 years depending on the reason for borrowing funds	Overdrafts must be authorized in advance or can be a very expensive way to finance. Interest will have to be paid but there will be no dilution in ownership. Interest rates can fluctuate and have an impact on interest payments and cash flow. Some sophisticated loan packages have been created such as SWAPS. These are creative but complex and controversial
Debentures	These are fixed interest loans made by firms or individuals	As above but interest is usually fixed. Debenture holders usually have first claim on a firm's assets if the company is put into liquidation and bankruptcy proceedings are started
Venture capital	This is volatile capital made available by individuals or institutions to be put into potentially profitable but risky projects	Venture capital has been cast as a hero (e.g. the Grameen Bank has sourced venture capital from the developed world) and as a villain (fuelling the unsustainable dot.com boom of the late 1990s). Some critics have argued that in the pursuit of short-term profits, venture capitalists may exert too much influence over a firm's objectives
Business angels	Sometimes referred to as providers of informal investment, business angels are usually affluent individuals who seek out potential investments and provide start-up capital in return for some ownership or equity stake in the new business	Venture capitalists are usually represented by groups and are arguably more aggressive in their dealings with providing finance. Venture capitalists may demand a greater say in decision-making. A business angel is generally more hands-off. Increasingly we are seeing business angels attracted to more socially responsible or ethical business models as a source of finance

Table 3.1.1 Internal and external sources of finance

Short-, medium- and long-term finance (A01)

The timescales involved for these three types of finance are:

- short term – to meet immediate liquidity needs and those for up to the next six months
- medium term – to achieve an objective within a period of the next six months to two years
- long term – to finance a longer-term strategic plan.

Appropriateness of source of finance (A03)

A firm will wish to use a number of different sources of finance depending on the purpose behind the need to acquire more funding. These can be broken down into:

- purpose and time considerations
- the cost to the organization
- the issue of the debt versus equity dilemma.

We will discuss each in turn.

Purpose and time considerations

Firms will have short-, medium- and long-term needs for finance. The source they choose will depend on the time frame under consideration.

For immediate liquidity concerns, an extension to a bank overdraft may be all that is required. For other short-term finance, internal methods may give quicker access to funds, such as using previous profits or reserves, rather than trying to raise new additional external finance. An extension of credit or the use of a debt factor may be appropriate.

For medium-term financing, a business may look to raise finance from debentures or other external sources with a fixed rate of interest.

For longer-term strategic uses involving sums that can run into millions of dollars, an organization will have to conduct a financial SWOT analysis and involve financial institutions or management consultants in order to source the most appropriate, cost-effective method of obtaining funds. The fees from such expertise can run into thousands of dollars, so it is assumed that only the largest organizations can afford these services.

As a general rule, if the purpose or objective to be financed is considered to be long term (over a number of years) then the most appropriate method of finance will also be long term. If the purpose is short term, then a short-term funding solution should be found. Accountants call this process "matching".

Cost considerations

Planning and size are important factors in determining the cost of finance. If a firm has poor planning and runs short of cash to pay immediate invoices then a hastily arranged overdraft can be expensive due to punitive interest rates. Unauthorized overdrafts will annoy any financial institution lending funds and are considerably more expensive for the borrower.

Loans from financial institutions may also carry high interest rates if the purpose behind the loan is not carefully articulated to the bank or financial institution lending the money. Discussions and the creation of a business plan will be needed at this point.

Finally, larger firms have the advantage of financial economies of scale over smaller firms and are able to borrow large sums of money at greatly reduced interest due to their size and the amount of collateral they can offer the lender as security.

The debt versus equity dilemma

A critical analysis will need to take place when an organization considers the choice of financing large, long-term projects. The author calls this the debt versus equity dilemma.

In response to a new strategic plan or aim, does a large organization issue more shares, and consequently dilute ownership for existing shareholders? (We assume that the shares will be targeted at new potential owners rather than existing ones.) However, issuing fresh shares avoids the need to borrow and of course pay additional interest. The risk of undertaking the new strategic plan is also "shared" among the new owners.

Or does the organization allow more debt onto the balance sheet to finance this new strategic goal and take on additional longer-term financing? However, if the new strategic move is poorly received, the organization keeps the existing level of control, there is no dilution and potential threat of a takeover is less likely.

Therein lies the debt versus equity dilemma.

Link to concept 3: Innovation and concept 1: Globalization

As we have seen with the creation of the Grameen Bank and organizations such as Kiva, the Internet is leading the way in creating new sources of finance for start-ups in the developed world. For example, analysis of the 2008 US presidential election revealed that Senator Obama raised nearly 50% of the $603 million needed to fund his campaign from donations of less than $200 collected from supporters who visited his website and transferred funds electronically.

Formed in 2009, Kickstarter has led the way in creating a new platform for creative projects and artists to raise funds through the Internet which otherwise would not be available to them. The organization is run in the United States but funding opportunities to receive and to donate are establishing themselves globally. www.kickstarter.com provides an illuminating experience as the organization tries to fulfil its mission of allowing creativity to grow.

This new funding platform has not been without its critics. One recently funded project about a live action film incorporating the very popular online community "Minecraft" was cancelled after it appeared that the creative director of the project had not sought approval to use the Minecraft logo and intellectual property.

Costs (AO2)

Table 3.2.1 defines, explains and gives an example of each different type of cost.

Type of cost	Definition	Explanation	Example
Fixed or indirect	These are costs that have to be paid but are not dependent on the level of output. They are also referred to as overhead costs	These costs are incurred if the firm produces zero output	Rent and rates on the premises, insurance
Variable or direct	These costs are output dependent	As production increases, so do variable costs	Raw material costs, wages of production workers
Semi-variable	These are costs that may have a fixed charge initially but after a certain level of usage may rise depending on production levels	(See definition)	Electricity and telephone charges. Some Internet fees are semi-fixed depending on the plan used

Table 3.2.1 Different types of cost

Total revenue and revenue streams (AO2)

We can define revenue as the amount of money generated from trading activities: selling goods or services to customers. In accounting terms, revenue may be counted as money earned even if physical cash or electronic transfer has not been received. The amount of debtors listed under current assets on a balance sheet can be counted as a form of deferred revenue (transfer of cash not yet received).

A company can earn revenue from activities other than trading in the goods and services for which the business was created (such as dividends from investments or shares owned). This is referred to as non-operating income.

Revenue streams

A revenue stream is a method or range of mechanisms – often automated – that a company, organization or individual uses to collect revenue from users of their products or services.

In *Web 2.0: A Strategy Guide* (2008) Amy Shuen identifies six types of revenue streams for an online business:

- subscription payments
- advertising fees from other companies advertising on the website
- transaction fees
- volume and unit selling
- franchising
- sponsorship and co-marketing partnerships from other online businesses.

IB Learner Profile

Inquiry ?

Here is an inquiry question often asked by students and teachers. How does Google make its money (or, to be more precise, how does Google generate revenue streams), when it gives the majority of its products away for free?

Google revenue in 2012	
Google is used for 83.18% of all worldwide searches	
Total revenue = $33.3bn (97% coming from online ads)	
Online ads can be classified into two categories:	
Approx. 70% revenue = Adwords. Adwords ads allow businesses to advertise after key words and searches have been created by using Google	The top eight searches are: 1. Insurance ($54 per click earned by Google) 2. Mortgage ($37) 3. Attorney 4. Loans 5. Credit 6. Lawyer 7. Donate 8. Degree
Approx. 30% revenue = Adsense. This allows businesses to link Adwords to particular websites	Some of the most expensive sites to advertise on include: CBS ($70 cost per thousand views from the On Demand Mad March site) Hulu ($35 cost per thousand views) American Online (AOL) "Homepage takeover advert" costs £500 000–700 000
Of the remaining 3% revenue earned by Google some is earned from a number of acquisitions (takeovers)	Examples of these acquisitions (takeovers) by Google are: YouTube, Android Operating Systems (OS) and Smartphones (e.g. Motorola Mobility)
Revenue streams to come in 2014–15 include the launch of Google Glass and Google "Driverless Cars"	

Table 3.2.1 Some of Google's revenue streams

Source: Best Accounting Schools: Rankings and Reviews of Top Accounting Degree Programs

Setting the scene

Break-even and contribution analyses are important decision-making tools and concepts for business management.

As an example, consider this: Should organization X release a new improved version of an existing product? This question will require an analytical approach before a solution can be found. Market research will need to be undertaken and analysed, for example.

However, before data collection begins in earnest, a business will often carry out a simple break-even calculation to see roughly how many units of the new improved version of the product the company will need to sell before it covers the costs of introducing it. This figure will only be an estimate and could be loosely based on previous experience, but it will give an indication of whether this opportunity is worth considering further. If current sales of the product are 50 000 units and the estimate calculated to break-even for the new version is 60 000, then the company may choose not to proceed.

Another issue arises if we consider the following. Although this new improved version of the product may not generate a large profit given that the estimated break-even point is higher, what if the new version provides a contribution to fixed or indirect costs of the business and makes a small loss? Would it still be sensible to produce this version? What if this new improved version may provide a benefit for a business in the form of a longer-term competitive advantage?

Break-even and contribution analysis can be used as ways to begin the decision-making process for an organization. We will consider break-even analysis first and then look at contribution briefly. Then, in unit 5.5, we will look at a more considered analysis of decisions about whether to buy-in or make items.

IB Learner Profile

Inquiry ?

Introduction to break-even

The article below is a rare insight into the finances associated with a major media or sporting event featuring a globally recognized personality. It neatly introduces the importance of using break-even analysis at the start of the decision-making process.

> ### QUESTIONS FOR REFLECTION
> - A previous match between a team featuring David Beckham was successful in 2007. Why do you think this latest match was unsuccessful?
> - What does the article suggest are the difficulties in trying to predict revenues even for an event that has been successful in the past?
> - Given the example below, how useful do you think break-even analysis is for an organization?

Break-even analysis: theoretical review

Straightforward break even quantity

$$= \frac{\text{fixed costs}}{\text{(price - variable cost per unit) or contribution}}$$

Below is a summary of the important elements of break-even analysis.

Consider Figure 3.3.1.

Break-even quantity with a profit target

If the firm is looking to try and guarantee a minimum level of profit, perhaps to satisfy shareholders or ensure a sole trader's salary, fixed costs will need to be adjusted. The profit target effectively becomes an overhead and must be included. The break-even quantity will have to rise accordingly.

$$\text{Break-even quantity} = \frac{\text{fixed costs + profit target}}{\text{contribution}}$$

Auckland Regional Council (ARC) paid $2.9 million on David Beckham's LA Galaxy and lost $1.7 million.

The ARC spent $2.91 million on travel, accommodation and promotion for the ill-fated football match between LA Galaxy and the Oceania All Stars in December 2008, a report has shown.

It was also revealed yesterday that the ARC banked on David Beckham's "world superstar" status drawing Auckland's Asian community to its football game that lost $1.7 million.

"Beckham is a phenomenon in Asia and with Asian people", councillors were told in a pitch from staff for staging the LA Galaxy fiasco at the ARC-owned Mt Smart Stadium.

The proposal for LA Galaxy versus an Oceania All Stars team match was pitched as a concept devised so that a wide range of people of differing ethnic descent would be attracted.

The Auckland Football Federation was to help by promoting the event to its 20 000 registered players and clubs.

"Therefore, it was not expected that there would be too many problems in attracting a healthy crowd for the event", said the report.

The "break-even" crowd needed was 25 000 and considering a similar event in Wellington had attracted 31 800 people in 2007, the report said it was unlikely that this crowd size would not be achieved. Auckland has nearly four times the population of Wellington.

The report suggested the ARC set ticket prices for a 30 000-seat capacity, with 29 000 paying ticket sales.

A profit of $484 350 was expected if 30 000 tickets were sold.

On the night only 16 587 people turned out. As for their tickets, "a portion of these were complimentary or were offered in a two-for-one deal, resulting in lower revenue".

Mr Winder's review of what went wrong is highlighted in the following details:

There was a loss of $1.79 million.

Costs of $3 057 602 were $151 052 or 5.2% above expectations.

Revenue of $2 075 599 was 61% lower than expected.

Expected revenue from ticket sales was on the day of the match 70% less than hoped for.

What went wrong?

Mr Winder said the ticket price was set too high, the marketing effort was ineffective and the Oceania team were not good enough to be considered a creditable opposition against Mr Beckham's team. It was likely that any future matches of this kind would not occur.

Source: Adapted from the *New Zealand Herald*

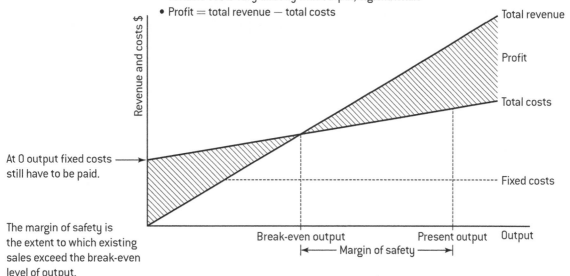

Break-even is the output at which revenue equals costs, i.e. no profit or loss is made.
- Total revenue = price × quantity
- Total costs = fixed costs + variable costs
  Fixed costs do not change with output, e.g. rent
  Variable costs vary directly with output, e.g. materials
- Profit = total revenue − total costs

At 0 output fixed costs still have to be paid.

The margin of safety is the extent to which existing sales exceed the break-even level of output.

Figure 3.3.1 Break-even analysis

The margin of safety level of output

This is the amount by which the demand for a firm's product can fall before a firm incurs losses. Alternatively, it measures how close the firm is to the break-even level of output.

Current level of demand × break-even output

Break-even quantity, profit, margin of safety (AO2, AO4)

Effects of changes in price or cost on the break-even quantity (AO2, AO4)

Graphical and quantitative analysis

When we consider changes in the price of a product charged or an increase in costs, then the impacts on break-even analysis should be obvious. Consider the following example.

Firm X has fixed costs	= $3 000
Price of the product	= $10
Variable costs	= $7
Current level of demand	= 1500
The break-even quantity	$= \dfrac{3\,000}{3}$
	= 1 000
Margin of safety	= 1500 - 1 000 = 500
Profit	= total revenue - total costs
	= (1500 × 10) - [3 000 + (1500 × 7)]
	= 15 000 - 13 500
	= 1 500

If the firm cuts the price by 10%, the quick complacent answer is that the break-even quantity will need to rise by at least 10%.

The answer is actually 50%!

If the price falls to $9 from $10 and variable and fixed costs remain the same, the new break-even quantity will be calculated from:

new break-even quantity $= \dfrac{(3\,000)}{2} = 1\,500$

margin of safety = the new break-even quantity = zero.

The business has reached maximum capacity.

New profitability = (1 500 × 9) − [3 000 − (1 500 × 9)] = loss of 3 000.

From this straightforward example a number of issues arise:

- Making price cuts is not always the most effective method to generate increases in revenues or profits. This method only works if demand for the product or service is expected to rise significantly more than the price increase in percentage terms.

- Is a 50% increase in demand achievable even with the price cut?

- Will a price cut affect the perception of quality of the product?

- What if competitors (if any) follow this price reduction? What will be the impact on quantity demanded?

- Could additional demand required be produced quickly without significantly raising short-term variable costs, i.e. is there spare capacity in the organization? If not, fixed costs may need to increase if the firm needs to finance additional capacity.

The benefits and limitations of break-even analysis (AO3)

From the above example and the case study featuring Beckham's LA Galaxy we can analyse a number of limitations of the break-even model.

It is assumed that the firm can sell as much as it wishes at the same price. This is unrealistic. In order to sell higher quantities, the firm may have to reduce prices significantly and we have seen the inverse impact on revenue and profitability.

The law of demand, which assumes a negative relationship between price and the quantity demanded, **does not result** in a linear total revenue curve. It is shaped like a parabola.

On the cost side, the assumption that variable costs rise in a linear fashion can also be challenged. If large production runs are required then a firm's costs may fall due to economies of scale or rise due to diseconomies of scale. As Figure 3.3.2 illustrates, this could lead to a multiple number of break-even points.

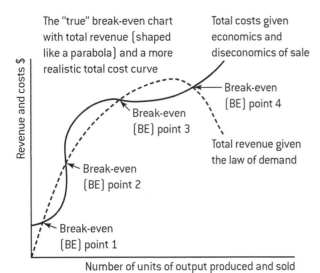

The "true" break-even chart with total revenue (shaped like a parabola) and a more realistic total cost curve

Total costs given economics and diseconomics of sale

Break-even (BE) point 4

Break-even (BE) point 3

Total revenue given the law of demand

Break-even (BE) point 2

Break-even (BE) point 1

Revenue and costs $

Number of units of output produced and sold

Figure 3.3.2 Multiple break-even points

Break-even analysis is an important element in the decision-making model but there are a number of drawbacks. We can use the case study of Beckham's LA Galaxy to highlight these.

From the case study, we can note that the ARC's use of break-even analysis was correct. However, the council did not take into account a number of other external factors.

Non-financial factors outside the control of the users of break-even analysis will need to be considered once the break-even quantity and margin of safety have been calculated. There is some evidence from the case study that the ARC underestimated these.

A break-even analysis should not be static, but different break-even points under different cost, price and revenue scenarios should also be examined. Some writers refer to considering these

different scenarios as "What if…?" analysis. It is clear that the ARC may have not prepared these.

The pricing of one-off events needs to be carefully considered. Promotions, which are used to test, and boost, the level of demand should be costed carefully and also subjected to "What if…?" scenarios.

Total contribution versus contribution per unit (AO2)

We saw that with the break-even calculations, a formula can be used to provide a quick confirmation of the break-even point after the diagram has been drawn. This formula includes the calculation of the contribution per unit.

It is worth repeating here:

contribution = price of the product – variable cost per unit.

To calculate total contribution we can either multiply the contribution per unit by the number of items sold or we can calculate:

total contribution = total revenue – total variable costs.

The importance of contribution can be illustrated using the following example.

A business making a range of products may have one product that is not making a profit. Even so, the business may decide to continue with that product because the total contribution it makes towards fixed costs, and ultimately profit, may make this worthwhile.

Simply, if a product is making a loss, contribution analysis along with marketing and operations considerations may provide justification for continuing to produce it.

The importance of contribution will be discussed in greater detail in unit 5.5.

Note that the material on depreciation in this section is HL only.

Setting the scene

In the new IB Business Management course accounting topics are now focused on how accounting can support organizations in making effective tactical or strategic decisions. Much of the process of accounting creation and calculation is now left to new technology with software programs such as Mind Your Own Business (MYOB) or Internet or cloud-based systems (e.g. those offered by start-ups such as Xero). These programs are not incorporated into the IB Business Management course but could be part of a tertiary or university degree.

The process of accounting has become more automated for most organizations than in the past. The challenge for accountants or finance departments is to make use of accounting data in a manner that supports other departments such as operations (unit 5), marketing (unit 4) and the organization's managers.

How this accounting data is interpreted and used will depend on the stakeholders who are using the accounts and their interests towards the business. Two notes of caution, however, are added. First, given that published company accounts rarely give more than a snapshot of financial figures, their use may be limited. Second, the Enron scandal, which we will refer to in due course, has questioned the principles and ethics of accounting practice. Can we trust the figures? In the new era of transparency this question is surely more relevant than ever.

The purpose of accounts for stakeholders (AO3)

The main purposes of accounts linked to stakeholders are as follows:

- By referring to its accounts, an organization can analyse its performance in terms of profitability, liquidity, efficiency and gearing in combination with accounting ratios (see units 3.5 and 3.6). Given this, accounts allow **senior managers** to make adjustments to a strategic direction if necessary.

- Accounts satisfy legal requirements in the case of publicly traded companies and thus allow calculation of corporate tax liabilities demanded **by the government**.

- Accounts allow a degree of transparency on the company's financial position to **external stakeholders such as potential investors, lenders and suppliers**.

We now consider more detailed use of published accounts, in particular:

- Current and potential investors will be especially concerned with the profitability and gearing aspects of the balance sheets. They may also wish to view financial accounts over a time period to build up an overall picture of financial performance.

- Lenders of funds will be an issue for creditors, who will be concerned with liquidity, profitability and existing levels of gearing, and perhaps the amount of fixed assets for collateral purposes if the firm is looking to borrow additional funds.

- Suppliers will be interested and concerned with liquidity issues arising from the current assets and liability sections of the balance sheet.

Conclusion

Final and published accounts can provide an invaluable source of information in the decision-making process. However, they must be taken in good faith and accepted on trust. Different stakeholders will view the accounts with different perceptions depending on each stakeholder's objectives and motives.

With any consideration of quantitative information provided by financial accounts, stakeholders will also have other issues to consider. These include qualitative or non-financial information, in addition to information about the external environment in which the firm operates.

With the growth of globalization and online trading, we must also acknowledge the difficulty in collecting accurate data, financial figures and forecasts. (This difficulty arises when an organization extends itself across a number of economic regions with alternate accounting systems and tax treatments.)

The importance of final accounts to stakeholders

The final accounts given in this guide are also published accounts available on company websites or in the financial media. Students often make the mistake of thinking that the company is "giving away secrets" by publishing final accounts. It is not, and it would be impossible to run an organization by using these accounts, as they are merely outlines or sketches of the performance of the company.

Internal accounts, sometimes referred to as managerial accounts, are much more detailed and revealing. It is not surprising, therefore, that these accounts are not made available to competitors or other external stakeholders.

We must remember that published accounts refer to the past. They should be used with caution when trying to predict future performance. The dot.com boom of the late 1990s provides us with a renowned example of investors throwing large sums of capital at Internet start-ups. These investors hoped to achieve what turned out to be fictitious profits calculated from over-optimistic balance sheets, cash flow forecasts, and profit and loss accounts, which were based on only the flimsiest of business plans.

Specifically, you could investigate the fate of pets.com. This was one of the high-profile casualties of the dot.com boom. It lost an estimated $300 million in less than two years of trading.

Principles and ethics of accounting practice (AO3)

The following inquiry task will give you an insight into how Enron abandoned principles and ethics in accounting practice.

IB Learner Profile

Inquirers and knowledgeable

Link to concept 3: Innovation and to ethical behaviour in accounting

Watch the documentary film "Enron – The Smartest Guys in the Room".

No study of ethical accounting would be complete without a review of one of the bleakest episodes of financial mismanagement in recent years by a large organization. "Enron – The Smartest Guys in the Room" is essential viewing, not too difficult to follow and very entertaining. However, it remains a worrying parable of our times, where greed and inappropriate accounting practices create an unethical and unpalatable mix.

Questions for discussion

- How was Enron innovative in an ethical manner? (Think of how the company took full advantage of changes in the natural gas and electricity generation markets.)

- Was Enron unethical in its accounting procedures? (You may wish to look at mark-to-market accounting and the ability to book virtual future profits on projects which had yet to yield any current profits.)

- How did the organizational culture driven by Jeff Skilling (the CEO of Enron) lead to the unethical behaviour of other managers such as Andy Fastow and the Enron traders?
- How much of Enron's organizational culture led to Enron and Arthur Andersen practising unethical accounting practices?
- What are they key lessons to be learned from the Enron scandal to assist in our knowledge of the principles and ethics of accounting practice?

You are encouraged to find your own answers to the questions in keeping with the IB learner profile.

Final accounts (AO2 and AO4)

To gain an understanding of balance sheets and profit and loss accounts, carry out the following research.

IB Learner Profile

Inquiry ?

You are strongly encouraged to research companies of your choice to view real-world balance sheets and profit and loss accounts. The information from companies' websites is extensive and at times overwhelming but can provide a great starting point in the study of this unit. For example, Apple's website is extremely informative and provides a whole range of financial information.

The balance sheet and profit and loss account (AO4)

Worked example

The following example uses a firm called Gemel Ltd. It shows the construction of profit and loss accounts and adjustments to them.

Again, note that depreciation does not appear on the SL syllabus. The worked example was originally set for HL students. SL students should note the format of the profit and loss account only.

(The exact structure required for the profit and loss account and balance sheet is given on pages 195 and 196 of the *IB Business Management Guide*.)

Table 3.4.1 shows forecast financial information for Gemel Ltd for 2008 and 2009.

	2008 ($000)	2009 ($000)
Turnover	485	870
Cost of stock sold	245	450
Expenses	91	138
Non-operating income	11	13
Interest paid	20	55
Tax	35	60
Dividends	60	75

Table 3.4.1

Gemel Ltd's fixed assets were valued at $200 000 on start-up. The assets would have a useful life of four years and an estimated scrap value of $40 000.

(a) Using straight-line depreciation, calculate the annual provision for depreciation that the accountant omitted. (The topic of depreciation is HL only.)

(b) Using the financial information provided for 2008 and 2009, prepare profit and loss accounts for the two years, adjusting the figures in the table above to include the provision for depreciation and recalculating the tax payment to equal 25% of net profit before tax.

$$\text{Depreciation} = \frac{\text{historic cost} - \text{scrap value}}{\text{number of years of useful life}}$$

$$= \frac{\$200\,000 - \$40\,000}{4}$$

Depreciation charge per annum = $40 000 (HL only)

Table 3.4.2 shows the revised profit and loss account for 2008 and 2009.

	2008 ($000)	2009 ($000)
Turnover	485	870
Cost of stock sold	245	450
Gross profit	240	420
Expenses (including new depreciation charge)	131	178
Total operating profit	109	242
Non-operating income	11	13
Net profit before interest and tax	120	255
Interest paid	20	55
Net profit before tax	100	200
Tax @ 25%	25	50
Net profit after tax	75	150
Dividends	60	75
Retained profit	15	75

Table 3.4.2

Presentation of balance sheet and profit and loss account (SL/HL)

Where balance sheets and profit and loss accounts are given in case studies or examination questions, they will be presented in the format shown below. Students should be familiar with this layout. Please note that while profit and loss account is also known as income statement, the term profit and loss account will be used in assessment.

ABC Ltd

Balance sheet as of 31 May 20**

	$m	$m
Fixed assets		
Fixed assets	500	
Accumulated depreciation	20	
Net fixed assets		480
Current assets		
Cash	10	
Debtors	12	
Stock	35	
Total current assets	57	
Current liabilities		
Overdraft	5	
Creditors	15	
Short-term loans	22	
Total current liabilities	42	
Net current assets (working capital)		15
Total assets less current liabilities		495
Long-term liabilities (debt)	300	
Net assets		195
Financed by:		
• share capital	110	
• retained profit	85	
Equity		195

Depreciation (AO2, AO4) HL

Depreciation: straight-line method (AO2, AO4)

Depreciation is a poorly understood topic. Many students, when asked for a definition of depreciation, reply that it is "the wear and tear" of an asset being used. Although this answer has some merit, it is not correct.

Firms depreciate assets for two main reasons. One is that assets lose value due to use over a period of time. The other reason is that the technology incorporated in the asset becomes obsolete or out of date.

Strictly speaking, however, depreciation is the process of allocating the historic cost (or price paid) of a fixed asset less any residual or scrap value, over the number of years that the asset is deemed useful. This is also known as "writing off" the value of an asset.

This method of depreciation is sometimes referred to as the straight-line method:

depreciation charge per year
$$= \frac{\text{(historic cost – residual or scrap value)}}{\text{number of estimated years of useful life}}$$

When charging this expense to the profit and loss account, there is no physical movement in cash. Instead the depreciation charge for the year is set against the profits earned by the company and the book or current value of the asset is automatically reduced. For the straight-line method, the amount charged to the profit and loss account is a constant amount each year until the whole historic cost has been written off.

Depreciation: reducing-balance method

The reducing-balance method of depreciation is another possible way of spreading the cost of a fixed asset over its useful life. The fixed asset is depreciated by a constant percentage each year, e.g. 20% of the book value.

Comparison of the two methods of depreciation

Going back to the example of Gemel Ltd, we can compare the depreciation of the firm's fixed assets under the two different methods of straight-line and reducing-balance depreciation.

The depreciation charge on a fixed asset costing $200 000 with a residual value of $40 000 over four years of useful life is $40 000 per annum. Let's depreciate the same asset by, say, 40% per year on the remaining book value at the end of the year.

Table 3.4.3 highlights a number of important considerations.

Straight-line depreciation is aptly named as the book value of the asset reduces by a constant amount. This is shown in Figure 3.4.1.

The reducing-method of depreciation is shown in Figure 3.4.2.

Strengths and weaknesses of each method (AO2)

We can see that for the reducing-balance method the initial depreciation charge to the profit and loss account in the first couple of years of an asset's useful life is higher than for the straight-line method. It is impossible to reduce a number by a percentage less than 100% and arrive at zero, so with the reducing balance method it is impossible to "write off" the value of an asset completely.

With straight-line depreciation if the residual or scrap value is zero then it is possible to spread the cost of the asset precisely over its useful life. Straight-line depreciation is easy to calculate and assumes that there will be some scrap value left over for an asset. Of course, it is possible that the scrap value or resale value of an item may be zero. However, for products which may become technologically obsolete very quickly, such as personal computers or mobile phones with increasing shorter product life cycles, the reducing-balance method of depreciation is more appropriate.

Finally, for a few fixed assets neither method is appropriate, for example aeroplanes or other forms of transport which add productive capacity to an organization. Rather than the number of years of useful life of an aeroplane, we should focus on the number of hours the asset is in use as this will have more impact on "wear and tear".

Year	Opening value of asset: straight line	Depreciation charge for that year	Book value at the end of the year
1	200 000	40 000	160 000
2	160 000	40 000	120 000
3	120 000	40 000	80 000
4	80 000	40 000	40 000
5	40 000	0	Asset sold
Year	Opening value of asset: reducing balance	Depreciation charge or that year	Book value at the end of the year
1	200 000	80 000	120 000
2	120 000	48 000	72 000
3	90 000	36 000	54 000
4	44 000	17 600	26 400
5	26 400	10 560	15 840

Table 3.4.3 Straight-line and reducing-balance depreciation compared

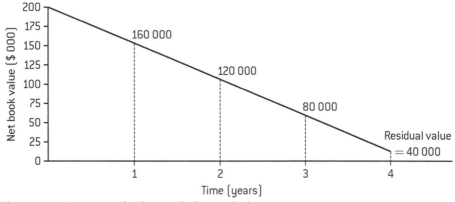

Figure 3.4.1 Depreciation by the straight-line method

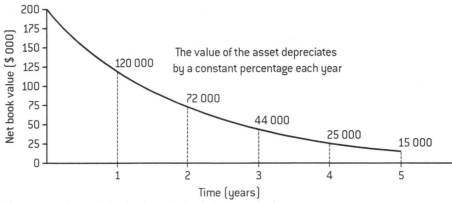
Figure 3.4.2 Depreciation by the reducing-balance method

Different types of intangible asset (AO1)

An intangible asset is one that cannot be physically touched or seen. However, as we will shall see in our study of branding in unit 4.5, intangible assets are an important component of balance sheets of large multinational organizations, valued in millions of dollars.

A brand provides a company with a product that can represent a personality trait. Brands are the trade names associated with a product so, for example, we speak of Coke (the brand) when in fact we are referring to the product (cola). However, brands now come to define individuals, given the clothes and shoes that they wear or mobile phones or music devices they listen to. There will be much greater detail on branding in unit 4.5.

In addition to branding, there are a number of other common intangible assets. The two most important are goodwill and patents.

Goodwill is an asset. It can take a number of forms. It is normally created when an organization changes ownership and the price paid by the acquirer exceeds the book value of a business; it is usually calculated by looking at the balance sheet of a company. The new owner is rewarding the previous owner by paying more than the book value in recognition of the previous owner's past efforts in establishing a strong brand presence in the market-place. For example, it is believed that Nestlé paid over $1 billion more than the book value to acquire Rowntree with its roster of famous confectionery brands including top-selling KitKat.

In the public or not-for-profit sectors where there may be no change of ownership or sale and purchase of a business, goodwill can be identified by the skills of the workforce or willingness to work additional hours for no extra pay (the education or health sectors are good examples). These skills do not show up in the balance sheet but they remain a valuable asset of the organization.

Patents provide entrepreneurs who may have created a new good or service with exclusive rights to use, sell or control their new invention which will hopefully turn into an innovation. Depending on the country of issue, patents can last from 5 to 20 years. Once the patent has expired, then competitors may be able to 'copy' this innovation. (The book value of a patent will diminish each year as this expiry date approaches but a full accounting treatment of patent values is beyond the scope of this guide and not included in the Business Management syllabus.)

Setting the scene

In unit 3.5 we will use ratio analysis to help us understand the performance of an organization as measured by criteria such as profitability and liquidity. Efficiency and gearing will be covered in unit 3.6. It has been decided to combine these two topics into one unit although please note that efficiency analysis is for HL only.

Please note that the ratios used here have been taken directly from the *IB Business Management Guide* on page 207, as these are the formulae that will be issued to students on a separate sheet before the start of the exam.

IB Learner Profile

Thinkers and open-minded

A useful introductory activity to ratio analysis is to discuss, in groups, issues related to the following questions.

From the greatest sportspeople to accounting ratios

Who is the greatest sportsperson of all time?

Justify your answer with relevant examples of the sportperson's success. Be specific – give dates of the person's achievements and degree of competition faced, and other possible classifications of his or her success.

Questions for discussion

These questions are for discussion in your group then for sharing with the rest of the class:

- Why is it so difficult to come up with a "definitive" answer to the question of the greatest sportsperson of all time?

- Why is it difficult to compare different sportspeople and reach a final judgment given that they have been successful in different sports during different periods of history?

- Are there any cultural influences on your suggestions for the greatest sportsperson of all time?

- What is the "best and fairest" way to reach an final answer in your whole class?

As this exercise illustrates, it is very hard to justify why one particular sportsperson should be considered as the greatest sportsperson of all time. Any criteria of success could be chosen but the justification should be based around performance, which is easily measurable via the use of results or available statistics.

There is no definitive answer though. Discussions would probably include the problems of comparing individual performances over time, the degree of difficulty and competition present in the sport, the degree of media exposure, the training facilities and diet available, and other numerous external factors.

Relevance to business and financial ratios

We could easily extend this analysis to business management by asking these questions:

- Which organization is the best in the world at present?

- Which organization is the most successful of all time?

One way to measure performance of an organization is to calculate financial ratios. Using these we can try to decide which business is experiencing profit growth, a sustainable liquidity and debt position, and is being efficient in its use of resources for productive means.

However, the greatest sportsperson exercise highlights one of the most important issues of using financial ratios to define and measure organizational performance. Taken in isolation (i.e. ratios derived from one year's set of financial accounts) and without consideration of the prevailing external environment or competitors' performance, ratios are meaningless indicators of business success or failure.

Profitability ratios

We will try to keep the analysis brief, focusing on the role each ratio plays in informing stakeholders.

The two key profitability ratios are gross and net profit margin.

Gross profit margin

$$\text{Gross profit margin} = \frac{\text{gross profit}}{\text{sales revenue}} \times 100$$

- **Key stakeholders** using this margin are line and senior managers.

- This ratio identifies the profit a firm achieves from trading – the buying and selling of goods.

- Assuming that selling prices and purchase prices remain constant over a trading period, this ratio should also be constant.

- If the ratio starts to deteriorate, the implication is that sales are not being transferred successfully into trading profits – a potential cause for concern. Firms may wish to look at their purchases of stock to see if the cost of stock sold is rising.

- For this reason, this ratio can also be viewed as an efficiency ratio.

Net profit margin

$$\text{Net profit margin} = \frac{\text{net profit before interest and tax}}{\text{sales revenue}} \times 100$$

- **Key stakeholders** using this margin are senior managers, and current and potential investors.

- The ratio signals the capacity the firm has to generate profits after overhead or indirect costs have been taken into account.

- The net profit figure excludes interest or tax and is the favoured ratio of managers as the final ratio will be higher than net profit margin after tax, which of course is a compulsory payment to government.

- The ratio should be constant over a trading period. If it starts to fall, it implies that overhead costs are rising faster than sales and an investigation should be carried out.

- Given the above, the company may need to change suppliers or, for example, look for alternative insurance quotes to cover premises or vehicles to reduce fixed costs.

AN APPROPRIATE LEVEL OF MARGIN PER UNIT SOLD?

There is an important link between the gross profit margin per unit sold, the industry the firm operates in and the rate of stock turnover (see below).

Supermarkets and increasingly e-commerce retailers can afford to set lower margins per unit given the faster stock turnover these firms experience. In industries where turnover is slower, especially in niche markets, much higher gross and net profit margins per unit sold are the norm.

Return on capital employed (ROCE)

$$\text{ROCE} = \frac{\text{net profit before interest and tax}}{\text{total capital employed}} \times 100$$

- **Key stakeholders** using this ratio are current and potential investors, media groups, CEOs and the government's tax department.

- This ratio is listed in the syllabus as an efficiency ratio because it looks at how efficiently an organization uses its capital or total assets to create goods and services that are in turn used to create profits.

- An alternative way of looking at the ROCE is as a measure of reward (in the form of profit) for risk-taking by entrepreneurs.

- An entrepreneur has to take the somewhat difficult decision to combine and finance the factors of production such as capital, land and labour into a profitable enterprise.

- The ROCE is the reward for taking this risk, given that an alternative opportunity could have been considered, such as a low-risk investment offered by a financial institution.

Liquidity ratios

$$\text{Current ratio} = \frac{\text{current assets}}{\text{current liabilities}}$$

$$\text{Acid test ratio} = \frac{\text{current assets - stocks}}{\text{current liabilities}}$$

- **Key stakeholders** using these ratios are lenders, potential lenders and suppliers.

- The acid test ratio is a stringent measure of liquidity as stocks of unsold goods are not included in current assets.

- Some writers have argued that firms should consider calculating **a "cash ratio"** where current assets have stock *and* debtors removed from current assets as we cannot guarantee that all monies from debtors will be paid, given the existence of bad debts.

EFFICIENCY RATIOS |HL|

Stock turnover can be calculated in two different ways.

$$\frac{\text{Cost of goods sold}}{\text{average stock}}$$

- This gives the number of times the current level of stock is "turned over" or sold.

$$\frac{\text{Average stock}}{\text{cost of goods sold}} \times 365 \text{ (days in the trading year)}$$

- This formula converts the first figure into a number of days.

- **Key stakeholders** using these ratios are line managers or heads of departments, for example involved in purchasing.

- The importance of this ratio will depend on the type of industry the firm operates in and the nature of the product itself.

- In fast-moving consumer goods (FMCG) industries, stock turnover will need to be quick or the firm may find itself with stockpiles of unsold goods. This will be critically important if the firm is supplying perishable goods such as dairy products, fruit or vegetables.

GEARING |HL|

The gearing ratio is measured by observing how much of the firm's capital employed in the business is provided by long-term lenders.

$$\text{Gearing ratio} = \frac{\text{loan capital}}{\text{total capital employed}}$$

- The figure is usually expressed as a percentage.

- A "high" gearing ratio such as 50% of capital employed, perhaps compared to other firms in the industry, indicates that the firm is vulnerable to changes in interest rates or external factors which may make credit more difficult to obtain.

- If the firm has sufficient liquidity to pay short-term interest costs, then a high gearing ratio may not be a major concern to some stakeholders. A number of high-profile takeovers have been instigated and financed by new owners (for example in the takeover of English Premiership soccer clubs) taking on additional borrowing collateralized against the newly created company's assets.

- However, if we return briefly to our point about the debt versus equity dilemma (see page 58), we must be tempted to ask the question whether other stakeholders would be concerned about the level of gearing and the degree of ownership of the firm. Do we wish for a company to be predominantly controlled by the firm's management or by long-term lenders such as financial institutions?

- **Key stakeholders** using these ratios are current and future lenders of funds, and shareholders.

Additional efficiency ratios

Debtor and creditor days

$$\text{Debtor days ratio} = \frac{\text{debtors}}{\text{total sales revenue}} \times 365$$

$$\text{Creditor days ratio} = \frac{\text{creditors}}{\text{total sales revenue}} \times 365$$

- **Key stakeholders** using this ratio are suppliers and creditors, and department heads.

- The relationship between these two formulae is critical and has important implications for working capital and liquidity. We have already noted the degree of interdependence between credit received from creditors and credit allowed to debtors. It is important that these two cycles are matched as closely as possible, ideally with debtor days being fewer than creditor days so that on average a firm receives payment for goods sold before it has to pay its suppliers.

Financial ratios and stakeholders

We have seen that the key stakeholders involved in using ratios in decision-making processes include current and potential shareholders, lenders, suppliers and senior managers.

We stress again that a single ratio in isolation without comparison to other firms, or the current state of the external environment or over time is not a basis for making a considered financial decision.

TOK

We could consider other stakeholders not yet covered.

First, the lessons from the collapse of Enron, in particular, reveal that huge importance has been attached to a firm's ability to deliver increasing profits. It would appear to many that profitability is the only important measure of performance.

Even when in the case of Enron, these profit figures were mere fantasy, stakeholders such as the financial media, potential investors and financial institutions continued to believe the illusion. There are a number of important TOK issues here which would provide the basis for a good discussion. (If the financial figures look too good to be true, then they probably are.)

Second, the increased need for greater transparency of company financial reporting (perhaps a lesson learned from the Enron collapse) has allowed consumers to access information such as gross profit and net profit margins, regional sales figures, etc.

This new knowledge should be used to try and inform customer decision-making especially when there have been concerns about the high prices which some brand-driven companies charge for products such as fashionable clothing or footwear. The ease of acquiring this new information quickly and at little cost has been a key driver in the growth of ethical and socially responsible consumer behaviour.

Evaluation

Below is a brief summary of how a firm may evaluate possible financial and other strategies to improve the values of ratios. Some of these ratios such as gross and net profit margin, current and acid test ratio and ROCE are HL/SL. The remaining ratios are HL only.

Ratio	Possible strategies with discussion to improve the value, and links to other topics
Gross profit margin	If the ratio is falling the firm may have to look at stock control and purchasing decisions. If the cost of stock sold is rising, managers may have to consider alternative supply chain management strategies (unit 5.5 – HL only). There may also be significant marketing factors to consider such as the effectiveness of the current promotional mix (unit 4.5), although, of course, altering this could raise costs
Net profit margin	If the ratio is falling, the firm will have to look at its overheads and indirect costs. Could the firm outsource some production to reduce overhead costs? (unit 3.2)
Current and acid test ratio	See the section on dealing with working capital and liquidity issues (unit 3.7)
ROCE	A fall in this ratio relative to competitors' ROCE over time may signal discussions among senior managers about pursuing a new strategic direction, especially if the fall is sustained, to try and regain lost market share (unit 1.3). The firm may also consider restructuring (unit 2.2) to try to reduce variable costs
Stock turnover	The rate of stock turnover needs to be appropriate for the industry and for the nature of the product, and has links to gross and net profit margins. The firm may need to review pricing methods and the marketing mix in general if stock is consistently not being sold (unit 4.4)
Creditor and debtor days	See the section on dealing with working capital and liquidity issues (unit 3.7)
Gearing ratio	Further borrowing may transfer some control away from shareholders, towards financial institutions. The firm may need to compare its gearing ratio with competitors' gearing ratios and take appropriate action if it is deemed too high. In addition, the firm may have to look at asset sales or introducing sale and leaseback schemes (unit 3.1). Changing the gearing ratio for a business has implications for the debt versus equity dilemma (unit 3.1).

Setting the scene

One could argue that the best way to learn about a cash flow problem is to experience one. Setting up and establishing a real-life business, the handling of cash inflows and outflows, forecasting future cash requirements and cash flow planning are essential life skills as well as important skills for creating a sustainable organization.

In some countries, there are opportunities for students to gain an understanding of the value of working capital and cash flow through taking part in Young Enterprise schemes or other entrepreneurial-based business simulation programmes. These opportunities could form part of a powerful creativity, action and service (CAS) opportunity.

> An excellent video explaining to "non-accountants" the role of final accounts, including cash flow forecasts and the role and importance of working capital, is "The Balance Sheet Barrier", a rather grainy 20-minute film produced in the late 1970s starring John Cleese and Ronnie Corbett. It has been updated recently but its cost is prohibitive as its target is the corporate market. It may be possible to borrow it from a library. (As of July 2014, only a teaser trailer is available on YouTube.)

The difference between profit and cash flow (A02)

Here is an example definition taken from yahoo answers:

> Cash flow refers to the amounts of cash coming into and going out of a business while profit is the difference between income and expenses.

Cash flow and profit will not be the same because items are often bought and sold on credit and there are many non-cash expenses such as depreciation.

Without using too much accounting "jargon" the difference between profit and cash flow is as follows. Cash flow allows a business to purchase resources, transfer them into finished products and deliver to customers. Then, on receipt of payment from the customer, the firm hopes to enjoy a small profit (assuming that the payment more than covers the firm's costs of supplying the order).

Figure 3.7.1 explains this process.

Unlike the Enron example, profit is realized or recorded after the final payment is received from the customer. Accounting rules dictate that costs and losses should be provided for before profits are taken by a business. This is a rule that Enron clearly violated with its preference for mark-to-market accounting.

The relationship between investment, profit and cash flow (A02)

The relationship between investment, profit and cash flow will depend largely on the nature of the investment undertaken, the level of risk in the investment and the level of profit expectation. An example from the film industry based on the author's own inquiry should illustrate these points, it is hoped in an engaging manner.

> ## PRODUCING A MOVIE
>
> Making a film or movie to be shown at a multiplex is a risk. Of every 10 films produced in the United States, 5 will lose money, 3 will break-even after DVD rentals are taken into account and 2 will make significant profits. The problem for Hollywood movie producers is that to quote one famous scriptwriter – William Goldman – "Nobody knows anything." Even with extensive market research, a famous actor or director and a great script, not one movie studio executive can say for certain what combination will constitute a success.
>
> See the case study on "The Lone Ranger" in unit 4.2, page 81.

Movie studios make significant **investments** in actors, directors, producers and technology often with no real guarantees that the movie they are going to produce will be a success or will return a **profit.** Studios have to spend considerable sums before the movie is released to create the **investment** opportunity. It is not unknown for a movie studio to use its **cash flow** to fund an investment in a new project up to three years before the movie is released. Cash outflow during this period is significant while cash inflow may be zero. (We have noted one example of this already: Disney's intention to produce an additional three "Star Wars" films by 2020.)

Even after the principal filming to create the movie has finished and the actors, directors and producers have moved on to new projects, it may take up to a year for the film to be released, despite rapid changes in film-processing technology. Moreover, the movie studio will begin an extensive marketing campaign with trailers and interviews before the movie is released in order

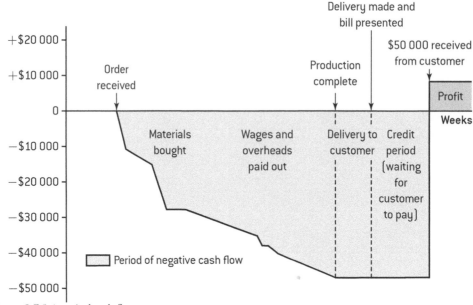

Figure 3.7.1 A typical cash flow process

to try and generate audience "buzz". Social media are also used. Again, this marketing effort, which can be up to one third of the total costs of the movie, needs to be funded out of cash flow before cash inflow is received.

Once the film is finished, market research or sneak previews are conducted to see what the initial audience reaction will be. In many cases, movie studios shoot additional scenes or even whole endings, if advance word-of-mouth reaction from these screenings is not positive. Again, any additional changes will need to be paid for by the movie studio with no cash coming in. These additional scenes or alternative endings are usually included on DVDs or Blu-ray releases to "add value" once a movie is released in this format.

Once the film is released to the general public, the cash inflows will be earned and the hope is that costs of production will be recovered and profits earned. For every ticket sold at the movie box office roughly half of the revenue will go to the studio and the rest to the distributor (to the multiplex where the movie is being shown and to the government as goods and services tax). In this context, a movie that cost $100 million to make and advertise will need to take $200 million at the box office *just to break-even*. The movie business really is a risky business.

The link between investment, profit and cash flow can be summarized as follows:

- Investments require finance and an organization's cash flow will be used to pay for this.

- Profits are not guaranteed from an investment but it is certain that an organization will experience significant cash outflows before cash inflows are earned.

- The organization will hope to earn profit after all cash outflows have been recovered. It may take considerable time to collect all cash inflows.

- In the case of an investment, if a new movie is looking likely not to yield a profit, then additional marketing funds may be required. This will add to cash outflow and reduce the possibility of the movie earning a profit.

Working capital and the working capital cycle (AO2)

Working capital

Working capital is the difference between current assets and current liabilities, and has a number of alternative names such as day-to-day finance or circulating capital. Its role is to bring the other factors of production such as land, labour and man-made capital into productive use. Without working capital being spent on resources such as raw materials, power or stationery, these factors would be idle and not productive.

Second, working capital provides cash and credit opportunities to allow businesses to trade with other firms. (Cash in our context refers to money which the firm has at its disposal for immediate use. This could be notes and coins but is likely to be electronic cash transactions or bank transfers.) Many transactions in business are settled in cash but many firms rely on being able to pay for raw materials or finished goods up to two months after they have been delivered.

A firm can be a creditor to its customers who have not yet paid and a debtor to its suppliers who have allowed the firm to receive raw materials without paying in advance. Credit is a vital source of working capital.

The working capital cycle

A version of the working capital cycle of a spoon manufacturer (as featured in the video "The Balance Sheet Barrier") follows, to help students understand the process. We also comment on the possible cash flow implications for a firm. This will lead us neatly into the importance of cash flow forecasts.

Cycle stage 1

A firm purchases raw materials such as metal plating for pressing spoons and equips two workers to carry out this work.

Cash flows out or credit is received to pay for this.

Cycle stage 2

The firm processes raw materials (sheet metal) into spoons and begins to take orders. The firm may pay the suppliers of the sheet metal.

Cash flows out with possible credit allowed to customers as orders are received.

Cycle stage 3

The firm fulfils orders and delivers.

Cash flows in from customers and invoices are sent to customers with delivered orders. A truck is hired with a driver to deliver. Cash flows out.

Cycle stage 4

The firm follows up on unpaid orders. Payment is received by debtors. The firm pays its creditors. Profit from sales is kept in reserves. New orders are received.

Cash flows in from debtors and out to remaining creditors. New orders are received and the process begins again.

IB Learner Profile

Reflection Я|R

Too much working capital or too little?

It is hoped that the simplified example above clearly states that enough working capital must be present in an organization to allow production to take place. If a firm has too little working capital then it will be difficult for the company to trade with other companies and inevitably liquidity problems will result.

What is perhaps not so obvious is the opposite situation. Having too much capital tied up in raw materials or finished goods with substantial reserves of cash in a bank account may imply that the firm is missing out on potential profitable opportunities. If the firm is holding too much stock, this may create additional cost problems.

One recent criticism of Apple is that the company accumulated too much cash, which was "sitting" on the organization's balance sheet and it was argued was not being used productively. It was estimated that in 2011, Apple had over $100 billion in cash as part of its current assets. This was estimated to be more cash than the US government had at that time.

Cash flow forecasts (AO2)

Table 3.7.1 is a template for a fictitious small firm forecasting cash flow from January to June 2010. The figures are not given as only the structure is being presented. The structure of the template shown is just one possible version. There could be variations in the ordering of rows.

Item	Jan	Feb	Mar	Apr	May	Jun
Opening balance						
Cash inflows						
Cash received						
Sale of assets						
Total cash available						
Cash outflows						
Rent						
Rates						
Materials						
Wages						
Total cash outflows						
Total cash available – total cash outflows						
Closing balance						

Table 3.7.1 Template for cash flow forecast

The closing balance at the end of the month will become the opening balance for the next month. Cash flow forecasts are used as follows:

- They are presented at the centre of a business plan for new start-ups.
- Lenders will wish to see whether future cash flow issues can be anticipated.
- Liquidity problems will be potentially easier to solve if they can be foreseen.

(Of course, the cash flow forecast cannot predict the unforeseen.)

Dealing with liquidity problems

Before evaluating strategies for dealing with liquidity problems we need to define what we mean by a liquidity problem and then try to offer a solution. There is some overlap here with ratio analysis (which was covered in unit 3.5).

Table 3.7.2 focuses on four short-term liquidity problems. Longer-term financing issues were covered in unit 3.1.

Liquidity problem	Solution	Discussion
The firm has run out of cash to pay immediate expenses such as wages	A bank overdraft extension is needed to tide the firm over until further cash is received from customers (improving cash inflow)	Using a bank overdraft in this case is a suitable but expensive way to borrow funds
The firm is unable to pay creditors	The firm tries to extend the credit period (reducing cash outflows)	The business world is interdependent. The firm's creditors may also have debts to pay. Careful negotiation is necessary. The firm may have to pay interest for late payment
The firm is waiting for debtors to pay	Discounts can be offered for payment but if the situation persists the firm may have to employ a debt factor (additional source of finance)	If the situation is critical then some money received is better than none. With debt factoring only a proportion of the debt is recovered
The firm has unsold stock which is taking up shelf space and tying up valuable working capital	The firm may be left with no option but stock clear out (improving cash inflow)	Deep discounting is undesirable as profit margins will be cut. This could affect perception of the firm due to low prices. However, costs of goods going out of date or fashion must be recognized if left unsold. These goods will become worth less as time passes

Table 3.7.2 Examples of short-term liquidity problems

Setting the scene

Example of an investment appraisal decision

One appropriate way to study this topic and cover the requirements of the syllabus for HL and SL is to work through a recent past exam question (adapted from May 2005 < paper 2, question 2).

Lev Yashin and Alexi Kirov are partners and racehorse owners. They are looking to move into new sports activities and have begun to look into the possibility of owning a football team to increase their range of businesses and increase their commercial success.

They have identified two potential teams, both public limited companies, which may provide potential takeover and investment opportunities. They have prepared financial estimates of returns and costs of each proposal.

We must assume that the costs of financing the opportunity have been included. We do not know if the two investors have borrowed the capital or are using private funds.

Figures ($m)	Team A	Team B
Cost of takeover	200	70
Expected returns Year 1	-30	15
Year 2	-2	18
Year 3	76	21
Year 4	96	24
Year 5	150	30

Calculate to two decimal places and analyse your results for:

- payback
- accounting or average rate of return (ARR)
- net present value (NVP) assuming that the discount factor is 6% (HL only).

We shall calculate the values first and then provide some suggestions on how we can use these to help us analyse an investment decision.

Investment appraisal

This is the process consisting of a set of techniques designed to determine whether an investment opportunity should be taken. In the case of multiple opportunities, investment appraisal can be used to rank projects in order of desirability in quantitative terms only. External and qualitative factors are not considered. The three techniques to guide decision-making are payback, ARR and (HL only) NVP.

Payback (AO3, AO4)

Payback is defined as the time period required before an investment opportunity "pays back" (recovers) its initial investment cost.

For team A the cost of the takeover is $200 million.

Team A will return $290 million in 5 years:

$(-32 + 76 + 96 + 150) = \$290$ million.

It will return -$32 million after year 2 and $172 million after year 4, a total of $140 million.

Hence for team A to pay back the whole $200 million, $60 million of year 5's $150 million is required.

Assuming that this money is received evenly throughout the year, we can expect the $\frac{60}{150} \times 365$ days in 146 days or 4.8 months.

Now calculate the payback for team B and confirm the figure of 3 years 243 days or 3 years and 8 months.

Analysis of payback

Payback is a straightforward way of looking at an investment opportunity. It assumes that expected returns are received evenly throughout the year and that a dollar received in one year's time has the same value as a dollar received today. Both assumptions can be challenged. NPV provides a more rigorous appraisal of the time value of money.

A closer look at the expected returns from each takeover reveals that for team A the majority of returns are expected to arrive in years 3, 4, 5. The biggest returns are forecasted much later where their value cannot be guaranteed. For team B, the expected revenues arrive earlier in the five-year investment horizon with only $30 million expected to arrive in year 5. This has important implications for decision-making especially as it is difficult to predict the influence of external factors in five years' time, after the initial decision has been made.

In common with simple break-even analysis, payback is useful when carrying out brief or rough calculations to see if a particular investment is warranted. However, for a more considered approach we must consider NPV.

Average rate of return (ARR) (AO3)

The formula for this calculation will be given on the formula sheet at the start of the exam.

$$ARR = \frac{\text{average profit per year}}{\text{cost of the opportunity}}$$

For team A, the expected average profit over five years:

$$= \frac{290 - 200}{5} = \$18 \text{ million}$$

For team B, the expected average profit over five years:

$$= \frac{108 - 70}{5} = \$7.6 \text{ million}$$

$$\text{ARR for team A} = \frac{18}{200} = 9\%$$

$$\text{ARR for team B} = \frac{7.6}{70} = 10.86\%$$

In common with payback, the ARR assumes that a dollar received in one year's time has the same value as a dollar received today. This assumption will be challenged when we consider NPV and discounting.

Considerations when using ARR

The ARR and other ratios, as we have seen in units 3.5 and 3.6, are not useful in isolation. The ARR will need to be compared with other investment opportunities such as a risk-free savings account in a financial institution to see if the additional return given by the opportunity is justified for the level of risk taken. Of course, the attitudes of the investor with respect to risk and the external environment will need to be considered in combination with the calculations.

Analysis in terms of the question asked

- From the payback and the ARR calculations it would appear that team B should be chosen.
- It has a lower cost and a quicker return of the initial investment.
- It has a lower overall profit but a higher ARR.
- However, before making a final call, we must consider the time value of money, which both payback and ARR ignore.

INVESTMENT OPPORTUNITIES USING NPV (AO3)

Both payback and ARR calculations ignore the time value of money. So far we have assumed that $1 received today from an investment opportunity is the same as $1 received in one year's time. In reality, this will not be so.

Towards the final NPV

NPV = future discounted returns added - cost of the investment opportunity

From the table, the discount factors over 5 years at an interest rate of 6% are: Year 1: 0.9434, Year 2: 0.89, Year 3: 0.8396, Year 4: 0.7921, Year 5: 0.7473.

We can now calculate the NPVs for the two investment opportunities.

Full workings are not given. It will be up to you to check your arithmetic to make sure you understand the process described above. Negative figures are in brackets.

Years	Team A	Team B	Discount factor	Present value A	Present value B
Cost today	(200)	(70)	0 (as this is today)	(200)	(70)
Expected return Year 1	(30)	15	0.9434	(28.3)	14.15
Year 2	(2)	18	0.89	(1.78)	16.02
Year 3	76	21	0.8396	63.61	17.63
Year 4	96	24	0.7921	76.04	19.01
Year 5	150	30	0.7473	112.1	22.42
Total of present values				21.87	19.23

Analysis

The NPV for team A is higher than for team B. Hence with the time value of money taken into account and assuming an interest rate of 6%, team A will yield higher expected returns than team B as an investment opportunity. This contrasts with the findings from the payback and ARR calculations.

An alternative way of looking at NPV is that both opportunities offer a smaller return than the firm could achieve by putting a lump sum of – in the case of team A – $200 million in a low-risk bank account.

The time value of money

A dollar received today and invested at an interest rate of 10% would be worth $1.10 in one year's time. In two years' time, assuming that the whole amount is invested again at 10%, a dollar invested will be worth $1.21 (1.1 + 10% of 1.1).

Alternatively, we can find out the true value today of $1.10 received in one year's time. This is called the present value of $1.10.

In situations where a firm is receiving future amounts in 125 years' time, these amounts will need to be discounted by a factor in order to arrive at the present value. These discounted amounts will be compared with the cost of an investment opportunity (which we know at today's value) to calculate the NPV.

In order to calculate the present value of $1.10 received in one year's time at an interest rate at 10% we must apply a discount factor of 0.91 to two decimal places, from the discount table, which is available in your textbook or the formula sheet that will be provided as you begin the final exam.

Present value = $1.10 × 0.91 = $1

To calculate the present value of $1.21 received in two years' time at an interest rate of 10%, we apply a discount factor of 0.83 to two decimal places.

Present value = $1.21 × 0.83 = $1

Check your understanding by calculating the future amounts of $1 invested at an interest rate of 10% over three, four and five years. Then discount these amounts using factors from the discounting table.

Taking it further

The question that needs to be asked to complete our discussion is whether the risk reward of $21.87 million for investing in team A over the initial cost is suitable for the investors. This will depend on the degree of risk the investors wish to take.

Conclusion

Investment appraisal is a scientific approach to decision-making based on a number of assumptions. Assumptions are made about expected future capital flows resulting from a new project (which are estimates) compared to initial costs today (which are more certain). If a long time period is under consideration we must treat the final NPV calculations with some caution given the rapid changes in the external environment that have been a constant theme throughout this guide.

Setting the scene

From our movie theme in unit 3.7, linking in the idea of investment, cash flow and profit, you will be familiar with the role of a movie director. This is the person who creates the scenes and instructs the actors where to stand, how to act and react, in the process of transferring the finished script to the screen.

What is not so commonly known is the role of the producer. Put simply, the producer's role is to find the finance, hire the key talent (including the director) and make sure that the film meets its budget, which has probably been allocated to the producer by a senior executive unconnected to the film. The producer is also the first person to inform the studio financing the movie of any cost overruns or, to use a business term, "variances" from the budget. With many major movies from Hollywood now having budgets running to over $100 million, a movie producer's role as the "babysitter of the budget" is a demanding and stressful one.

Definition

Budgets are financial targets or predictions of how much a firm is expected to spend or receive in a given time period.

The importance of budgets (AO2)

The above example introduces the importance of budgets, their role and relevance to strategic planning. It will also help us to understand the concept of variance analysis.

Budgets perform a number of crucial functions for an organization. They can be particularly important if the culture of an organization does not have strong accountability (as opposed to Handy's Apollo structure – see unit 2.5) and flat hierarchies. With laissez-faire leadership styles, budgets are an essential method of financial control.

Budgets have been described as a "route map" in helping an organization achieve its objectives for a predetermined period. Budgets have the following uses:

- They can impose financial discipline on departments and require managers to become accountable for every dollar spent. This process is sometimes referred to as zero budgeting.

- Budgets provide financial motivation (and thus rewards) to divisions or managers if they are empowered to meet certain targets or forecasts.

- Budgets allow senior managers to control and monitor spending and through variance analysis perhaps highlight or pre-empt potential problems.

- They also allow senior managers to review performance if a new strategic plan has been introduced (see below).

VARIANCES (AO2) HL

A variance occurs if a figure, such as advertising expenditure for a firm, calculated at the end of the financial period is different from the budgeted or forecasted figure. These differences can be favourable:

(actual > budget in the case of revenue or budget > actual in the case of costs)

or they can be adverse:

(actual < budget in the case of revenue or budget < actual in the case of costs).

The example given in Table 3.9.1 will help to clarify understanding. (Note that for the new syllabus specific knowledge of actual variances is not required.)

Cost or revenue item	Budgeted figure	Actual figure	Variance
Sales revenue in host country	42	40	2 Adverse
Overseas sales	17	21	4 Favourable
Material costs	24	21	3 Favourable
Advertising	6	11	5 Adverse

Note: All figures are millions of dollars.

Table 3.9.1 Adverse and favourable variances

The advertising account has overspent by $5 million. It will now be up to the senior managers to investigate further the causes of this variance.

Budgets, variances and strategic planning (AO2)

As we saw previously, businesses have aims and objectives and will need periodically to make changes and decide on a new course of action. The decision to be made could be either a tactical or strategic one.

Once a decision has been made on a suitable course of action, it is good business practice to monitor progress periodically, perhaps in terms of sales increases or cost reductions – whatever the original objective was behind the decision.

The setting of budgets and the calculation of variances could be important elements in this review process to see whether the strategy is meeting forecasts, or is in need of adjustment. If early indications reveal that the new strategy is not going according to plan then variances will help.

These are possible areas of inquiry to see whether the tactical or strategic change is on course:

- Were new sales targets met? Are they above or below expectation?

- Did the company overspend on above-the-line promotion?

- Has the new strategy resulted in a fall in labour costs below target?

Depending on the nature of the strategic plan, its scope and time frame for completion, budgets and variance analysis can be used to see whether the new direction is "on track". If variances in particular look likely to be grossly adverse, immediate corrective action in the strategy could be taken. It would not be sensible for an organization to wait too long before deciding whether to change if the strategic direction is off course.

Jack Trout, in his book *Big Brands, Big Trouble* (2001), sums up this view on strategic planning very succinctly:

Remember the Titanic.

Cost and profit centres (AO1)

Some businesses organize themselves in such a way to split divisions, departments, products or brands into self-contained autonomous units. These are called cost centres or profit centres and allow a business to identify costs and revenues easily:

- **Cost centres** are allocated their own **direct costs** and can set their own budgets to control and monitor efficiency.

- **Profit centres** are similar to the above, but profit centres (usually separate divisions or departments) are allocated costs and revenues for the purpose of calculating individual profit. Unilever took a decision recently to convert all its major brands into dedicated profit centres for this reason.

We must also remember that the centre, whether cost or profit, will be expected to absorb some of the overhead cost of the whole organization.

The role of cost and profit centres (AO2)

The creation of these cost and profit centres has been driven by the idea that empowering managers of these units **may lead to motivation** via increased delegation. The cost or profit centre must now be accountable for its own actions and this **may lead to greater efficiency and productivity.**

The main drawback from creating specific centres is that when individual managers are responsible for individual centre performance then potentially the centre may set objectives that are different from the overall objectives of the organization. There could be a significant conflict of interests between centres.

We can use the case study featuring TK Pictures to revisit and review some of the themes and ideas we have been analysing and discussing in this unit.

EXAMPLE OF PROFIT CENTRES IN ACTION

TK Pictures is a movie company which has been in the film industry for 40 years. TK currently aims to produce 20 movies with its output in a typical year being:

Division or department	Number of films produced in 2014
Action/drama	8
Family/musical	6
Comedy	4
Debut	2

Steven Abrams manages TK. As a young movie director he found it hard to get his movies made. TK offered him a chance in 2008 to develop his own project and he became hugely successful. In 2011, as the newly appointed CEO, Abrams created the Debut division with a vision to encourage and support other young filmmakers. Debut wanted to be the Pixar of the real rather than animated movie world.

However, Abrams is worried about recent falls in profitability and especially escalating direct costs, specifically actors' salaries. He is also frustrated that the Debut department three years on has not "discovered" a great new talent. Many of Debut's films are loss-making projects.

Abrams feels that turning the four departments into individual profit centres may be the way forward. This would mean greater accountability and would also make the profit centres responsible for raising their own sources of finance.

Debut's manager, George Romero, has urged Abrams to reconsider this idea, arguing that although the Debut division has been struggling, it still provides a contribution and has an important role to play in discovering new talent. Abrams is not too sure and has been approached by an independent producer, Harvey Tarrantino, about a possible sale of Debut.

The case study highlights a number of points that have been raised in this unit:

- Should TK continue to support Debut even though it is a loss-making department and has not as yet found any new innovative or creative talent?

- Should TK keep Debut to block potential rivals from entering into this market and keep its contribution?

- Should the firm sell Debut and receive a one-off cash boost from the sale and then use this to support the other divisions financially?

- Could the creation of its own cost or profit centres allow Debut the opportunity to manage itself and with this increased empowerment and responsibility allow it to be more successful?

- Will the creation of cost and profit centres change the culture at Debut and impose a financial discipline, which will limit innovation further?

- Should Debut seek additional funding through Internet sources such as Kickstarter, Indiegogo or other crowd-funding websites?

Setting the scene

To quote from the *IB Business Management Guide*:

Marketing is an essential business function: it creates a bridge between an organization and its customers. In our everyday speech, the word marketing *is often associated with advertising and finding innovative ways of getting people to buy a product or service.*

However, as this unit will show:

effective marketing requires consideration of everything from product quality to consumer perception and increasingly, engagement with people's everyday lives to uncover needs that customers may not be aware of themselves.

As has been said before, marketing is simply not just selling a good or service.

In an increasingly connected globalized world and with technological change resulting in multiple distractions and demands on people's time, either at work, at home or on the move, delivering an effective marketing message can be very difficult. For this reason, organizations regard marketing as a **dynamic process** with a need to constantly **evaluate** and **review** performance then change marketing practices if necessary. In this section of the syllabus, we will be incorporating a significant number of AO3s and you must be aware of this when you come to study specific units. In some of the learning outcomes, you will have to carry out research of your own, in order fully to evaluate some of the topics discussed, given that you are stakeholders in the marketing process.

As part of our evaluation, we will make reference to a number of points raised by Jack Trout, who has written extensively on marketing, market research, product positioning and strategy. By way of introduction and to set the scene we will look at some of his research.

Jack Trout "the tyranny of choice"

Trout's work discusses how difficult marketing has become given the explosion of choice in almost all markets both on a national and global level. For example, Trout (2001) highlights that in the consumer goods industry:

- An average US supermarket has 40 000 items.

- An average US family gets 80–85% of its needs from only 150 of those items.

- The person shopping for this average US family will routinely ignore the other 39 850 items.

Clearly with this "tyranny of choice", a good deal of marketing effort is going to waste. Even in small niche markets such as the luxury sports car market, which used to be dominated by Ferrari, choice and competition have emerged in the shape of Porsche, Lamborghini, Bentley and Aston Martin, and most recently the Mercedes SLR range.

The tyranny of choice has had an impact across a range of markets, as Table 4.1.1 reveals. One noticeable exception is that the number of menu items available at KFC between the early 1970s and late 1990s has only increased by seven. Researching McDonalds and other globalized fast food outlets would reveal similar findings. As we shall see in unit 4.7, the key to developing a global brand and presence across a range of markets may lie in product and service standardization and not always product variation.

Product	Number of items in the US market – early 1970s	Number of items in the US market – late 1990s
Sports utility vehicle (SUV) styles	8	38
Software titles	0	250000
Bottled water brands	16	50
Milk types	4	19
Mouthwashes	15	66
Dental floss	12	64
Over-the-counter pain relief drugs	17	141
Contact lens types	1	36
KFC menu items	7	14

Table 4.1.1 Number of items in a range of US markets in the 1970s and 1990s

IB Learner Profile

Knowledgeable and balanced 📖 ⚖️

Trout's work has been influential in shaping the marketing strategies of a number of high-profile US organizations in response to this explosion of choice. However, we can argue from a completely different viewpoint that in fact although globalization is apparent, a number of large trans-national organizations continue to have significant influence over what we consume.

Consider the figure on the following web page: http://elitedaily. com/news/world/illusion-choice-10-companies-responsible-virtually-every-product-market/. This illustrates the illusion of choice, an idea created by Redditt.

Questions for discussion

- Do we really have unlimited choice given the small number of large companies controlling some of the world's most popular brands?

- What are the implications of the illusion of choice figure for a new business considering developing either a new chocolate bar, breakfast cereal or soft drink?

- How is entry for a new business in these global markets possible and how can marketing help? (As we indicated earlier, the marketing function for an organization operating in a global environment is much more difficult than it first appears – this last question for discussion is probably rhetorical.)

Marketing's relationship with other business functions (AO1)

Marketing is defined as the process of identifying and satisfying consumer wants and needs in line with the objectives of the organization. One updated version of this definition is that it is the role of marketing to anticipate, identify and **create** new needs and wants.

We must not treat marketing in isolation from the other sections of a business. Consider the following issues or conflicts for a company in the competitive snack food industry:

- The finance and operations departments have criticized the marketing department for insisting on a new TV advertising campaign to "buy one pack, get two free". They argue that the company cannot produce the large quantities of snack food required; nor can it afford the cost of the proposed TV commercial involving a famous media figure.

- The sales director is not enthusiastic about the marketing department's insistence on developing a cheese and vinegar flavoured potato chip. His sales team lack enthusiasm for this tactical move and it also does not fit with the organization's strategic decision to move into new overseas markets.

We could have highlighted a number of other issues. The key is that marketing has to fit within the constraints placed on it by the organization. The marketing department must also be aware that its actions may have significant implications for other parts of the organization.

Marketing goods and marketing services (AO2)

There are differences between marketing goods (products) and marketing services. In the following example, the product is a moisturizer and the service is a facial.

- Product benefits are "embedded" inside the product and/or packaging and can be delivered to customers through distribution channels. A skin care product may claim certain benefits on the outside and inside it will have certain ingredients.

- As services are location-based activities, customers have to travel to the service location. In our example this may be a beauty salon or spa.

- Customers like their products to be standardized, for example in terms of features and packaging, but they like their services to be customized to suit their individual needs.

- Products are tangible so customers can inspect them and, in some cases, sample them before committing to buy. Services on the other hand are experienced and once carried out may not be reversible. A moisturizer can be sampled at home or in a store but it is not possible to return a facial or properly sample one without the activity being completed.

To overcome some of the issues with service-based delivery as opposed to the marketing of products, many beauty salons provide **physical evidence** to assist with the marketing effort and **process** and they provide trained **people**. We shall return to this aspect in a later unit on the additional three Ps in the marketing mix for services in unit 4.6.

Market orientation versus product orientation (AO2)

Theodore Levitt (quoted in Russell-Walling, 2007) provides an example of the difference between market orientation and production orientation:

Movie companies do not make movies but they provide entertainment. In the 1950s, the American movie studios dismissed television and ignored its influence. They lost their customer focus and became too product orientated. They have barely recovered from the impact of television. It took them too long to see television as an opportunity for market growth (through market orientation) and not a threat.

A few established companies, including Rolls Royce and Apple, are able to operate profitably by concentrating solely on the strength of their product and effectively ignoring the needs of the market (production orientation). Most organizations, however, have to try to satisfy an increasingly demanding consumer base empowered by knowledge and information from the Internet. These organizations must conduct research and develop an understanding of market trends and respond accordingly. This is the very essence of market orientation.

Commercial marketing and social marketing (AO2)

Commercial marketing

If we adjust our definition of marketing at the beginning of this unit, we can identify a definition of commercial marketing:

Marketing is the process for an organization to help identify and satisfy needs and wants of consumers profitably.

Some definitions of commercial marketing include reference only to marketing activities in the private sector and not the public or government sector. The increasing use of public-private partnerships (as discussed in unit 1.2) may in some countries demand a revision of the commercial marketing definition.

Commercial marketing is justified on this basis: if a firm is going to take a risk, create a new product and try to use marketing to help the product become sustainable, then profit must ultimately be the reward of the business activity.

Social marketing

The emergence of a more ethical and socially responsible external environment has given rise to a new breed of "social marketing". Both the private and public sectors have embraced this. The focus is on communicating the existence of and extolling the virtue of "merit goods" such as education and health while, for example, raising awareness and aiming to reduce the consumption of demerit products (such as alcohol, cigarettes and "junk food") given that these products can have significant impacts on the wider community. Any profit generation is of secondary importance. In social marketing, the message is the aim.

IB Learner Profile

Risk-taking and caring

The author challenges you to find a better example of social marketing than the one created by the Tranz Metro in Australia. Watch "Dumb Ways to Die" – a YouTube clip (and now App) – which in 2013 won a global creativity award for marketing (but also created some controversy in Russia). The aim of the clip is to alert passengers to the dangers of using public transport, especially the danger of crossing railway lines at stations.

The campaign by Tranz Metro went viral and has led to a number of imitators. Its effectiveness in raising social awareness issues has led some commentators to remark that social marketing must, like its commercial cousin, be innovative and forward looking in anticipating future needs.

Market characteristics (AO1)

From our study so far, we can see that some markets, such as the branded consumer household goods market shown in the illusion of choice figure (sometimes referred to as the fast-moving consumer goods market or FMCG market) is dominated by 10 firms. This market would be classified as a "red ocean" (see concept 5: Strategy). Market share is distributed around a number of large organizations. It would be difficult for a new firm to enter this market given the brand, purchasing and marketing barriers to entry which exist.

For uncontested markets or "blue oceans", there is a possibility of creating a market place where there is very little competition. However, as we have seen, creating a "blue ocean" will require research and development, innovation and some good fortune.

If we are to take a global perspective, we could argue that many markets outside the FMCG market are becoming more open – or to use an economics term – contestable. This includes the airline industry, telecommunications and perhaps the best example, the online retail environment. Where once large organizations such as Amazon dominated the virtual market-place, we are now seeing the creation of a whole range of online shopping opportunities, fuelled by the growth of the world wide web and the ever-increasing mobile commerce (m-commerce) or mobile applications available through the smartphone.

Market share (AO4)

We can calculate market share for an organization using the following formula.

Market share is defined as the sales of the individual firm expressed as a percentage of total industry sales.

Market share
$$= \frac{\text{total revenue the firm generates}}{\text{total revenue the whole industry generates}} \times 100$$

Market size = the total sales of all the producers within a market.

Another way of stating this is by using the total amount of revenue generated. The US personal computer market was worth $15.8 billion in the fourth quarter of 2013.

Market growth is also an important consideration. Market growth is identified in the column on the far right in Table 4.1.2. It is interesting to note that even in the deteriorating global economic environment some companies have gained market share (Acer, Apple and Toshiba) at the expense of the market leaders.

The importance of market share and market leadership (AO3)

Table 4.1.2 confirms that despite claims by some media commentators that Apple is the dominant force in the computer industry, in terms of market share it still lags behind HP and Dell in the desktop computer market. However, in terms of market growth, we can see that Apple is "gaining fast" on its rivals. It would be interesting to see what Table 4.1.2 would look like in five years' time.

Having significant market share allows an organization to influence pricing in that market. Revenue growth will also be possible and these additional funds could be invested into improving the marketing effort even further, consolidating its position and market share into the future. Enjoying growing market share can effectively be a self-fulfilling prophecy.

As we will argue in later units, however, Apple enjoys **market leadership** and market share in those markets such as the smartphone (iPhone), mobile devices (iPad) and music players (iPod Touch, Nano and Shuffle) through the creation of "blue oceans".

The iPad has been particularly important for Apple in terms of market share and leadership even though (as we shall see in unit 5.6) when the product was released in 2010 many consumers were unsure exactly what it was for. The iPad's influence on leadership in the tablet market is undeniable, as Figure 4.1.1 shows.

However, we must sound a note of caution. The experience of Nokia we considered earlier and the example of BlackBerry remind us that market leadership in a rapidly changing technological world cannot be taken for granted. In 2007, Nokia and BlackBerry were important players in the mobile and hand-held computer device markets. The arrival of the smartphone, the iPhone and the renaissance of Samsung as a communications company soon altered the "playing field" leaving the mobile phone business of Nokia in tatters. Only seven years later, BlackBerry is still looking for a buyer to save itself from extinction.

Before iPad ↑

After iPad ↓

Figure 4.1.1 The influence of the iPad on the tablet market

Company	4Q13 Shipments	4Q13 Market share (%)	4Q12 Shipments	4Q12 Market share	4Q13–4Q12 Growth (%)
Hewlett Packard	4 179	26.5	4 657	27.3	−10.3
Dell	3 602	22.8	3 355	19.7	7.4
Apple	2 168	13.7	1 688	9.9	28.5
Lenovo	1 526	9.7	1 474	8.6	3.5
Toshiba	1 143	7.2	1 327	7.8	−13.9
Others	3 178	20.1	4 567	26.8	−30.4
Total	15 795	100.0	17 068	100.0	−7.5

Table 4.1.2 US personal computer sales, market share and market growth in millions of units

Source: Gartner Inc. from www.macrumors.com

Marketing objectives in for-profit and non-profit organizations (AO3)

Our definition of marketing (on page 77) was careful to acknowledge that marketing is a process to satisfy needs and wants, to fit in with the firm's objectives. Not all firms are profit maximizers and, as we highlighted in unit 1.3, a number of other corporate objectives exist.

Maynard argued in an article in 2009 it is important for non-profit organizations to establish a well-defined niche; while most are not selling goods, they are selling their mission, their ideas, their vision and their services. We cannot assume that the non-profit organization (however ethical or socially responsible) will sell itself based on its inherent worth and the goodwill generated in the community. Key points are as follows:

- Identify your target audience: define key stakeholder groups.
- Maintain consistent communication.
- Create a strong visual identity: use logos.
- Use message repetition wherever possible: create a slogan.
- Employ multiple communication tactics (Maynard, 2009).

One could argue that for-profit organizations need to mirror the marketing objectives of non-profit organizations.

IB Learner Profile

Inquiry ?

This exercise aims to deepen your understanding that non-profit organizations are increasingly following marketing objectives aligned with those of their for-profit "cousins". Visit the Oxfam website to investigate this topic.

Questions for reflection
- What do you notice about Oxfam's website?
- Compare Oxfam's website to the website of a for-profit organization which has a global presence, such as Coca-Cola or McDonald's. Are the marketing objectives of the for-profit organization so very different from those of Oxfam?

Marketing strategies and customer preferences (AO3)

How marketing strategies evolve when customer preferences change (AO3)

Given changes in social trends, it can be hard to identify at the time of writing (2014) exactly which changes in customer preferences are occurring and how these are having an impact on marketing strategies. We must also remember that our perspective in these matters will be altered depending on whether the consumer is living in the developed or developing world. Even a quick search on Google Zeitgeist (an excellent resource) fails to yield what are the key consumer preferences in 2014.

For our purposes, we could identify the following changes that could have an impact on evolving marketing strategies for an organization:

- Consumer preferences are moving towards purchasing online rather than from retail stores. (This will be covered in unit 4.8 on e-commerce.)
- There is growing consumer awareness of the need for organizations to be more ethical, socially responsible and transparent (which we have considered in unit 1.3 on organizational objectives).
- There is widespread adoption of m-commerce in many countries through an improvement in mobile phone technologies. This aspect will be considered in unit 4.5 when we analyse the impact of changing technology on promotional strategies such as viral marketing, social media marketing and networking.

Clearly, for an organization to be truly market-oriented, in its marketing strategies it will need to take changing consumer preferences into consideration. Of course, this will involve significant costs and set-up delays in adjusting current strategies. Unlike a marketing tactical change, such as a change in the price of a product or a new short-term promotional offer, changing a marketing strategy can take detailed planning and organizing and use up valuable resources (financial and human) in the process.

Moreover, although changing a marketing strategy may benefit some customers, what about those customers who resist change? An organization may lose significant brand loyalty from existing customers if it changes too quickly the marketing mix of a good or service.

Coca-Cola Company's decision to change the taste of Coke, and launch "New Coke", in 1985 caused significant stakeholder dissatisfaction. It led to the return of "Classic Coke" some six months later. This should serve as a warning that changing a marketing strategy is fraught with danger, even if market research has informed the organization that a particular change is warranted.

Setting the scene

We now begin a number of units focusing on specific marketing issues such as the marketing plan, the marketing mix, market segmentation, and product differentiation and positioning. The amount of marketing terminology used is considerable and you are encouraged to check your understanding frequently to ensure that your knowledge is relevant and up to date.

One way of doing this is to apply a student-led inquiry approach to the learning of marketing by asking a number of questions about your own approach to marketing as a consumer of a product (a stakeholder). Questions to ask might include the following:

- How does this marketing idea apply and appeal to me as a consumer?
- How do I respond to marketing messages such as online advertising?
- What are the factors influencing me to purchase a particular product or service?
- How do I judge the effectiveness of a marketing mix of a product I enjoy, or one I do not enjoy?
- Can marketing influence my own preferences or perception of a new product or do I decide on a product's value by some other method?
- How important an influence is social media marketing on my consumption of goods and services?

The elements of a marketing plan (AO1)

We can add to our knowledge of planning taken from unit 1.7 by identifying some additional specific elements relevant to developing a marketing plan. The marketing plan should include:

- a marketing budget for promotional activities to be undertaken
- the strategy employed to fulfil the overall objectives of the organization
- tactical methods, for example the elements of the marketing mix such as the product, price, placement and promotion, to increase consumer awareness
- a breakdown of expected revenue and costs earned by the new product
- a time frame or time line to monitor and review progress of the plan
- contingencies or action plans to be used if the original marketing plan fails to achieve its objectives.

The role of marketing planning (AO2)

The purpose of the marketing plan is to ensure that the organization's marketing strategy is put into operation. Ideally, the plan will have a number of short- and long-term objectives to achieve. It is also important that managers of all departments understand the reasons and timings for the plan given that (as we saw earlier) finance, operations and human resources will all be affected; otherwise conflicts could occur, jeopardizing the overall strategy.

On the positive side, good marketing plans allow for:

- adjustments in the external environment to be incorporated into the plan to make it realistic
- an understanding of the competitive environment in which the organization is operating, which will have a direct influence on the marketing mix chosen.

A note of caution, however, is that marketing plans, which stretch over a number of years, will need to be updated regularly especially if the business is operating in a rapidly changing market place. As we saw earlier, Nokia failed to anticipate the impact of the iPhone in 2007 (see unit 4.1).

Monitoring marketing plans and updating them can take additional time and financial resources.

The four Ps of the marketing mix (AO2)

The marketing mix has been an important framework for developing an understanding of the "ingredients" required to successfully create an economically sustainable product in a competitive market. Students of the IB Business Management course should be very familiar with the basic elements of product, price, promotion and place. Each element is critical to ensure marketing success but a common misconception is that they are all equal parts of the mix (see Figure 4.2.1).

Figure 4.2.1 The four Ps of the marketing mix are all important ingredients

Filmmakers blame the critics as Disney reports a loss of $190 million on "The Lone Ranger"

Walt Disney's hopes that "The Lone Ranger" would prove box office gold quickly crumbled as audiences failed to fall for the western hero resurrected for the big screen.

The studio admitted this week it faces losses of up to $190 million (£124 million) on "The Lone Ranger", which stars Arnie Hammer in the title role and Johnny Depp as his trusty sidekick Tonto.

So who is to blame for this debacle? The actors and producer pointed their fingers squarely at the critics, claiming they pre-wrote negative reviews on social media that sunk the movie.

The 2013 incarnation of the Lone Ranger brought back the much-loved character portrayed on the radio, books and television that first appeared in the 1930s.

The finished film has been criticized as overlong and overwrought. *Time Out* dubbed it "Frustrating, lazy and lifeless", while *Rolling Stone* gave it one star out of four.

"Why is 'The Lone Ranger' such a huge flop at the box office?" its critic Peter Travers asked. "Because the movie sucks, that's why."

The production was plagued with difficulties and was delayed when the ballooning budget threatened to get out of control.

The film's producer Jerry Bruckheimer added that the critics were reviewing "the budget, not reviewing the movie".

Source: Adapted from the UK newspaper, *The Independent*, 7 August 2013

Some writers argue that increasingly given the "**tyranny of choice**" described in unit 4.1, the product itself and its perceived quality by stakeholders must be at the core of the marketing mix, ably supported by price, promotion and place. Without a quality product, the mix will not be effective despite creative pricing methods, extensive promotional activities or widespread distribution channels.

Again, the movie industry provides an excellent example linking to the knowledge gained in unit 3.9.

"THE LONE RANGER" – CONCLUSION

As we saw in unit 3.9, the producer effectively is in control of the finance and operation of the film. Jerry Bruckheimer and Johnny Depp are successful and well-regarded stakeholders in the movie industry; the director of the movie was Gore Verbinski who also directed Johnny Depp in the very successful "Pirates of the Caribbean" franchise which has grossed over $2 billion.

Even with this successful "management team" behind the production, the product was perceived as poor by word-of-mouth promotion on its release and even at sneak previews. Disney would have embarked on an extensive promotional campaign on TV and social media to direct audiences to the film and its distribution channels (movie theatres) would have been extensive across the United States and in global markets. The price of movie tickets is determined by the distributor although some special offers and promotions are possible.

This example reiterates the point that the product stands at the core of the marketing mix and the other elements, although important, must take a supporting role otherwise the marketing mix is unlikely to be effective. As we shall discuss further, if initial word-of-mouth is poor then social media marketing will provide the final judgment on a product's chances in the market-place and fatefully even before a product has been officially released.

Achieving marketing objectives via the marketing mix (AO3)

The discussion above clearly indicates that for a marketing mix to be effective the product at the core of the marketing mix needs to satisfy consumer needs and wants, but the ingredients of the mix need to work together. For example, a good-quality product perceived by the market may fail if not supported by:

- an appropriate price, either aimed at the target market or trying to appeal to a new one
- a promotional campaign that raises awareness of the product in the consumer's mind and again is appropriate to the target market
- a distribution channel (place) that allows the consumer to purchase the product quickly and avoids frustration.

There are, of course, exceptions to these rules.

One organization that has created a unique marketing mix, which for some commentators defies "traditional" business and marketing practice, is Apple. The product we will look at is the Apple iPhone. A discussion of the marketing mix of the Apple iPhone 5s follows.

Product

The Apple iPhone is perceived by the mobile phone industry as an iconic global brand. This is the case even though, according to industry commentators, the iPhone has significant competition, and fewer features than products from rivals such as HTC and Samsung.

Price

The iPhone is priced considerably above its rivals in the marketplace with price discounting rare. The final price of the iPhone to customers will depend on a whole range of factors including the telecommunications subsidy given by the phone carrier, local goods and service taxes and the size of the market being sold to. However, the iPhone is price-skimmed (see page 100 for a definition of skimming) in all of its markets and remains the "must have" gadget for many young consumers. Economists speak of a phenomenon called **conspicuous consumption** and the iPhone is certainly priced to meet this expectation by consumers.

Promotion

The promotional techniques used by the organization are unusual. Secrecy around product launches (on Steve Jobs' insistence) was and still is legendary. Websites and blogs have been created not necessarily to promote Apple iPhones *per se* but to reveal sneak photographs of potential products or new innovations. (Much of the Apple information referred to in this guide to help our understanding was taken from www.macrumours.com.)

Apple's advertising is limited to a few TV commercials throughout the year. Sales promotions are very rare on iPhones. One example is the newly created Black Friday promotion which usually occurs on the day after Thanksgiving in the United States (and has been copied in the UK) but reductions are hardly generous at a maximum of $50.

Place

Famously, despite pent-up demand and considerable consumer anticipation, Apple does not make the new version of an iPhone available to all global markets on the same day. Staggered product launches are the norm. Some consumers may have to wait weeks or even months to receive their new iPhone. Such is the excitement surrounding the launch of an iPhone that Apple's supply chain is pushed to the limit. Media coverage of queues of consumers waiting in line outside stores for a number of days to purchase the new product only adds to this frenzy and of course generates significant free publicity for Apple.

Conclusion

One could argue that Apple's marketing mix has been extremely successful although it is unique. Most business textbooks argue that all marketing mixes are unique but even in its own industry Apple has consistently not "played by the rules".

One could argue that the marketing mix of the iPhone and iPad for that matter is an example of a "blue ocean" strategy (see concept 5) and it clearly is effective in achieving its marketing and organizational mission to put a "ding in the universe". The big question is of course: under the leadership of Tim Cook, how long can Apple sustain this?

IB Learner Profile
Balanced ⚖

Based on the following article, has Apple made its first major mistake with the iPhone 5c?

New data suggests iPhone 5C has been a disaster

Umeng, China's largest app analyst, has produced a chart of iPhone activity on its network following the launch of the iPhone 5, the iPhone 5S and the iPhone 5C.

It's a disaster for the iPhone 5C. Four months after the launch of the iPhone 5C, activations remain way below those of the 5S. The chart shows what percentage of users is on which device.

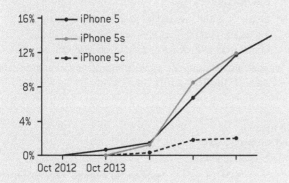

The 5C is on only 2% of devices on Umeng, the company says. It draws its data from 75 000 developers and 210 000 apps on its network. The 5S is on 12% of devices – or six times as many.

The good news for Apple is that the iPhone 5S is way more popular than the iPhone 5 was. And the 5S is much more expensive than the 5C. So Apple's "problem" here is a high-class one.

Nonetheless, when Apple gets something wrong, it's so unusual that it makes headlines. There has been a wave of rumors recently that the iPhone 5C has essentially failed, and that CEO Tim Cook will cancel the product later this year.

First, Cook admitted on his most recent financial conference that the company had predicted demand for the iPhone 5 incorrectly:

"... the mix was something very different than we thought. It was the first time we'd ever run that particular play before, and demand percentage turned out to be different than we thought."

He added that Apple would be unsentimental about making "a change" to the lineup if required: "if we decide it's in our best interest to make a change, then we'll make one". Then came an unconfirmed report from the Asian news site DigiTimes that there were warehouses in Taiwan that had 3 million unsold iPhone 5Cs in them.

Source: Business Insider, 17 March 2014

Update on 21 March 2014: Apple introduces a new 8GB of the iPhone 5c with a reduced price. This model is only available outside of the United States.

QUESTIONS FOR DISCUSSION

- In what ways can the marketing mix of the iPhone 5c be considered to be responsible for this "disaster"? Should the actual product shoulder the majority of the blame?

- Apple has just released a new version of the iPhone 5c with a smaller memory. By the time you have read the article above, a new range of Apple iPhones will have been released. If the iPhone 5c is withdrawn from the market, can we claim that this version of the iPhone has been a disaster?

- Compare the marketing mixes of the new Samsung Galaxy 5 with the new iPhone released in October 2014. Which is the more effective?

Target markets and market segmentation (AO2)

Now we will look at the difference between target markets and market segmentation and the creation of consumer profiles (AO2). Target markets and market segmentation are very closely linked.

Market segmentation is the process of classifying customers with similar needs and wants within a whole market. Once this classification has taken place, a business may try to determine an appropriate **target market**. This will allow the organization to direct financial resources and the marketing effort more effectively to avoid waste.

Once a target market has been established, it is likely that an organization will closely monitor consumer preferences and any changes that occur. The organization will need to monitor its own marketing effort to ensure that this is still relevant to the target market.

With the world wide web and social media marketing, the growth of **consumer profiling** is inevitable as organizations attempt to

form "virtual relationships" with their stakeholders. Attempts to form these relationships have led to the creation of a number of loyalty or customer relationship programmes offering special deals or privileges, but it has also led to an increase in "spamming". As we shall see in unit 4.4, a number of important ethical considerations must be taken into account when using online databases as a way of profiling customers and identifying market research opportunities.

Possible target markets and market segments (AO4)

Possible market segments could be identified and constructed from the market research undertaken by a business. This market research might gather data from a sample of customers regarding various characteristics, for example:

- age
- gender
- geographical location
- lifestyle, including family background
- occupation or income level.

The benefits of segmentation leading to targeting specific markets are principally built around the ability to focus the marketing effort on a group of consumers who share similar characteristics. Firms could focus on a segment where there may currently be limited competition or even a need that has yet to be filled, leading to a market gap. Segmentation may allow specialization and the opportunity to achieve economies of scale, which could allow greater price flexibility through reduced unit costs.

However, segmenting a market needs to be carried out with care and thought. Considerable problems will occur if a firm tries to segment its market in too many ways. Segments, unless carefully separated from each other with a different product and price – effectively creating a distinct marketing mix for each segment – may end up leading to the phenomenon of market cannibalization. One could argue that the iPhone has cannibalized the market share of the iPod Touch, as we will argue when we consider Boston Consulting Group (BCG) matrix in unit 4.5.

What if there is too much segmentation?

The "tyranny of choice" (Trout, 2001), which began our investigation into marketing in unit 4.1, has also not been kind to segmentation, especially in some markets such as the music and movie industries. If you were to enter a music retail shop in the 1970s, popular music would have been classified as just that. There might have been a classical and jazz department but the segments would have been limited. Today, there can be up to 15 different jazz classifications including traditional, blues, fusion, smooth, avant-garde, classic, funk, acid and so on.

IB Learner Profile

Inquiry ?

A quick visit to iTunes or Amazon will confirm that excessive segmentation is present in the music industry. As of March 2014,

the iTunes store in New Zealand was listing 23 different categories of music. Amazon.com was listing 25 different categories of music, which included some genres not listed on the iTunes site. Amazon had 19 different classifications of jazz.

Check the number of categories of music available online in your country. (You could include Spotify or other online music providers in your country.)

Questions for discussion and further reading

- How many categories of music available online exist in your country?
- What are the marketing implications for an industry such as the music industry of excessive segmentation?

For further reading turn to *The Long Tail* by Chris Anderson. This excellent book considers the impact of the Internet on the creation of new market segments and, by assumption, closer target markets.

How organizations target and segment their market and create consumer profiles (AO4)

Consider the financial data from Apple shown in Table 4.2.1.

Issues arising from the data

- If the objective of Apple **is to boost market share**, then which "operating segment" should the company target?
- How did you make your decision that Apple should target this market?
- By carrying out a consumer profile exercise or cultural intelligence (CQ) exercise, how could Apple use this information to increase its market share in China?

We shall also be using the product information in unit 4.5 when we consider the BCG matrix.

Apple Inc.
Q1 2014 Unaudited summary data
(units in thousands, revenue in millions)

Operating segments	Q1'14 Revenue	Q4'13 Revenue	Q1'13 Revenue	Sequential change Revenue	Year/Year change Revenue
Americas	$20 098	$13 941	$20 341	44%	-1%
Europe	13 073	8 005	12 464	63%	5%
Greater China (a)	8 844	5 733	6 830	54%	29%
Japan	4 948	3 341	4 443	48%	11%
Rest of Asia Pacific	3 633	1 980	3.993	83%	-9%
Retail	6 998	4 472	6 441	56%	9%
Total Apple	**$57 594**	**$37 472**	**$54 512**	**54%**	**6%**

Product summary	Q1'14 Units	Q1'14 Revenue	Q4'13 Units	Q4'13 Revenue	Q1'13 Units	Q1'13 Revenue	Sequential change Units	Sequential change Revenue	Year/Year change Units	Year/Year change Revenue
iPhone (b)	51 025	$32 498	33 797	$19 510	47 789	$30 660	51%	67%	7%	6%
iPad (b)	26 035	11 468	14 079	6 186	22 860	10 674	85%	85%	14%	7%
Mac (b)	4 837	6 395	4 574	5 624	4 061	5 519	6%	14%	19%	16%
iPod (b)	6 049	973	3 498	573	12 679	2 143	73%	70%	-52%	-55%
iTune/Software/Services (c)		4 397		4 260		3 687		3%		19%
Accessories (d)		1 863		1 319		1 829		41%		2%
Total Apple		**$57 594**		**$37 472**		**$54 512**		**54%**		**6%**

(a) Greater China includes China, Hong Kong and Taiwan.

(b) Includes deferrals and amortization of related non-software services and software upgrade rights.

(c) Includes revenue from sales on the iTunes Store, the App Store, the Mac App Store, and the iBooks Store, and revenue from sales of AppleCare, licensing and other services.

(d) Includes sales of hardware peripherals and Apple-branded and third-party accessories for iPhone, iPad, Mac and iPod.

Table 4.2.1 Financial data from Apple: Q1 2014

The difference between niche and mass markets (AO2)

It is interesting to note that the Apple organization has grown from a "niche" player in the computer market into a market leader in the consumer electronics industry. A niche market is a smaller segment of a much bigger market. A niche market may try to "capture" a particular segment of a market that has been under-served by established firms. In the hi-fidelity industry, established suppliers such as Sony and Panasonic leave the supply of highly technical and expensive hi-fi equipment costing thousands of dollars to niche organizations such as Linn, Naim, Rega and Krell.

Organizations operating in a niche market must make their profits from small sales volumes. Given that overhead costs are fixed, they must charge relatively high prices to compensate. Niche products therefore must offer significant "value" to customers in order to be successful.

Mass markets attempt to create products that have national or global appeal. Rather than targeting a specific customer, mass marketing aims to reach as many as stakeholders as possible. Both profit and not-for-profit organizations can be mass market, as the examples of Coca-Cola and Oxfam show.

Mass marketing requires significant budgets for organizations to develop a brand presence in a number of different segments. Niche marketing will inevitably have to be carried out with fewer financial resources, as consumer targeting and profiling can be very helpful in this process.

Positioning, perception and differentiation from the competition

The topic of positioning, perception and differentiation from the competition is popular among examiners. It is a demanding topic – perhaps one of the most conceptually difficult areas of marketing for students to grasp. Positioning is a complex term to define and you are encouraged to read then reread this section carefully. We will be covering a good deal of ground and, in order to make this material accessible and up to date, we will make extensive use of examples and analysis by Trout (whose work we have come across already).

We will begin by quoting one of Trout's famous maxims (2001):

Marketing is not about a battle between products. It is about a battle of perceptions.

Positioning

Positioning is the process of creating a consistent and recognized customer perception. This perception may be about a company's brand, product and service or the company itself.

Positioning maps

Kotler's work in this area has been important. A two-dimensional perception or positioning map illustrates his analysis of the positioning of an instant breakfast drink relative to the variables of price of the product and speed of preparation (see Figure 4.2.2).

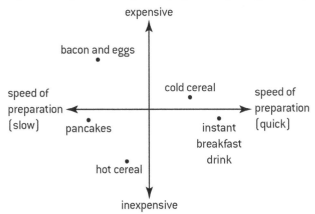

Figure 4.2.2 Positioning map for an instant breakfast drink

The importance of a unique selling point or proposition (AO2)

If Trout is correct, then clearly a strong marketing aim for an organization is to have a unique selling point or proposition (USP). Put simply, a USP is defined as **a summary of what makes a business unique and valuable to its target market.** A USP answers the fundamental differentiation question: How does a business or product benefit its clients better than any other organization or its product can?

If a product is perceived to have a USP in the minds of consumers then this can act as a very powerful marketing tool given the "tyranny of choice" that has often been referred to in this unit. This USP can also increase brand loyalty and awareness and have significant implications for the type of marketing mix pursued by the organization. For example, a USP may allow an organization to charge a much higher price than the competition.

Attribute ownership – USP in action

Some organizations, due to a number of differentiating factors which we will come to later, are able to create a perception in the mind of the consumer just by mention of their company name. Trout (2001) calls this **attribute ownership**. It is a very valuable quality and if sensibly marketed can lead to the creation of a USP. To clarify understanding, Table 4.2.2 gives some examples.

Company/Brand	Attribute
Volvo	Safety
Crest toothpaste	Cavity protection
Duracell	Long-lasting
Toyota	Reliability
McDonald's	Fast food and children's meals
Visa	Ubiquity
Evian	Pure water
Gillette	Men's shaving

Table 4.2.2 Examples of attribute ownership

Some companies have developed their perception so well that the brand has become generic in the minds of consumers and has entered everyday language. Some examples are:

- Xerox: "Can you Xerox this to head office, please?"
- Hoover: "I am going to Hoover the room".
- Kleenex
- Scotch Tape
- Gore-Tex
- Band-Aid
- Laundromat
- Zipper
- Aspirin
- Thermos
- Yo-Yo
- And of course, Google: "Let's Google the meaning of this".

Differentiation from competitors (AO3)

All marketing consultants and strategy specialists from Kotler to Trout would agree on the need for a firm to be able to differentiate its products or services away from those of the competition.

The creation of the art of differentiation is credited to Rosser Reeves in 1960, who in his book *Reality in Advertising* argued that advertising should create a USP for a product to convince a customer to buy a certain brand rather than a competitor's. His ideas on differentiation have been hugely influential.

Table 4.2.3 gives a definition of characteristics that students tend to assume must be differentiating (such as price and quality) and then provides a brief overview, suggesting some issues or problems. Interested students, looking for more detail, are encouraged to read Trout's comments in the book he co-wrote with Rivkin: *Differentiate or Die*.

Differentiating factor	Discussion points
Quality	Trout argues that using quality is a poor way to differentiate. Consumers expect good quality as standard. (Which consumers would knowingly accept poor quality?). He stresses that all firms have the same opportunity to implement quality management such TQM, so that "me too" products appear in the market-place all promising the same level of quality. This is hardly differentiating
Customer loyalty programmes (CLPs)	The differentiation impact here has been reduced by ubiquity. CLPs are easily imitated and not always cost-effective. The airline industry with its "air miles" programme is perhaps one of the most well-known CLPs. However, an air miles programme can: • reduce demand for some paid tickets • limit the availability of seats on popular flights which could have been sold at higher prices • irritate loyal customers who cannot "cash in" their air miles easily • lead to some ethical issues (as we shall see in unit 4.4 on market research)
Price	Consumers may have the perception that low prices have an impact on the quality of the finished product. Wal-Mart and Amazon have been able to maintain low price positioning by substantial supply-chain power to enforce low prices. This has given them unique cost advantages which a new firm would find very hard to match. Trout concedes that a high price differentiation strategy based on more than just quality can be successful if accompanied by a range of other factors such as being first in a market or by obtaining attribute ownership. He cites the Apple iPod, Rolex watches and North Face (Gore-Tex) as examples of products which have been successful with high price differentiation
Line extension	The range of products offered can be a differentiation point but size of selection is critical. Toys "R" Us and again Amazon have been very successful due to their focus and huge selection. New line extensions need to counter consumer scepticism that advertised changes may simply be cosmetic and not significantly different enough
Differentiation based on the company positioning itself as environmentally friendly or socially responsible	Trout argues that this could be a source of differentiation but we can note these points based on his argument: • The firm must find a willingness among customers to pay higher prices to ensure environmental quality. • Credible information must be available to the consumer at low cost about the environmental and social advantages of consumption

Table 4.2.3 Differentiating charateristics – issues and problems

Setting the scene

A number of marketing decisions require planning into the future, which is of course unknown. If an organization is going to introduce a new product into the market-place it will need to carry out market research. This is covered in greater depth in unit 4.4. However, in addition to finding out whether a new product could be successful, an organization will require some form of financial forecasting of future demand, costs and revenues. Financial forecasts may be made relating to a time period well beyond the date on which the marketing plan was created (e.g. they may cover a period two to four years from that date) and of course they will be subject to a number of unknown variables.

Making these forecasts is similar to the process of weather forecasting. External factors can influence a weather forecast only a few hours after it has been made. Forecasts can only be based on the information available at the time the forecast was made and weather patterns, in common with sales behaviour, can change rapidly.

Sales forecasts need to be realistic and conservative and as accurate as possible. However, if an organization is too risk-averse and under-produces, the risk of being short of supplies and missing out on valuable profit-making opportunities becomes inevitable.

This unit focuses on scientific methods of sales forecasting. We must though remember that some sales forecasting could be based on experience and intuition or "gut feeling". The type of forecasting method used will depend on the culture of the organization and the leadership style adopted.

Trout points out that there are no guarantees when making forecasts. However, our planning has to begin somewhere. Also, if a business wishes to attract additional investors to help finance the launch of a new products, sales forecasts made under different assumptions are vital.

Sales forecasting terminology

Before we begin the process of illustrating how a sales forecast can be created we need to define some important terms:

- sales trend
- seasonal and cyclical variation
- random variation.

Sales trend

The sales trend is the underlying movement or pattern of the data presented. In many sales forecasting models, the forecast sales of a product are given over a period of months or even years. This is called a time series. Figure 4.3.1 illustrates a set of sales data in time series form, and the trend. The trend is the underlying pattern of the data of this time series and is shown as the dotted line in the figure. In our analysis, the trend will be calculated using a method called the four-part moving average.

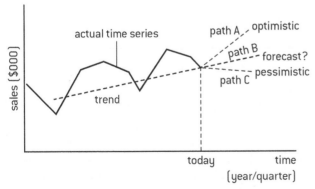

Figure 4.3.1 Sales data – time series and sales trend

Source: Powell (1991)

The sales trend line can be extended to forecast the future path of sales on the understanding that the trend of external factors will continue into the future (as shown by path B). However, with new information on external factors coming to light, a forecast may need to be adjusted either optimistically (path A) or pessimistically (path C). Whichever path is chosen, it is reasonable to say that the further the trend line is extended the more likely it will prove to be inaccurate.

Seasonal and cyclical variation

The trend may have regular variations. For example, sales of tents and camping equipment may traditionally peak in the warmer months. This is called a seasonal variation. However, over a much longer period of years, other variations in camping equipment sales may also be experienced. These longer-term swings are called cyclical variations as they depend on the various "ups and downs" that an economy inevitably goes through. The economic term for an "up" is recovery where consumer and business confidence is increasing. For a "down" the economic term used is a recession where output in an economy falls for two consecutive quarters, unemployment may increase and consumer confidence will decline.

Random variations

In addition to the regular movements of trend and seasonal factors, there are "one-off" events which can affect data. For example, events that occur every four years could include the feel-good factor generated with the election of a new president or a major sporting occasion such as the Olympic games or the soccer World Cup. These are termed random variations.

Constructing a four-part moving average, sales trends and forecast (AO4)

The following section shows the construction of a four-part moving average, sales trends and forecast, including seasonal, cyclical and random variation, using given data (AO4). Table 4.3.1 giving data about a bicycle manufacturer is adapted from an example given in a business studies book by Ian Marcousé *et al* (2007). This shows how to satisfy AO4.

Year	Sales of bicycles ($000)
2004	300
2005	500
2006	600
2007	550
2008	600
2009	750
2010	850
2011	1 100
2012	800
2013	1 100

Table 4.3.1 Sales data from a bicycle manufacturer

Step 1: Constructing a four-part moving average to identify the trend

We can see from the data in Table 4.3.1 that the underlying pattern of bicycle sales is upward. We can plot the data on a diagram (see Figure 4.3.2).

To identify the trend we must "smooth out" the raw sales data. It is possible to calculate a trend by using a moving average. The average can be taken for any period such as a year, a month or a quarter. We shall create a four-year average, as shown in Table 4.3.2.

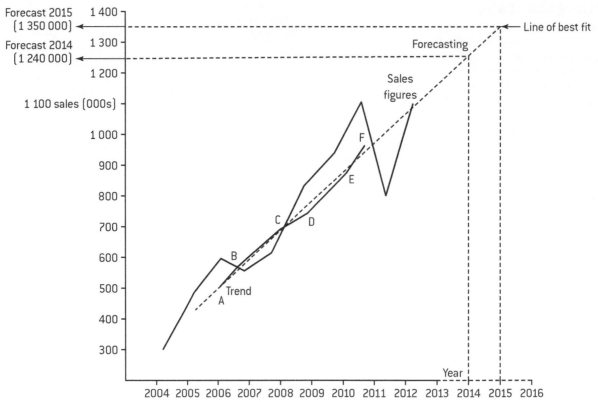

Figure 4.3.2 Annual sales for a bicycle manufacturer 2004–2013

Year	Sales	Four-year moving total	Eight-year moving total	Trend four-year moving average = eight-year moving total ÷ 8
2004	300			
2005	500			
		1 950		
2006	600		4 200	525
		2 250		
2007	550		4 750	593.75
		2 500		
2008	600		5 250	656.25
		2 750		
2009	750		6 050	756.25
		3 300		
2010	850		6 800	850
		3 500		
2011	1 100		7 350	918.75
		3 850		
2012	800			
2013	1 100			

Table 4.3.2 Calculating a four-year moving average for a bicycle manufacturer

To calculate the average for the years 2004–2007, we must add the totals, giving us a figure of 1950, then divide by 4.

One problem is that this average lies between years 2 and 3 and placing this figure between two years may result in misleading predictions in the future. The solution is to use **centering**. This uses a four- and eight-year moving total to find a mid point, as Table 4.3.2 indicates.

Plotting the moving average figures shows the underlying pattern or trend. The trend line is "smoother" than the line showing the raw data and gives a more obvious indication of the trend taking place by eliminating fluctuations.

Step 2: Predicting from the trend

Having identified a trend that is taking place with the sales figures presented, we can now use this information to predict what could happen in the future. Taking our lead from Figure 4.3.2, we could extend the trend by drawing a "line of best fit". This line, represented by the dotted diagonal line in Figure 4.3.2, matches

the general slope of all points in the trend and can be drawn "by eye". Extending this line carefully will give a fair prediction of future sales values in future time periods.

From Figure 4.3.2, we could predict sales for 2014 as 1 240 000 and for 2015 as 1 350 000.

Using a computer program, the actual forecasted values for 2014–2017 could be calculated using a process known as the sum of least squares. This method is beyond the scope of this guide and the IB Business Management syllabus.

Step 3: Variations from the trend

The trend we calculated in step 1 smoothed out variations in sales figures. To create an accurate prediction of sales in 2014, the organization will have to find the average variation over the period and incorporate this.

The variation is calculated by taking:

actual sales – trend value.

The results are presented in Table 4.3.3.

Year	Sales	Trend (four-year moving average)	Variation in (each year)
2004	300		
2005	500		
2006	600	525	+75
2007	550	593.75	-43.75
2008	600	656.25	-56.25
2009	750	756.25	-6.25
2010	850	850	0
2011	1 100	918.75	+181.25
2012	800		
2013	1 100		

Table 4.3.3 Actual sales – trend

Taking all of the available variations and dividing by the number of observations creates an average cyclical variation.

In this case the answer is

$$\frac{+75 - 43.75 - 56.25 - 6.25 + 181.25 + 0}{6} = \frac{150}{6} = +25$$

(or 25 000)

If the forecast or prediction based on the trend and line of best fit was $1 240 000, then adding $25 000 may give a more accurate predicted figure of $1 265 000.

Seasonal variations

So far we have considered creating a forecast based around yearly data for the sales of a bicycle manufacturer. For another organization, what might be of interest is to look at sales variations **within** a given year. Ice cream and tourism businesses are just two possible companies that may wish to look at sales across different months of a year to see whether there are seasonal variations. This information can be very useful to help with marketing and HR planning.

Table 4.3.3 indicates the quarterly sales of a business selling ice cream in the northern hemisphere where summer (the warmest time of the year) occurs in quarter 3.

Year	Quarter	Sales	Q4 moving average	Variation
2011	3	42		
	4	21		
2012	1	20	31	-9
	2	28	31.625	-3.625
	3	48	34.5	13.5
	4	40	35	5
2013	1	24	34.5	-10.5
	2	28	33	-5
	3	44	31.625	12.375
	4	32	32.25	-0.25
2014	1	21		
	2	36		

Table 4.3.4 Sales of ice cream

To calculate the expected sales value in 2015 quarter 4 (Q4), we could plot this data and create a four-quarter moving average trend and then by eye extend a line of best fit through the trend. As we saw from our analysis above, this trend is a smoothed-out figure. Calculating the average seasonal variation and adjusting our figure or reading from the graph could make a more accurate forecast for Q4 in 2015.

Average seasonal variation Q4 $= \dfrac{5 - 0.25}{2} = \dfrac{4.75}{2} = 2.375$

Hence if the forecasted value for sales in 2014 Q4 was 40 000

a more accurate prediction would be $40 000 + 2 375 = 42 375$.

Benefits and limitations of sales forecasting (AO3)

In setting the scene for this unit we have already highlighted some of the benefits of sales forecasting:

- Sales forecasts allow a marketing plan to have an objective or aim which is much more quantifiable than just "increasing sales revenue".
- Financial stakeholders such as investors or banks will clearly wish to see predictions of sales forecasts (e.g. if an organization is looking to introduce a new product into the market-place additional finance will be required). To act as a form of security that their financial assistance is going to be used

effectively, financial institutions will require sales forecasts that are as accurate as possible.

- Sales forecasts allow an organization to plan its future cash needs and pre-empt possible cash shortages. As we saw in unit 3.1, banks are much more willing to grant overdrafts to solve cash flow problems at cheaper rates rather than encourage unauthorized or poorly timed overdrafts.
- Sales forecasts allow monitoring of a marketing plan to see whether objectives are SMART (see page 17). These forecasts could be taken in three- or six-monthly steps to heighten the control process and to ensure that financial targets are realistic. Sales forecasts can also help with the issue of over-purchasing of raw materials which if not sold will lead to waste and jeopardize future profits.

However, sales forecasts have the following limitations:

- The limitations of sales forecasts are closely aligned with the difficulties of predicting future cash inflows and future monetary benefits used in the decision-making process.
- In a rapidly evolving market-place with changes such as new competition and other external threats occurring at such a pace, sales forecasts cannot ever hope to keep up.
- As any publicly traded company will know (and our knowledge from the Enron debacle shows us) any organization that continues to over-predict its sales forecasts or provide inaccurate overly optimistic figures to appeal to market analysts and thus become less transparent will run the risk of the "wrath" of the markets when the truth is known. Forecasts are necessary but not sufficient for a successful marketing plan.

Setting the scene

Market research is the gathering, recording, analysing and presentation of information or data in order to assist in the marketing process. There are two major types of market research.

Primary market research is where an organization will try to ascertain first-hand knowledge directly from the market-place about a potential new product or consumer reaction to an existing one. This information will not have been collected before.

Secondary market research is data published by an external stakeholder in an industry. In unit 4.1, Table 4.1.2 (see page 79) provides the sales data on the number of personal computers sold to US customers between 2012 and 2013. Gartner – an independent market research agency with a particular interest in the consumer electronics industry – collected this data.

This should immediately illustrate a key difference between primary and secondary market research. The former is up to date and the latter could be a few months (or years) out of date. However, which one is the easier to collect and most relevant to an organization's needs? This unit aims to discuss these important issues.

Why and how organizations carry out market research (AO2)

The "why" part of this learning outcome can be referred to by considering some of the marketing fundamentals defined and highlighted in unit 4.2. Market research is used to ascertain the current **market size**, the current **competitive nature of the market** via **market share** and the potential for **market growth** and will be essential information for an organization looking to enter an existing market.

For a completely new product or market, this information will not be available. Instead, organizations will need to identify trends or behaviours revealed by consumers and other stakeholders that may indicate that a potential market gap or niche is available. Research of this kind will take time and use up financial resources but will be invaluable if the organization is, for example, looking to introduce a new product to solve a problem it encounters during the research process. Even more preferable is that the market research data reveals a new problem **yet** to be solved.

Analysis of market research

In the following comment, Trout and Rivkin (2008) advise caution over attaching too much importance to the role of market research.

Marketing people are pre-occupied with doing research – getting the facts. They analyse the situation to make sure the truth is on their side. They sail confidently into the marketing arena; secure in the knowledge that they have the best product and that ultimately the best product will win.

It's an illusion. There is no objective reality. There are no facts. There are no best products. All that exists in the world of marketing are perceptions in the minds of customers. The perception is the reality.

This may be an incomplete view as Trout and Rivkin also advise businesses to carry out market research in order to identify a point of difference from the competition. However, they are correct that conducting market research is no guarantee of creating and marketing successful products especially (as we saw in unit 4.2) if the customer's perception of a product is unfavourable.

The "how" part of the market research learning outcome is easier to explain. Either an organization can carry out the primary and secondary data collection itself or it can employ a specialist marketing agency such as Gartner to do this. The final choice will depend on a number of factors.

Objectivity and relevance

Given the inherent bias in collecting data, a number of large organizations do not collect primary or secondary market data themselves. Instead they prefer to employ a specialist market research agency to increase the degree of objectivity (or to reduce bias).

As we noted above, if a company is launching a new product in the market-place, secondary data collection will be difficult to find. Primary data may also be scarce if a questionnaire or interview is expected to reveal how a consumer "feels" about a product that currently does not exist. A specialist agency with experience may be able to overcome some of these difficulties.

Cost and accuracy

For small business start-ups, the cost of employing a specialist agency may be high, although the time saved could be considerable. The world wide web is a cheap, immediate source of secondary data but will this data be accurate and suit an organization's needs? Given that secondary data can date quickly as soon as it is published, especially in rapidly changing technological markets; primary data collection may be more accurate.

Methods of primary market research (AO2)

Surveys

These can include feedback from customers directly via online surveys such as www.surveymonkey.com or via company websites. A more traditional survey may include a person-to-person questionnaire or a telephone call asking for consumer feedback or reaction to a company's product or service.

Interviews

Interviews tend to be more in-depth than surveys but with fewer respondents. They can be costly to organize or set up. However, if properly conducted, an interview can reveal hitherto unknown information for a business to use.

One common theme of surveys and interviews is that extracting accurate and useful primary market research will depend on the ordering and quality of the questions asked; how they are phrased and how they are interpreted by the respondent.

Focus groups

Interviews may have the drawback that some respondents may feel intimated by a one-on-one interview. Focus-group sessions avoid this problem by asking groups of individuals – not always known to each other – certain questions about a new product or about their "feelings" towards on old one. This environment may allow participants to "relax" and spend longer in the primary market research process. Focus groups are also a good way to collect **qualitative** market research.

Observations

If location is an important consideration for a new business start-up, then some of the most productive primary market research could be obtained by an observation or visit to a possible site. If the start-up is located near a rival enterprise, for example, observers can view customer numbers.

Observations can be carried out fairly quickly and inconspicuously although there are implications here for bias and security. There may also be **ethical considerations** from observing for too long.

Methods of secondary market research (AO2)

Market analyses

The world wide web has provided a whole range of opportunities to find research from organizations, government institutions,

NGOs, concerned stakeholders, pressure groups and so on. The problem, of course, is deciding which market analysis survey is the most accurate and suited to an organization's needs.

Academic journals and government publications

These two types of publication are grouped together as there could be potential overlap: many academic journals could be financed from government research departments.

The government of most countries will publish census material on population and demographic trends every five years or so, depending on the size of the country. This information could be useful for businesses looking to target a particular market segment such as the 16–24-year-old population or the over 65s.

Academic journals may be published by universities or research institutes. These journals may contain specific information relating to a particular industry or market.

Media articles

Without media articles and the "rise of citizen journalism" through blogs or wikipages, this study guide would not exist in its current form. Media articles especially can provide balanced views to an issue or a business decision, which an official government publication may not. This is of course a generalization but it is important for a market researcher conducting secondary research into a range of topics, markets, opinions and trends to consult as wide a range of the available printed material as possible.

Qualitative and quantitative research (AO2)

The above point is critical when we consider the difference between qualitative and quantitative market research. Qualitative research is concerned with ascertaining motivation and attitudes towards buying habits of consumers. It can be difficult to quantify exactly. How would you measure objectively how you "feel" about a particular product or service?

Qualitative market research can be obtained by market research respondents taking part in group discussions such as in focus groups or in-depth interviews. Given the nature of these conversations about emotional connections to products or brands, a good deal of qualitative market research is collected by psychologists.

Quantitative market research is conducted mostly by researchers having pre-prepared questions which can be answered by large samples of the population. Answers to these questions are then collated and, using computer software, collected into a readily digestible form. The results of quantitative market research could be easily expressed by the following:

- In the age group of 16–20 years, 42% of people prefer low-sugar drinks to regular soft drinks.

- In the age group of 65 years and over, 82% of people would like to know how to use all the features on their smartphone.

The ethics of market research (AO3)

The need for market research cannot be underestimated. To summarize, in carrying out market research a firm needs to balance the degree of accuracy and objectivity required with the cost, purpose and time allowed to collect the data.

However, one critical consideration is that the market research process must be as non-judgmental or unbiased as possible. This aspect can create significant problems for market research organizations – even those with many years of experience.

For example, when conducting primary market research, the interviewer should not ask questions that may embarrass the respondent. An example could be: "Do you have bad breath? Would you consider using this product if you had bad breath?" It is a well-intentioned question but poorly phrased. Would a respondent really admit in public to having bad breath?

However, bad breath is a minor issue. Much more significant qualitative market research designed to ascertain feelings or attitudes on race, religion, sexual orientation or other personal issues may "cross the line" from being informative research to become being intrusive.

As Rosenberg and Daly (1993) indicate:

Behavioural scientists recognise that research is a probing process with the potential to infringe on subjects' rights. Despite their own sensitivity for the rights of others and the faith in their professionalism of their colleagues, behavioural scientists have come to recognise that a formal code of checks and balances is needed to preserve the ethical integrity of behavioural research.

For secondary market research where data may be collected from a range of sources, the ethical issues may intensify. As an example, consider the humble loyalty card issued by a number of retail outlets to encourage repeat purchases in return for member discounts or "privileges". The data collected from these repeat purchases can in many countries be legally purchased and used for market research purposes. Welcome to the world of junk and spam mail that has its origins in the purchase data collected by organizations offering loyalty schemes.

However, given the rapid changes in technology and increasing processing speed of computers, the issue of using secondary data collected from loyalty cards now has a global dimension. This is revealed in the newspaper article on the next page.

Methods of sampling (AO2)

The process of sampling is crucial and it saves costs and time. It would not be possible for an organization to carry out an investigation of an entire market or population within a reasonable time frame and for a reasonable cost. Instead, a firm may wish to take samples of consumers. There are a number of ways in which these samples can be taken.

Students also have to consider the benefits and costs of each sampling method. Key factors are time taken, cost, degree of accuracy required and of bias accepted (see Table 4.4.1 on page 93).

A full description of bias and its implications for statistical work is outside the realms of this study guide. However, we should note that researchers try to minimize bias as much as they possibly can.

Results from data collection (AO2)

Presenting market research data

Given the increasing availability of software packages such as Excel or Numbers, which allow students to generate sophisticated diagrams and tables, there is no need to explain the different forms of data presentation here. (Descriptions of each method of statistical presentation should be covered in other parts of your IB Diploma such as another group 5 subject.)

However, a skill that is worth considering is looking at the reasons **for a particular choice** for displaying different types of data. This choice will have an impact on the presentation method selected.

IB Learner Profile

Reflection Я|R

Using prior knowledge to develop understanding in business management

Following the newspaper article (on the next page) are review questions on presenting data from previous study or prior knowledge of statistics. It is not the intention that you should answer these questions in class but they are listed to offer a way of checking that your prior knowledge of statistics is applied to the IB Business Management course.

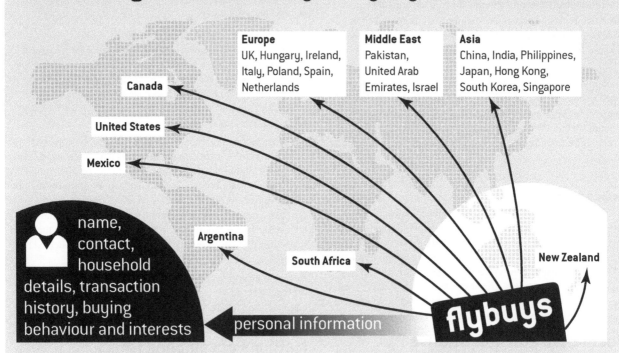

The data gold mines How your flybuys data is shared

Europe
UK, Hungary, Ireland, Italy, Poland, Spain, Netherlands

Middle East
Pakistan, United Arab Emirates, Israel

Asia
China, India, Philippines, Japan, Hong Kong, South Korea, Singapore

Canada

United States

Mexico

Argentina

South Africa

New Zealand

name, contact, household details, transaction history, buying behaviour and interests

personal information

flybuys

Coles shares personal flybuys and online data

Customers using the Coles flybuys loyalty card or online shopping service are having their personal details sent to up to 30 other companies owned by the same corporation and to third parties in at least 23 other countries.

Customers were told that by using flybuys or online shopping they consented to a privacy policy that allowed data collected to be shared with other companies in the Wesfarmers group, including Kmart, Bunnings and Officeworks. But the retail giant also revealed that the personal information it collects on its customers might be sent to nations such as China, Pakistan, the Philippines, Mexico, the United Arab Emirates, the United States and Britain.

Under the Coles policy, personal information, defined as data that identifies someone or allows a person's identity to be ascertained, can be used in conducting risk assessments for credit and insurance. This can include name, contact and household details, transaction history and buying habits.

A spokeswoman said Coles' global commercial partners had the highest standards of data security and that Coles followed all regulatory requirements and best-practice disclosure. In line with the new legislation, Coles' policy enables customers to access or correct personal information it has collected about them.

The Australian Privacy Foundation vice-chair David Vaile said companies such as Coles should have for years been revealing where data was being sent and it was unlikely Australian customers would have any comeback if their data was misused overseas.

University of Technology Sydney marketing lecturer Ingo Bentrott said "data mining" "sounds very Big Brother but if it's done ethically and you're giving the customer what they want then I think it's OK".

Source: Adapted from an article in the Australian newspaper, *The Sydney Morning Herald*, 9 March 2014

Read more at www.smh.com.au/national/coles-shares-personal-flybuys-and-online-data-20140308-34efw.html#ixzz2xPXmI2xx

(a) Why is it important to display data collected from market research carefully?

(b) Explain why bar charts are useful in presenting data.

(c) Explain two problems when using a pie chart to present data.

(d) Explain how pictograms can be useful in representing certain types of quantitative data.

(e) You are given the sets of data listed below. In each case, decide how you would best illustrate the data bearing in mind the appropriateness of the presentation method and how to make your chosen method the most effective to the reader:

(i) the sales figures for a soft-drink company over the last 10 years

(ii) data to show the number of industrial accidents and injuries in large businesses over the past two years

(iii) the male/female ratio in your current class

(iv) the numbers of different nationalities present in your school

(v) the income or wage levels of 10 different occupations.

(f) A senior manager in a record store Rare Retro is looking at the sales figures of three music departments. He is trying to decide which department is "doing the best". Assume that the current external environment has affected all three departments in the same way.

Year	2010	2011	2012
Jazz	1.2	1.8	2
Rock	2	2.4	2.1
Alternative (introduced in 2010)	0.2	0.4	0.8
Total	3.4	4.6	4.9

Note: Figures are in millions of dollars.

- The senior manager cannot tell which department is doing the best.
- The jazz supervisor says that his department has had the biggest increase in sales.
- The supervisor in New Zealand argues that rock music still contributes the most to sales.
- The alternative music supervisor argues that since his range was only released in 2012, his department has seen the largest percentage increase in sales.

Advise the senior manager as to which department you think is "doing the best".

Why does this exercise reveal that it can be difficult to interpret sales data collected accurately and decide who or what is "doing the best"?

Suggested answers to questions (e) and (f) are given on page 132.

Sample method	Description	Time taken and cost considerations	Accuracy and bias
Random	In a sample survey, there is an equal chance that any particular respondent will be chosen	This method can be time-consuming and skilled interviewers may be required. It can be very costly	Given that there are no preconditions, random sampling has the least bias. For niche or technological product surveys, random samples may not generate enough accurate data compared to quota samples
Quota	Respondents are segmented into specific groups, which share similar characteristics. The interviewer is then given a target to sample. For example, 10 males aged 18–25 are questioned. Once the target is fulfilled no more respondents are asked questions	Given the smaller number of respondents, the quota method may be cheaper than using a random sample. Time will be needed to set up segments	If a company requires respondents to have specialist knowledge, e.g. for technological products, then a quota method may be more accurate than the random method but bias is increased due to pre-selection of respondents
Stratified	This is similar to a quota but there are no targets. Respondents are randomly selected from segments	See "Quota"	See "Quota"
Cluster	Geographical areas are used as the group characteristic. Respondents are then randomly sampled	There are similarities to quota	Regional bias may exist, especially if there are significant economic and social differences between regions. Opinion polls based on regions need to be treated with caution
Snowballing	This is a method of sampling in which existing study subjects recruit future subjects from among their acquaintances. In 2014, Google is attempting to launch the Google Glass: the first commercial pair of glasses with a mini-micro processor attached which will allow wearers to record photos, make movies and surf the Internet through the lens. As part of a snowballing exercise, Google gave many of its employees samples of the glasses to try at home and at work and feed back the results. The employees were then encouraged to nominate other potential market research respondents who could then give feedback to Google	The time taken can be considerable. Given the small number of respondents, snowballing can be cost-effective	There could be significant bias in this method as influential stakeholders pass on the information about the product to "other" influential people. This could generate a very narrow range of feedback but of course this may be what was intended

Table 4.4.1 Key factors of different sampling methods

Product – setting the scene

Link to concept 2: Change, concept 3: Innovation, and context

We are now going to look at the marketing mix in more detail with a much greater analytical and evaluative approach. AO3 dominates the following topics.

We must also remember that our study of business content must be linked to the concepts introduced at the beginning of this study guide and a context that allows you to make connections or linkages between all three. From this, it is the intention that you will develop a much deeper understanding of business management, which will certainly help with your ability to discuss and evaluate. We shall also develop a much greater focus on a context by considering one of the paradigm-breaking organizations of our time.

We consider the first element of the marketing mix – product – which was deemed to be at the "core" and link this to two concepts: product **innovation** and technological **change**.

According to Marketing Intelligence Services Ltd, in 1987 there were 14 254 new products introduced into the United States. In 1998 the number of new products that year was 25 181, or 69 for every day of the year. Research from Nielsen in 2007 and 2008 indicates that in each of these years 122 000 new products were introduced.

Most of these products were neither new nor innovative. Trout and Rivkin (2008) refer to the majority of them as simply adding "bells, whistles and tweaks". They claim they were effectively modest extension strategies (see more on extension strategies later in this unit).

However, since 1998 and the application of **Moore's law** (see opposite) there has been an explosion of growth of new technological products aimed at the consumer. Product innovation has become very important to cash flow and even for survival. For example, it was estimated that for companies such as Hewlett Packard, new products created in the previous year exclusively generated 75% of global sales in one year. This imposes a huge burden on companies to be constantly innovative in a rapidly changing technological landscape.

Consider Table 4.5.1, which lists the changes to some of the product portfolio of the Apple Corporation since 1998. As we have established, Apple's philosophy has been built around innovative product design.

A product revision is defined as a cosmetic makeover, perhaps slightly altering the external features of the product. A reincarnation is defined as a completely new version of the product with changes made both internally and externally. In unit 5.6 we will refer to these revisions and reincarnations as adaptive creativity and innovative creativity respectively.

Apple product	First appeared	Number of revisions and reincarnations as of April 2014
iPod Classic	2001	6
iPod Mini (then Nano)	2005	9
iPod Shuffle	2005	4
iPod Touch	2007	5
iPhone	2007	8 including 4s and 5c and 5s
iMac (desktop)	1998	16 including Mac Pro
iBook then MacBook (laptop)	2003	16 including 6 MacBook Pro and Air variations
iPad	2010	5 including iPad Air
iPad Mini	2012	2 including Retina version

Table 4.5.1 Examples of Apple products launched since 1988

Source: www.macrumors.com

It is expected that by the time this study guide is published, Apple will have added a new updated version of the iPhone. We have already noted the introduction of a 8GB iPhone 5c. The iPod Shuffle and the iPod, however, may have reached the end of their useful life. We shall discuss this in more detail when we apply the Boston Consulting Group (BCG) matrix.

MOORE'S LAW – ITS IMPACT GIVEN RAPIDLY CHANGING TECHNOLOGICAL MARKETS

Moore's Law states that the number of transistors that can be placed cheaply on an integrated circuit board has increased exponentially, doubling every two years. This has enormous implications for processing speed and memory capability. In plain English, it would appear that technological products can do much more for much less every year – effectively doubling the processes' speed for half the cost. Apple and other manufacturers have clearly taken full advantage of this technical economy of scale with prices of new products falling a few months after their introduction to the market-place – apart from the iPhone of course.

The product life cycle (AO4)

It seems obvious that a product is developed, then launched and will go through various stages of growth, saturation and maturity before it enters the decline phase of the product life cycle. Decisions will then have to be made either to retain or to replace the product. If the latter, the cycle begins again with investment in research and development to create a replacement product.

The traditional product life cycle in an era of limited choice is given in Figure 4.5.1.

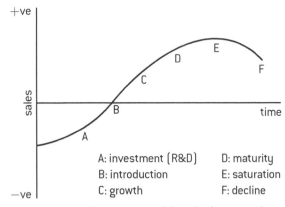

A: investment (R&D) D: maturity
B: introduction   E: saturation
C: growth   F: decline

Figure 4.5.1 Traditional product life cycle (focus on sales)

The reality today given the changes in technology and innovation is quite different. The traditional product life cycle is only an observation of the sales behaviour of a typical product. Some product life cycles experience a very brief existence when goods are withdrawn quickly. Others may take a much longer time to enter the growth phase and the product may experience a dip in sales before regaining market share.

In the new millennium with the "tyranny of choice" there has been considerable discussion on the shape of the new life cycle but broad agreement that, except for particularly loyal branded items, the product life cycle is becoming **shorter**.

The product life cycle, marketing mix and extension strategies (AO2 and AO3)

Table 4.5.2 indicates a possible link between the stages of product life cycle and possible adjustments to the marketing mix.

IB Learner Profile
Inquiry ?

A number of business textbooks make reference to a model that looks similar to the product life cycle. It is called the diffusion of innovations model, proposed by Everett Rogers, and it tries to explain at what rates technological change spreads through different cultures. Rogers (1962) identifies five particular cultures including consumers who will wish to adopt technological change quickly ("early adopters") and those who will wait until the end of the product life cycle before making a commitment ("laggards"). Research this model as it gives a valuable insight into the rate at which different cultural types adopt technological change.

Product life cycle and link to the marketing mix (AO2)

Table 4.5.2 lists possible adjustments that may be necessary to the marketing mix at various stages of the product life cycle. The list is not exhaustive and other appropriate action could be taken.

Extension strategies (AO3)

As a product enters the maturity or saturation stage of the product life cycle (some textbooks combine them both into one classification), a firm may decide to "breathe new life" into the sales of a product by introducing extension strategies. (An extension strategy does not occur at the introduction or growth phase of the cycle.)

Some popular extension strategies are outlined here:

- The first is a modification of the existing product with minor changes such as **repackaging** or the inclusion of additional new features. This is a popular extension strategy in the CD or DVD retail market. (The author is always a little sceptical of the inclusion of deleted scenes on DVDs or previously unreleased tracks on a CD – there must be a reason why these scenes were deleted or tracks not released in the first place.)

- At saturation, promotional spending on the product can be increased or reduced prices offered for a limited time period.

- A line extension to complement the existing product can be developed to boost sales of both products. For example, Gillette may add a new shaving cream to boost sales of its razors.

- The company might try to find a new market for the product (Ansoff's market development strategic method), perhaps by researching overseas markets.

- The product might be repositioned. This is risky and examples of outright success are rare. One successful case is GlaxoSmithKline's strategy to reposition the health drink Lucozade as a sports or activity beverage.

Selecting an appropriate extension strategy

- **Extension strategies should aim to be cost-effective and lead to an increase in profits.**

  There is little point in spending huge sums of money on a promotional campaign if the forecasted profits generated are too small, or if in the process the firm uses up all its cash reserves supporting just one product while neglecting others in its product portfolio.

- **New market research will be required before an extension strategy can be decided.**

  The firm will need to undertake new market research before investing in the extension strategy to identify an appropriate course of action. This will raise costs and take time. This market research will also have to be as relevant and up to date as possible. This point is reinforced if we consider our conceptual understanding so far that with innovation, rapid social and technological change and hyper-competition from globalization product life cycles have become shorter.

- **Trout argues that there is considerable consumer scepticism about the benefits of line extensions.**

  In the music industry, in order to extend the product life cycle of groups, record companies have released "new versions" of previously available albums with claims of these versions being either "remastered" or "remixed" or "digitally remastered" from the original tapes. Clever marketing phrases such as "from the vaults", "recently discovered" or "previously unreleased" can be used to entice loyal, long-suffering fans to re-purchase items they already own. (The author speaks from experience.)

The practice of offering slightly modified versions of the original product as an extension strategy is not confined to the music industry. The movie industry is full of examples and this does not include new formats which appear from time to time such as Blu-ray. Consider the following extensions:

- limited edition
- special limited edition
- ultimate limited edition
- ultimate collector's special limited edition
- uncut edition
- "what the censors did not wish you to see" edition
- "special edition with deleted scenes now added"
- director's cut
- director's extended cut.

Stage of the product life cycle	Adjustment to the marketing mix
Introduction	Heavy promotional spending on informative advertising is required. Distribution channels may be few. A price skimming or penetration pricing method (see page 100) is chosen depending on the product's technical complexity. A new innovation may be skimmed to gain **"early adopters"**
Growth	Distribution channels will need to widen if product sales grow rapidly. Price increases may be feasible if sales soar. Promotional mix may be altered to take advantage of this growth
Maturity	Sales growth slows down. Prices may need to be lowered as new competition enters the market. Promotion should focus on differentiation from the new entrants
Saturation	Sales growth has peaked and a decision needs to be taken about extension strategies (see below)
Decline	Strategic or tactical decisions need to be made about the future of this product. Price should be at lowest possible, possibly to attract the "laggards". Promotion spending should be reminder-oriented. Product repackaging will be possible although this will add to costs. Some distribution channels will need to be closed

Table 4.5.2 The marketing mix at different stages of the product life cycle

Extension strategies revisited

The long tail and the return of the long-playing record (LP)

Anderson (2006) argues that the Internet has provided businesses with a method of identifying new markets for previously popular products which may have entered the decline phase of the product life cycle. For example, social media's power in bringing together a multitude of consumers from different cultures to "like" a particular product or group has led in many cases to the reforming of musical groups from the 1980s, encouraged by a devoted fan base, and also created new ones.

From its *zeitgeist* in the 1970s and early 1980s before the introduction of the CD player (which nearly wiped this product from the retail shelves) the LP record or vinyl LP lives on. The third Saturday of every April has been designated as World Record Day. Vinyl record sales in 2014 are increasing at exponential rate mainly due to significant numbers of "early adopters" and "laggards" frustrated by the sound of CDs or MP3 players who are flocking to vinyl.

One could argue that the conclusion from this analysis is that an organization should never give up on a product. There will always be someone out there who will savour the memories and cherish the experiences the product delivered to them. With the world wide web, we know have a mechanism to connect consumers to their past, present and future. Amazon and eBay have been particularly successful in building e-commerce models around "the long tail" with almost an infinite number of products matched and geared to an infinite number of potential customers via the world wide web. May the vinyl record be revived once more!

Product life cycle, investment, profit and cash flow (AO2)

The first stage of a product's life cycle is often overlooked. Figure 4.5.1 (on page 94) indicates that, in the early stages, a product may be a drain on cash flow as the research and development costs need to be paid. This phase is often referred to as the investment part of the product's life cycle. Figure 4.5.2 shows a new product life cycle with focus on cash and sales.

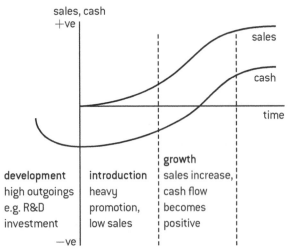

Figure 4.5.2 New product life cycle (focus on sales and cash)

Given the traditional shape of the life cycle, we can expect that even after the research and development costs have been paid, the firm can expect cash to be leaving the business until the point when significant growth in sales is achieved. This is because during the introduction phase the firm will need to support the product with promotional spending, especially on informative advertising.

The cash flow position of a product relative to its product life cycle is given in Figure 4.5.3.

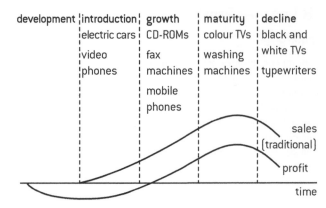

Figure 4.5.3 New product life cycle (cash flow and profits)

Finally, assuming that the product enters the growth phase without the company having to use all its reserves of cash to fund the promotional effort, sales of the product will start to rise at an increasing rate. Assuming also that the firm can confidently manufacture the product in larger production runs, the firm should start to experience some economies of scale and, with profit margins rising, the company should start to reap the reward for taking the risk of launching the product in the first place – profit.

The amount of profit will depend on the length of the growth phase before the maturity and saturation stages are experienced. It is also important to consider that other competing firms may be attracted into this market by the thought of making profit themselves. Depending on the nature of the patent and other barriers to entry, the original firm may find that it faces competition. This will erode the opportunities for the firm to continue to make large profits.

The Boston Consulting Group (BCG) matrix (AO3, AO4)

	High relative market share	**Low relative market share**
Market growth high	Star	Problem child
Market growth low	Cash cow	Dog

Table 4.5.3 The BCG matrix

The BCG matrix is one of the most powerful tools a firm can use to assist strategic decision-making when it produces a range or portfolio of products. We return to an example from some of the material we have considered so far on Apple to see how we can apply this model.

Applying the BCG matrix

The Apple product portfolio mix

In this section we discuss the Apple product portfolio mix introduced in unit 4.2. From the brief snapshot given in Table 4.5.4 we could argue that the iPhone is entering a phase of the **cash cow**. It is a popular product but with increasing competition from Samsung (the market leader in the smartphone category) and HTC, its pre-eminence in the market is not quite as strong as the public may perceive. The release of the iPhone 5c was designed to give the iPhone new "life" but as we have seen, the marketing mix of this product may have "backfired". As this iPhone is a cash cow, we will probably see a new version of it late in 2014, but with other new innovations being craved by the market, such as the rumoured iWatch, the iPhone may need a significant redesign and performance boost to maintain its current market position.

The iPad is clearly a **star**. This is a product with high market share (over 84% of the tablet market in some countries) but given that it was launched in 2010, there is still room for more growth, as its revenue figures testify.

Apple Inc.
Q1 2014 Unaudited summary data
(units in thousands, revenue in millions)

Product summary	Q1'14 Units	Q1'14 Revenue	Q4'13 Units	Q4'13 Revenue	Q1'13 Units	Q1'13 Revenue	Sequential change Units	Sequential change Revenue	Year/Year change Units	Year/Year change Revenue
iPhone (a)	51 025	$32 498	33 797	$19 510	47 789	$30 660	51%	67%	7%	6%
iPad (a)	26 035	11 468	14 079	6 186	22 860	10 674	85%	85%	14%	7%
Mac (a)	4 837	6 395	4 574	5 624	4 061	5 519	6%	14%	19%	16%
iPod (a)	6 049	973	3 498	573	12 679	2 143	73%	70%	-52%	-55%
iTunes/Software/Services (b)		4 397		4 260		3 687		3%		19%
Accessories (c)		1 863		1 319		1 829		41%		2%
Total Apple		**$57 594**		**$37 472**		**$54 512**		**54%**		**6%**

(a) Includes deferrals and amortization of related non-software services and software upgrade rights.

(b) Includes revenue from sales on the iTunes Store, the App Store, the Mac App Store, and the iBooks Store, and revenue from sales of AppleCare, licensing and other services.

(c) Includes sales of hardware peripherals and Apple-branded and third-party accessories for iPhone, iPad, Mac and iPod.

Table 4.5.4 Financial data from Apple: Q1 2014, product summary

The Mac computer is currently the third best-selling home computer (based on our Gartner research in unit 4.1) and its market growth is evident. However, given the increasing use of mobile devices such as smartphones, tablets and "phablets," could we see the Mac computer as a **problem child**? Should Apple continue to support this product or should it divert research and marketing funds to new potential products such as "wearable teach" (the much rumoured iWatch) or the new Apple TV?

The iPod (Touch or Classic) seems destined to be a **dog**. Market share is falling and revenues dwindling. Could it be that the iPhone and iPad have cannibalized the iPod?

Some applications of the BCG refer to a product being a **guard dog**. By keeping the iPod available, Apple blocks potential competition from operating in this market segment for MP3 players with no phone.

Conclusion

The BCG matrix provides an engaging way to link our understanding of the product portfolio of an organization to identify possible tactical and strategic decisions which may need to be made. A particular product might require support, whether that be "financial support" to boost market share and growth, "life support" to maintain its market share or "counselling" if the product is to be terminated.

The classifications used in the BCG matrix are not exact. We could make the claim that the Mac computer is the cash cow of Apple as this was the product that defined the company Jobs and Wozniak created. It has held its market share against such corporations as Microsoft and IBM and with modifications is continuing to reach new market segments.

Aspects of branding (AO2)

Defining a brand can be a difficult task. In the 1950s and 1960s, a brand could easily be defined as a **product name**, a **trademark** or even just a **logo**. In 2014, our definition needs embellishing. Trout (2001) refers to a brand as:

the sum of all experiences and values associated with a particular product.

A brand now has to encapsulate values, perceptions and experiences in terms of qualities such as health, luxury, quality, reliability and youthfulness. In recent years the Apple brand has developed to become the "epitome of cool and belonging", of luxury and necessity, and of acceptance and difference. How can a single brand encapsulate all of these values successfully?

IB Learner Profile

Open-minded

Branding has become a complex and to older consumers sometimes a puzzling topic. It would be revealing for students to have a conversation with an older person about the role and importance of brands. How does the older person regard or perceive Apple? What about Nike? Or Heinz Tomato Ketchup?

Aspects of branding applied to sports teams

Increasingly, as part of their strategic planning and marketing, sports teams now regard themselves as "brands" which can be used to raise **awareness,** create commercial **value** and develop **loyalty** through a mission or vision. Figure 4.5.4 is taken from a blog by Kenneth Cortsen to show the links between these four elements for a Premiership soccer club.

Brand awareness allows the sports team to retain and attract new customers. **Value** is created through the development of **loyalty** programmes that can allow members to access privileges and exclusive deals. This will unlock further value especially if the team is performing successfully or winning competitions.

The importance of branding (AO3)

There is general agreement that a strong brand identity can create awareness and customer loyalty, despite the "tyranny of choice" identified in unit 4.1.

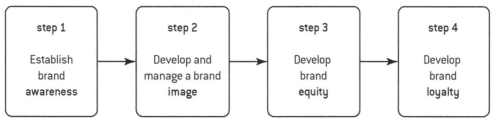

Figure 4.5.4 Four elements of branding in the context of a soccer club

Source: http://kennethcortsen.com/football-economy/guest-blog-arsenal-football-club-brand-strength/

- Loyalty through branding can enable companies to charge higher prices and therefore enjoy greater gross and net profit margins.
- Higher margins will influence distribution channels, as potential suppliers will be eager to stock "premium priced" items.

Through loyalty programmes, an organization encourages customers to develop a "relationship" with its brand, thus deepening the "connection" between company and customer and unlocking future value. In the context of soccer, generations of fans will come from the same family as traditions of supporting certain teams are passed down. In global markets, the UK Soccer Premiership "brand" has successfully penetrated the lucrative Asian-Pacific markets to the extent that English Premiership soccer is shown live across a range of territories, boosting this relationship aspect even further. Teams from the Premiership now regularly take part in exhibition matches or tour extensively to increase brand awareness.

Other benefits of branding

- If the brand of an existing product in the same industry has become well established, this reduces the risk of launching a new product under the same brand. For example, Sony has benefited enormously from its association with the Walkman, Discman and PlayStations to increase sales of TVs and DVD players.
- Branding can create powerful intangible assets for a company and increase the value of the company's balance sheet, allowing it to borrow or attract additional funds for expansion.

Clearly, therefore, the power of a successful brand in the minds of consumers cannot be overstated. This explains why many companies spend millions of dollars each year reminding, persuading and reassuring customers that their brand is the one to go for.

This is one of the key arguments against the rise of global branding especially in that ultimately consumers are paying the cost of all this promotional activity through higher prices for branded products. For example, the cost to manufacture a Nike pair of running shoes is a small percentage of the overall retail price. One of the critical fixed or overhead costs contributing to this significant mark-up over manufacturing cost is the advertising cost of maintaining a brand image.

Finally, as we saw in unit 4.1 (with "the illusion of choice"), branding by established organizations creates a very high **barrier to entry** for new entrants into an industry. In our example from the fast-moving consumer goods (FMCG) industry that is dominated by major transnationals, branding represents an almost impenetrable barrier. This perceived lack of competition, it could be argued, could also raise prices to consumers.

The importance of packaging (AO3)

The endless repackaging of classic movies on DVD or Blu-ray has been noted earlier as an extension strategy of somewhat dubious real value. However, it should be noted that packaging of a product can add considerable value, as the following examples will show.

Packaging of FMCGs such as breakfast cereal or chocolate bars, for example, allow a product to create a strong brand identify through its labelling. The ability to stack a product easily on shelves in supermarkets or other retail outlets is also important. In supermarkets, eye-level shelf space is often referred to as prime "real estate" in the retail market. Having a strong brand identity in a market with a number of choices could be critical in the purchasing decision of customers.

Although perceived by some as wasteful, the packaging of some items such as software programs can enhance value. Microsoft Office, for example, is effectively a software program stored on a disk. It sells in many countries for hundreds of dollars. The disk is usually housed inside a strong cardboard box, which acts to increase the perceived value (although for some this still does not justify the price). Given widespread piracy of software,

the external packaging of Microsoft Office may act as a signal of "reassurance" that the consumer is actually purchasing the genuine product. Disney has also carried out a similar exercise with the Disney logo appearing on the packaging of a product to reassure that it is not a pirated copy.

No discussion of packaging would be complete without reference to Apple's famous, simple, easy to use and consistent packaging of its iPhones, iPads, iPods, MacBooks, etc. These do not arrive with detailed instruction manuals common to other brands. Instead, in common with this study guide, a quick start reference booklet is given taking up minimal space. Even in something as straightforward as packaging, Steve Jobs' attention to detail is apparent to maintain the brand value of this innovative company.

However, we must note that not all packaging is effective and at worst it could be considered unethical. In 2011 Australia became the first country in the world to advocate the "plain packaging" of cigarettes. Despite clear health markings on the side of the packets indicating that cigarettes can cause cancer, sales of cigarettes were still considered too high. The move to plain packaging came into force to reduce the number of cigarette smokers to 10% of the population by 2018. An example of the packaging is shown in Figure 4.5.5.

Figure 4.5.5 Plain packaging for cigarettes sold in Australia

Naturally, the cigarette manufacturers countered the actions of the Australian government and set up their own "task force" to refute the government's claims that plain packaging would lead to a significant fall in the number of users. They also claimed that valuable dollars had been spent in the creation and development of these brands which would be now lost. One tobacco manufacturer claimed that its intellectual property had been "stolen" given the Australian government's decision.

The debate is still continuing and, as significant financial resources are available to the tobacco companies, it is likely that further legal delays and court hearings are likely. After Australia's decision, which was upheld by its own High Court, a number of other countries are considering following this lead.

The appropriateness of particular pricing methods (AO3)

There are a large number of pricing methods for organizations to use. The chosen method will depend on a number of factors including the organization's objectives, the degree of market competition, the nature of the product and the characteristics of the external environment in which the business is trading.

Although we use the term "pricing strategy", strictly speaking a number of these pricing ideas are methods, especially the cost-based ones. These pricing methods are used as part of an overall marketing mix to help guide a marketing strategic direction. Table 4.5.5 lists these pricing methods according to the *IB Business Management Guide* and gives summary discussion points.

Promotion (AO2)

In this section we discuss the effectiveness of the traditional methods of above-the-line and below-the-line promotion.

Above-the-line and below-the-line promotion

The author was once asked by a student "What is the line and where is it?" – a valid question indeed. We define above-the-line promotion as promotional activities which are directed at consumers through different media such as the cinema, radio and TV. They can reach a large number of potential consumers at once, making the average cost of above-the-line advertising small. However, firms are not able to receive immediate feedback from consumers about the virtues or successes of a TV commercial or radio advertisement.

Below-the-line activities are focused on using promotional techniques that allow immediate consumer feedback, such as running sales promotions in stores, organizing public relations (PR) exercises (where there is direct contact with stakeholders), using direct mail, issuing store coupons and running competitions. Some of these methods of promotion can be successful and cost-effective activities for small firms that may not be able to afford to advertise by contracting media space. Online e-mail advertising direct to the customer's inbox may be regarded as below-the-line promotion.

We can summarize the key functions of promotion as those actions that inform, persuade or remind consumers about the potential benefits of purchasing a particular good or service. However, there is considerable debate as to the most effective way of achieving this. Promotional effectiveness and the choice of method used will depend on a range of factors such as budget, intended reach, frequency, desired impact and, of course, business objectives. We can start by looking at a recent example.

The promotional mix – an analysis

(See Table 4.5.6 on page 101.)

We shall use five criteria to analyse the effectiveness of promotion as part of an overall mix of activities to gain attention, persuade or to keep customers loyal. These criteria are:

- targeting: the ability of the promotional technique to target the right customers to avoid wasting the promotional method and marketing effort

- reach: the ability of the promotional method to reach the widest audience possible

- frequency: how often the advertiser wants the message to be repeated

- cost – measured by average cost per viewer

- the ability to provide instant feedback to the business to gauge the impact of the promotional method.

The impact of changing technology on promotion (AO3)

In this section we look at the impact of changing technology on promotional strategies (such as viral marketing, social media marketing and social marketing).

Traditional methods of promotion such as some of those in Table 4.5.6 have come under renewed attack. The creation of new media technology has created both opportunities and threats for organizations. The growth of the Internet and the proliferation of media channels through cable and satellite TV have given businesses many new ways to reach and target audiences.

However, some of this new technology has also become a threat. Consumers are becoming irritated by junk e-mail and the practice of sending spam emails. Digital TV, through facilities such as Sky

Plus, allows viewers to record TV shows to be watched when desired. The idea of prime-time TV, where advertisers promoted products, ensuring the highest customer reach, is now becoming an anachronism. In addition, DVD recorders can be fitted with software which allows consumers to skip TV commercials when they record programmes.

In 2014, in keeping with our theme of rapid social and technological change, the promotional landscape and opportunities for an organization have been altered irrevocably. In addition to the new "hardware" technology noted above, the emergence of Facebook and Twitter as social media marketing forms coupled with the increasing use of smartphones and m-commerce has allowed even more pervasive methods of reaching a target market.

These social media marketing messages have raised once again the issues of privacy and intrusion. Is it ethical that an organization sends you a message wishing you a happy birthday without you having told them the relevant date? Is it ethical that a business sends an email to a consumer wishing his or her first-born child a happy birthday on the child's first birthday and asking whether the consumer needs a set of nappies? (This happened to the author on his eldest son's first birthday.)

IB Learner Profile

Inquiry ?

Viral marketing – T-Mobile and "Dumb Ways to Die"

If a social media message is carried out successfully and goes "viral" then the reach of a particular promotional method can be significant extending beyond the target market for which it was intended. We have already mentioned (in unit 4.1) the excellent 'Dumb ways to die' social marketing message which has gone 'viral' on YouTube. The flash mob is another method of viral marketing which was used recently very effectively in the T-Mobile commercials in the UK and is a wonderful example of an ethical social media marketing message.

> View the T Mobile flash mob videos on YouTube. Two superb examples are the flash mobs at Heathrow Airport and at London's Liverpool Street Station.

Guerrilla marketing (AO3)

Using guerrilla marketing as a promotional method is more controversial. It is designed to be a cheap but provocative risk-taking form of promotion. It includes a mixture of traditional below-the-line methods such as distributing direct mail and newsletters and aspects of viral marketing as described above through social media messages. Guerrilla marketing is designed to provoke a reaction or simply sensationalize.

It has also been used by business start-ups that cannot afford to spend sums of working capital on promotional activities. Some companies, such as Hell's Pizza and 42Below in New Zealand, have used guerrilla marketing to gain attention but also to push the boundaries of the Advertising Standards Authority to the limit. One of 42Below's YouTube clips was derided in New York as insulting and derogatory. This immediately increased interest from passive stakeholders. Is there such as thing as poor publicity?

Older consumers have complained about some of 42Below's media campaigns while some younger consumers have applauded the company's efforts to be different and take calculated risks. Why not explore the 42Below website and make up your own mind?

It is difficult to be objective about this area of marketing. There will be a number of cultural and ethical influences acting on your perception.

Method or strategy	Description	Example of appropriate use	Other issues/problems
Cost-plus (mark-up)	Price is determined by calculating the cost of an individual product and a profit margin is added	This is used for expensive luxury items and one-off purchases in small niche markets (e.g. classic cars)	This is more of a pricing method rather than a strategy. Cost-plus pricing ignores market demand conditions
Price leadership	The market leader by market share sets the price	Asset-led marketing firms, such as British Airways or Singapore Airlines, can use this strategy	The market leader may enjoy brand loyalty and may make it difficult for other firms to follow high prices
Penetration (market-based)	A firm tries to undercut existing market firms with a lower price	An established firm trying to enter into a new market will use this strategy. Virgin Airlines has offered lower prices on popular routes as an entry strategy. Ryan Air and EasyJet are other examples	Substantial cash reserves are needed to support potential short-term losses. How easy will it be to raise prices once the firm is established without losing goodwill?
Skimming (market-based)	A firm identifies a group or segment and tries to target niche customers by charging high prices to attract early adopters	New technological products such as Blu-ray DVDs are priced in this way. This method is suitable for innovative products in niche markets to recoup research and development costs	Market growth may be limited until prices are reduced. "Me too" competition from other firms can be a problem once the patent runs out and can have an impact on pricing
Predatory (competition)	A firm sets a very low price with the intention to remove competition from the market	In the print media industry in the UK, News International has been accused of charging very low prices for some of its tabloid papers to try to buy loyalty in a competitive market and to remove rivals. No-frills airlines such as EasyJet and Ryan Air have taken huge slices of market share from British Airways on some routes	Setting very low prices can be illegal in some countries when it is classified as unfair competition. This strategy can lead to price wars, the so-called "race to the bottom". There have been some concerns over product quality and safety in the airline industry
Price discrimination (market-based)	A firm charges a range of prices for effectively the same product or service depending on the "price elasticity of demand" of the end user*	A movie theatre offers different prices for adults, students, families and the elderly. (Some movie theatres have segmented their audience market even further by offering reclining beds or couches with waitress service, or 3-D IMAX)	The firm must be able to prevent "leakage" or price discrimination will not be successful. Leakage is the ability of the end user to "cheat" (e.g. a small adult tries to buy a child's ticket). Leakage prevention (such as showing ID) should be low cost or gains from price discrimination will be reduced significantly
Loss leader (market-based)	A product is sold below cost to encourage consumers into a retail environment who (it is hoped) will then purchase other items with higher margins	The classis loss-leader approach is adopted by supermarkets that offer milk, bread or some soft drinks at below-cost prices	This is not a strategy that can continue indefinitely as losses are made. Many loss-leader goods are rotated periodically to maintain consumer interest and so that a brand is not "hurt"
Psychological (market-based)	The product is priced to break some psychological barrier to create positive word of mouth or is priced due to cultural factors. For example, in many places instead of a price of $2 or $4, $1.99 or $3.99 is used to make the product appear cheaper	This was used for the world's first $100 laptop: Xo. An Indian company, Tata, set the price for its base model car at US $2 200 in 2009 – well below the expected level. In Asia prices ending or beginning in 8 are considered lucky, prices beginning or ending in 4 are seen as unlucky. "Everything for £1" and $2 shops are based on psychological strategies to attract customers	Consumer and cultural perceptions may take time to change. Once the psychological barrier has been breached there may be limited opportunity to set a new price point in the short run. There are perception issues in that a very low price may infer low quality

Table 4.5.5 Different pricing methods

* Price elasticity of demand is not in the IB Business Management syllabus for the exam in 2016 yet it is an important term to understand with respect to price discrimination. See page 133 for more detail.

Promotional technique	Examples and discussion
Broadcast media	TV, cinema and radio.
	This can have a dramatic impact on a large audience (consider the average costs per viewer of advertising during major sporting events such as the Superbowl or the Oscars).
	It can be too expensive for small businesses or new start-ups.
	Firms are not able to gauge direct feedback.
	This method is under threat from new technology.
	Cinema has a captive audience and can be segmented by film genre.
	Frequency can irritate some consumers
Printed material such as newspapers and magazines	Using printed material allows close targeting as each publication has its own readership profile and audience.
	It is cheaper to advertise through printed material than on TV and there is high reach in countries with large populations.
	Printed material can be used to inform and convey a good deal of information
Point-of-sale material and company newsletters	These materials are cheap to produce and it is possible to receive immediate feedback if they are given out in store.
	These materials can be specifically targeted and updated quickly.
	Their visual impact is limited. Many may be discarded immediately if the consumer is not interested
Coupons, special offers, competitions	Money-off coupons can be very successful and are cheap to produce.
	These provide direct contact with the customer.
	Reach may be limited
Internet	There may also be privacy issues here with consumers receiving unsolicited emails.
	The Internet is very cheap to use and has potentially unlimited reach.
	"Spamming" and "phishing" is irritating for consumers.
	Internet promotions are easy for consumers to delete.
	The marginal cost is effectively zero
Sales promotions	These need to be short term or the customer will just wait for the sale and not purchase products with higher margins.
	Sales promotions need to be eye-catching to generate good word-of-mouth advertising. The costs of relabelling and altering store design can be high.
	Overuse may lead to consumer fatigue and scepticism.
	Goodwill will be lost if a sales promotion item is unavailable or the store is crowded
PR/word of mouth	PR exercises are sometimes referred to as uncontrollable methods of promotion because even with the most tightly controlled media event, the success of PR exercises depends on the perception of the stakeholders.
	Staging media events to generate goodwill is not cheap and reach may be limited unless backed up by broadcast media support on TV or radio or in the printed media. This cannot always be guaranteed.
	Word-of-mouth promotion is something that every company wishes to have but only if it is positive. There is an old saying: "If customers have had good service, then they will tell 5 friends. If they have had a bad experience, they will tell 15." The creation and growth of "viral marketing" has given word-of-mouth promotion new meaning (see below)

Table 4.5.6 Analysis of the promotional mix

IB Learner Profile

Reflection ЯR

Discussion point – Samsung, the Oscars and that superstar "selfie"

Here we look at probably the most famous recent example of guerrilla marketing – the superstar "selfie" that host Ellen de Generes took at the Oscars in 2014. As an aside, we should note that some claim that this was not an example of guerrilla marketing given that Samsung agreed to donate $1 for every retweet of the picture – the final figure donated was $2.5 million.

Ellen de Generes took the "selfie" with a Samsung smartphone during the Oscars ceremony. Within minutes of the photo being retweeted by thousands of Ms de Generes' followers, Twitter crashed.

It was revealed soon that the host had "organized" this photo before the Oscars ceremony and that Samsung may have paid for the right to have the photo taken in such a manner that its logo was clearly visible. Note that Ms de Generes' and Samsung's brand value increased dramatically after this was revealed.

In the true spirit of caring and balance in the IB learner profile, the "selfie" is not included here. (If you have not seen it, you can "Google" it.)

The question remains: was this effective guerrilla marketing or direct exploitation?

Place and channels of distribution

This element of the marketing mix is critical and businesses must get it right. Unfortunately, it is commonly misunderstood and overlooked by students, especially when they are asked to evaluate a marketing mix or strategy.

This section tries to provide a straightforward analysis of the main channels of distribution. You are invited to discuss in class the merits of each channel, based on your own experiences as end users, possibly studying in a country that is not your original place of birth. It is also worth noting that future sections on e-commerce and outsourcing have close links to distribution.

Channels of distribution

The channel of distribution describes how a final good or service passes from producer to end user. The end user is usually a consumer but we must not forget that we can also have industrial markets to supply through an activity called B2B that is considered in unit 4.8.

Several distribution channels are open to a producer. The channel chosen will depend on the nature and complexity of the good or service and on whether the target is a mass market or a niche market.

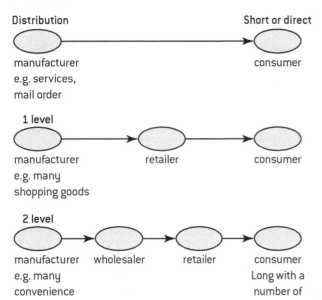

Figure 4.5.6 Channels of distribution

Examples of appropriate channels: two extreme cases

Baked beans are normally distributed via long channels. Wholesalers and retailers break down very large quantities of cans from the producer to take advantage of buying with economies of scale. The product is not complex and is easily transportable. This system of distribution allows baked bean manufacturers to target as many customers as possible (it is a mass market).

Industrial cranes for use in civil engineering are generally distributed via very short channels. The product is delivered by the producer to the industrial end user directly. The product is complex, difficult to move easily and serves a very small niche market segment. Training, installation and supervision may be required before the end user can successfully operate the equipment. The product will be very expensive and may require continued customer support.

The effectiveness of distribution channels

Wholesaling and retailing are the traditional way of distributing FMCGs. With large production runs and the possibilities of economies of scale, FMCGs are distributed to warehouses in bulk and then broken down into smaller quantities for retail producers. Naturally, there are purchasing and marketing economies of scale and also economies in a reduction of transport costs.

However, in some markets, such as the real estate industry or the luxury car market, agents have been used to provide local knowledge or expertise to ensure a smooth exchange between buyer and seller. In the case of the real estate market, important legal procedures may require the need for an agent to conduct the transaction. Agents are paid a commission on completion of work undertaken.

However, in the role of HR management, especially in the media and sporting industries, agents have been criticized for adding an intermediary function which may or may not ensure the smooth transition of an exchange between, for example, a soccer club (the buyer) and a potential player (the seller). Agents in these markets may delay the distribution process by, for example, bargaining for a higher price as their fee depends on the financial outcome.

In common with other distribution channels, the case for and against agents or other intermediaries will depend on the nature of the good or service being traded. Agents can add an extra step in the distribution process and this will raise costs to the final end user and reduce gross margins for producers. However, if a firm is looking to move into a new international market, it may be too expensive or risky to set up a distribution network in an untried region without local knowledge. An agent can provide this at lower cost than setting up a new offshoring facility.

An agent or intermediary with local knowledge can act as an efficient method to enable a firm to establish a market presence without spending large sums of money. There may be cost savings for primary data research as well as well as cultural intelligence (CQ) benefits. CQ may be provided with greater accuracy if the necessary tasks are carried out by an agent with knowledge of local market conditions.

The importance of place in the marketing mix (AO2)

Link to concept 2: Change and concept 1: Globalization

With the growth of online retailing on a local, national and global scale, and the prevalence of m-commerce, distribution channels have become a vital ingredient in the marketing mix and global marketing strategy. One could argue that for some large online retail organizations such as Amazon and Asos, a competitive USP has been created by the speed of delivery given the range of products on offer.

Globalization has lifted "place" in the marketing mix to be equally as important as the product given the hyper-competition which now exists in many markets.

At the time of writing this study guide, one online UK-based book retailer, Book Depository, was offering the service of **free delivery** to over 160 countries. How can local or even national book chains compete with this? Some answers will be discussed in the next unit.

Setting the scene

We saw in unit 4.1 the differences between the marketing of goods and services:

- Product benefits are "embedded" inside the product and/or packaging and can be delivered to customers through distribution channels.

- As services are location-based activities, customers have to travel to the service locations.

- Customers like their products to be standardized in terms of features and packaging, for example, but they like services to be customized to suit their individual needs.

- Products are tangible so customers can inspect or, in some cases, sample them before committing to buy. Services on the other hand are experienced. Once carried out a service may not be reversible and there will be no possibility of it being returned.

These points highlight crucial factors that service providers need to consider if they are going to satisfy consumer needs and wants. These crucial factors are the environment in which the service is provided, the process of service delivery and the interaction with customers.

An additional three Ps in a service provider's marketing mix (AO2)

In a service-based market, the marketing mix requires an additional three Ps (to create the seven Ps model). The additional three Ps were added in the mid 1980s to account for the differences in the marketing of goods and services. They were also designed to reflect that service delivery was much more customer-oriented than the marketing of most products at that time.

People

As a service is an intangible (you cannot take home the process of having a facial), the people delivering the service to the end user (the consumer or the industrial end user) must have **sufficient training** in order to ensure customer satisfaction. The people element in the mix may also include **after-sales** service. As we have seen, this element of the mix can be outsourced and offshored given the substantial improvements in ICT and the spread of globalization.

Process

A good can be purchased in store and paid for in a number of ways – using cash, electronic transfer or credit card. For some services this is not possible. A computer technician installing a new computer system for a company may take many days and is unlikely to be paid until after the work is completed. The process element in the marketing mix looks at how services are consumed and paid for. It is crucial in industrial markets when large sums of money are exchanged or large service providers undertake work stretching over many months.

Process has also been associated with the way in which employee–customer relationships are created and maintained in making the marketing effort more effective in an organization.

For example, this will include processes for handling customer complaints, processes for identifying customer needs and requirements, and processes for handling orders and checking that these orders arrive on the intended date.

Physical evidence

Some hairdressing salons are able to charge high prices for haircuts. The salon may include special lighting and music to provide relaxing surroundings for the customer. Often the customer can only tell the outcome of a haircut when it is finished (it may be impossible to start again). Physical evidence in the seven Ps marketing mix tries to cover these issues. The key is to ensure that the customer feels reassured that the service provider is competent. This could be achieved with demonstrations, reviews or endorsements by previous customers or images of successful styles that the salon has previously created.

Under threat of competition from online trading platforms, a number of retailers have tried to enhance the "retail experience" to lure customers back to the physical store and away from the Internet. "Westgate" shopping malls are common in many parts of the world. The extension of the three Ps is designed to provide a much more involving shopping experience with cinemas, food courts and other recreational activities in addition to actual shops. This physical evidence has been taken to the limit in the United Arab Emirates with one shopping mall (the Mall of the Emirates) having its own indoor ski field, and the largest mall in the world (the Dubai Mall by floor area) having its own indoor aquarium and ice hockey rink.

The capital invested into these new inclusive malls is substantial and they provide wonderful physical evidence, backed up by superb customer service. These malls, however, must always be in fear of the changing retail landscape. In Sydney the recent opening of a new Westgate mall was "spoiled" or "sabotaged" – depending on your point of view – when a perfectly legal billboard was hired and displayed nearby by a competitor containing the following ominous message: "Browse in the Mall – buy it on eBay".

Opportunities to develop the additional three Ps

In this section we consider the opportunities for developing the three additional marketing elements in an era of hyper-competition as part of a new strategic plan. As an example, we look at how one book retailer tried to position itself as a community bookstore and to be culturally sensitive to the stakeholders it served.

Linking content to context

In unit 4.5 we mentioned that Book Depository – which was acquired by Amazon – was offering free delivery on books to over 160 countries. How can a local bookstore in the United States retain its place in the market and still be economically sustainable? The following case study is one example of a new strategic direction involving the additional three elements of the seven Ps marketing mix.

Will Santa Barbara's Granada Books be swept aside by the tide of Amazon?

In June of 2013 – years after the rise of Mega-chain Bookstores and the explosion of online book suppliers such as Amazon and Abe books – one independent bookstore in Santa Barbara, California took a stand for small businesses everywhere. Granada Books' owner is Andrea McGregor.

Although Granada Books is only four months old, Andrea herself is by no means a newcomer to the book business. She was first involved with a small bookstore in Big Bear, California, she explains the store's struggle, "Things were so much harder there because we were fighting Amazon and big stores like Barnes & Noble at the same time."

Andrea describes Barnes & Noble's success in terms of forward thinking and their investment in the Nook (their e-reader, the equivalent of Amazon's Kindle.) However, Andrea agreed there is absolutely nothing comparable to holding a real book, though she did reluctantly admit to owning a Nook. Andrea travelled for work quite a bit during her time at Barnes & Noble; and it was during such trips that she discovered that e-readers don't make things that much easier. She also speculates that the role of print won't change too drastically in the near future.

Santa Barbara is not the only community to host this revival of independent booksellers. In 2012, over 35 independent bookstores set up shop across the country hoping to fill the void left by the disappearance of Borders Books and Barnes & Noble.

The American Booksellers Association reported a **7 per cent growth** of independent bookstores for the fiscal year.

One facet of independent bookstores' recent success came from the **"buy local"** movement. The movement originated from the theory that maintaining business locally results in better products, while also enhancing the town's economy. Andrea herself acknowledges the positive effect of the "buy local" movement.

"I think a lot of the independents are coming back because people want to buy from their own communities. We can't offer the same discount as Amazon **but we can offer you the ability to look at a book before your purchase. You can sit here and read all day and that's okay with us.** You can sample your books and you really can't get that online, plus if you shop **here you can support your community."**

Granada tells its customers that it's about more than just selling books. The store, though small, has something for every age and interest. Andrea says, "Everyone here is not only living in the community but working here too. **We want the community to feel at home here, the whole purpose is not only to come in here and shop, but to come in here and be."** She is truly dedicated to contributing to the balance of the Santa Barbara community. The "people" and physical evidence factors in the marketing mix are very important.

She also spoke briefly about her desire to occupy space. She explains, **"**I think you are right about the backlash of people who now need to occupy a physical space. I think the novelty of doing everything online will fade and people will want to find a space they can go and inhabit, and physically touch print."

Print is not the only thing making a comeback, recent studies show vinyl retailers around the country are also seeing an increase of sales. Senior Vice President David Bakula of Nielsen SoundScan reported that his company sold over 4.6 million LPs in the last year, a growth of 18 per cent from 2012.

Bakula argues that the resurgence in books and vinyl sales may have something to do with a need for of nostalgia and that book readers and vinyl collectors desire to have something valuable and permanent in their own home. "I definitely think there might come a time when it becomes a status symbol for someone to have a bunch of books or a pile of records. When I was growing up it was normal for people to have a large library in their home. I think books are becoming more decorative."

Whether books are decorative or informative, it seems that people are once again looking to their local bookstores to supply their books.

McGregor is asked what what her dream bookstore would look like. "I think my dream bookstore would have the ability to have everything in it. Everything for everybody. Some place where everyone can congregate and the community feel welcome." It looks like this has occurred at Granada Books.

Source: Adapted from www.vervesocialmag.com/independent-bookstores-fight-back-featuring-santa-barbaras-granada-books

QUESTIONS FOR REFLECTION

- Based on the information given in the article, reflect on how important the people and physical evidence parts of the marketing mix are for Granada Books as part of its service to the community.
- There are numerous references to "community" in the article. What are the key differences between a virtual community and a "real" community and how does the latter have an impact on Granada Books?
- Reflect on the possible organizational culture present at Granada Books. How important is the creation of this culture to the success of this business?

Setting the scene

No study of marketing would be complete without due consideration of the international or global context that now exists. With saturated and highly competitive markets at home, small and large organizations must now look overseas to take advantage of new opportunities that are becoming available.

In unit 1.6 we explored the growth of the Subway franchise, which has over 41 000 restaurants located in over 100 countries. We could have drawn on a number of other organizations that have experienced very fast growth by operating in a number of international markets outside the country of the organization's origin but Subway's growth has been spectacular and will be considered in more detail at the end of this unit.

Linking content to contexts

This topic will bring together some of the growth strategies examined in unit 1.6 and tactical and strategic marketing strategies which we have discussed in previous units. However, here we place these firmly in an international and global context.

Methods of entry into international markets (AO2)

There is no doubt that entering an international market involves some degree of risk. One obvious way would be for a business to "go it alone" and try and grow organically into international markets. This would be expensive and challenging, even if the organization carried out extensive market research and gained cultural intelligence (CQ). Of course the potential profits could be considerable from such an expansion. However, given some of the CQ issues we will discuss below, the ideas of a "partnership" or the involvement of local entrepreneurs to share the risks and financial burdens of entering a new market are outlined in this unit.

Franchising or licensing

Franchising the Subway brand to over 100 countries outside the United States has driven the enormous growth of Subway. The organization has been able to take advantage of local enterprise and capital and share the risk of developing brand awareness with an ever-eager group of entrepreneurs. As we shall see later in this unit, this method of entry into international markets requires careful scrutiny and consideration of local tastes and consumer preferences.

Licensing is a scheme similar to franchising. The intellectual property (the brand, logo, operations, etc.) of a product or service is licensed to an organization in an overseas market so that the local producer is allowed to produce the product or deliver the service on behalf of the global parent company. A good example of this occurs in the brewing industry where local brewers are able to produce "under license" beers that would not otherwise be available. Anheuser Busch InBev, the world's largest brewing company, famous for its lager beer Stella Artois, allows its famous brand to be brewed under license in Australia, Brazil, Hungary, the Ukraine and New Zealand.

The cost to Anheuser Bush InBev of organically growing the Stella Artois brand in these geographically and socially diverse markets would be prohibitive. Licensing allows a more cost-effective way of entering and penetrating international markets where local competition could be considerable.

Joint ventures and strategic alliances

There are two ways of sharing the risk of entry into international markets. One way is to create a joint venture with some ownership sharing through an equity deal. The other is to form a strategic alliance without an equity deal – an organization joins forces with another organization already operating in the international market of interest.

Forming a strategic alliance with a competitor located in an overseas market allows the possibility of sharing local CQ. This could also allow much faster entry into an international market than by doing so organically or by developing a franchising model.

To test the commitment of a new partnership, some joint ventures into new international markets may require that each partner take an ownership or equity stake in the strategic move. With a voluntary strategic alliance without equity, there may be some fear that if the early signs of entry into the international market are not promising, one partner could pull out, jeopardizing the whole entry strategy. The equity joint venture method gives some reassurance that the move into an international market will be for the longer term.

Acquisition

If a global organization is looking to enter an international market, a very straightforward way of achieving this is simply to take over an incumbent firm operating in the overseas market. Subject to government anti-monopoly laws that exist in the international market, this method of entry is perfectly legal. However, acquiring the overseas company may be expensive. There may also be the unwanted attention of pressure groups if the takeover is deemed to be "not in the best interest" of the stakeholders loyal to the locally acquired company.

Entry into overseas markets – opportunities and threats (AO3)

Opportunities

In previous units we have discussed some of the reasons why considerable opportunities exist for an organization that enters a foreign market:

- The organization can benefit from the growth and spread of globalization, and the potential cost savings which can be made by outsourcing some or all parts of the production process.

- Linked to the points made earlier about entering an international market, offshoring can also provide an opportunity to gain knowledge of these markets at a relatively low cost, before committing to entering the market fully. In this way offshoring helps to minimize the risk of entering.

- There is increased information and availability of training to understand local economies and cultural differences. An organization can minimize misunderstandings through an improved CQ approach.

- The Ansoff matrix growth model strongly advocates market development or differentiation to define a new competitive strategic position. Both could be achieved by operating in an overseas market.

- Improved ICT allows larger spans of control and the opportunity to structure an organization according to geographical region.

Threats

The following is a discussion of entry threats when operating in an international market. The aim of presenting this discussion is to improve exam answers.

The threats from moving into an overseas market can be classified as **weak** or **credible**. Weak threats regularly appear in exam answers where students have been asked to consider a number of threats to a firm moving into a new overseas market and have not thought through the discussion as part of their answer. With some clear and sensible management thinking, weak threats to international entry could easily be overcome, as the following answers will illustrate.

Credible threats need to be considered before a firm decides to take action and move into an international market. If these are evaluated, students can score very highly in external exams.

Weak threat 1

The firm will have to be aware of language barriers.

Management response: It is unlikely that a firm would not enter into a new market just because the managers were not fluent in the local language. It would be expected that an organization would hire translators.

Weak threat 2

The product may not be successful in this new market.

Management response: This could be true for any market, not just an overseas market. We must assume that, in order to understand the competitive nature of an international market, the organization will conduct extensive primary and secondary research before it enters that market. The organization could conduct a SWOT analysis or analyse STEEPLE factors. The Ansoff matrix does not assume that all market development will be risk-free.

Weak threat 3

There will be competition from local producers.

Management response: Again, we must assume that the organization thinking of entering a new overseas market will do its market research. Some form of competition is inevitable. If an organization is concerned about the level of competition, it should be able to determine the needs and wants of existing customers, and be able to determine whether a market gap exists and whether the market can grow significantly beyond its current size.

Credible threats, which constitute a more considered exam-type answer, include but are not limited to:

- the legal frameworks or constraints that exist in an overseas market
- economic and political instability
- exchange rate volatility and capital controls.

Legal frameworks or constraints

Firms entering overseas markets must ensure that they comply with local rules and regulations regarding the conditions of work and employment (particularly if they wish to bring in expatriate managers on work visas) and any minimum wage legislation. They will need to consider local taxation rules such as those relating to corporation tax and indirect tax.

Economic and political instability

Organizations looking to penetrate overseas markets will need to be aware that some developed countries have launched "buy local" campaigns in favour of locally produced goods rather than imported products. This move has been discredited by some writers as being counter-productive as a "buy local" campaign may jeopardize potential export markets due to retaliation by other countries.

However, perhaps more significantly, economic recession can lead to political instability in some overseas markets as governments struggle to tackle the growing list of problems created by the "credit crunch" and the global downturn. Political instability can have a considerable impact on a firm's ability to be successful in a new international market.

Exchange rate volatility and capital controls

Although very large firms can protect themselves from currency fluctuations by buying and selling forward in the financial markets known as "futures" or "derivatives", there still exists a danger for firms moving into new markets. Financial gains could be lost when funds are repatriated from the overseas market back to the country of origin if exchange rate volatility is present.

In more extreme cases, if the economic environment deteriorates as dramatically as it did in South East Asia during the financial crisis of 1997, or the euro crisis of 2012, some countries could impose capital controls on the movement of funds. This could present firms with an insurmountable threat if they have already invested heavily to develop a presence in international markets.

Strategic and operational implications (AO3)

Now we will look at the strategic and operational implications of international marketing, incorporating cultural differences and globalization (AO3). Linked to the above points concerning entering international markets are the strategic and operational implications of international marketing once an organization has achieved a foothold. Entering an overseas market will present challenges but remaining a sustainable business in this market will present even more.

We noted in concept 6: Culture that it is important for organizations to research the culture of the overseas market they wish to operate in. Significant cultural mistakes (or "misalignments" to use the proper business term) can be made if an organization fails to take into account language or cultural differences which may exist between countries and which are not incorporated into the marketing message.

The role of cultural differences now has a profound influence on international marketing given the increasing integration of world markets through globalization. Consider some of the following issues that could also be considered as ethical dilemmas for an organization with respect to international marketing:

- Should all forms of promotion for alcohol and cigarettes be banned? Australia has led the way by attempting to ban all branding on tobacco products and ruling that they should be sold in plain packaging.
- Should retailers who market and sell violent video games such as Grand Theft Auto IV to minors face prosecution, as happens in Thailand?
- Should fast-food companies be more open about the amount of saturated fat in their products, as saturated fat is linked to obesity and heart disease?
- Was the French government right in January 2009 to ban all mobile phone advertising during children's programming?

IB Learner Profile
Inquiry ?

Issues surrounding international and global marketing practices

You may wish view the DVD "McLibel" about the legal challenge by two human rights campaigners against misleading and unethical marketing by the McDonald's Corporation. Two campaigners, Helen Morris and Dave Morris, distributed a leaflet entitled "What's wrong with McDonald's".

The case was heard in the UK where libel laws are considered to be much tougher than in the United States. In the UK, the company accused does not have to "prove" anything. It is up to the human rights campaigners to prove "wrong doing" by the organization. In this case, the onus of proof was on two unemployed activists who had neither the budget nor the legal experience to handle the case.

The essence of the case was that McDonald's had "lied" in certain claims it had made, particularly in its international marketing. These included claims about the nutritional value of McDonald's food, working practices and conditions for employees, marketing to children and other unethical practices.

The outcome of the legal case – the longest libel trial in UK history up to that point – was that the judge in summing up agreed with the majority of the campaigners' claims. This was little short of remarkable given the financial resources and legal expertise of McDonald's. The organization had one of the most expensive legal teams at its disposal. The two campaigners defended themselves.

Since the judgment the campaigners' leaflet has been translated into seven different languages.

International marketing of a global brand

This section looks at the strategic and operational implications of international marketing involving a global brand. In unit 1.6 we considered Subway, one organization that has taken one of the most direct paths to realizing the opportunities available from globalization.

Subway's Chief Development Officer, Don Fertman (who incidentally appears as an undercover boss in the US TV series available on YouTube) was recently interviewed for an article about how his company went global. He reveals some of the key aspects that have made Subway the largest fast-food brand, in terms of number of outlets, in the world.

The whole article is available at: www2.qsrmagazine.com/articles/interview/138/don_fertman-4.phtml

Here are some of the highlights. The article provides a fascinating look at the challenges of developing a global brand through international marketing.

How Subway went global

Subway's chief development officer explains how the brand transformed into an international icon and which markets he's watching for the future.

What do you attribute to Subway's international success? "The secrets to our success are probably not secrets. I think they're really obvious and it has to do with the fact that people want something that tastes good, that's good value, and is something that is hopefully good."

Subway's original top 10 high growth-potential territories	
Australia	France
New Zealand	Germany
United Kingdom	Puerto Rico
Spain	Japan
Italy	The Benelux countries (Belgium, Luxemburg, Netherlands)

Initially, Subway identified 10 major markets that the company was focusing on internationally. Are those markets still the focus? "We're looking at a number of markets. We've moved beyond the 10 markets that we had the big focus on because we found that other markets are growing, surprisingly rapidly."

Is there something that culturally is going on that makes expansions into those countries easier? "There's an opportunity for changing pace, and I think it goes back to what I was saying originally. If we've got something that tastes good, we've got something that's good value, something that's convenient and appropriately adapted to the local taste without losing our original concept, then we have an opportunity to grow in those markets.

Another thing that's been of interest to us is in India you have quite an entrepreneurial spirit. It seems like there are many, many business people in India running either very small businesses or on the street. That entrepreneurial spirit is perfect for Subway because that's still the way we do business. We look for entrepreneurs who are excited about the brand that want to take it and make it grow."

Is it hard to maintain menu and brand consistency across so many units? "When we started in Japan the concept was changed originally to the point that a Subway customer from North America would walk into a store and look at the menu and really not know what to order because it wouldn't be familiar to them.

It was still sandwiches, but the sandwiches were very much changed from what we had originally intended. They have since come to understood that what made Subway great was those six-inch, foot-long sandwiches and basic menu structure. I was just there last spring and I am pleased to report that they had some terrific sandwiches that were just like what you or I would have and they had their own version of sandwiches that appeal to the local taste."

In the global rebalancing that follows the recession, analysts are pointing to BRIC countries (Brazil, Russia, India, China) as the catalysts for future financial success. Here's what Subway has planned for those territories.

Brazil "We have just less than 400 stores, so that's a rapidly growing country. And we have some terrific developers and franchisees in place, so that will be one of our top markets."

Russia "It's up to 75 stores and our developer there has just announced plans to get to more than 1 000 stores by the end of 2015. But they're looking at the economics in the market and they can see that Russia is a much bigger market than was originally anticipated."

India "It was interesting; we got into India with relatively low expectations. We hit the 100-store mark, we slowed down a bit. We're now at the 150-store mark and all of a sudden things have turned around and we're seeing a lot of acceleration there. We have another 100 franchises in development, and I see a lot of green lights."

China "It continues to grow – we have 140 stores in China right now, but I'm looking at Yum! Brands. I'm looking at some of the other folks that have made tremendous progress there."

Even though Subway is in 104 countries, does the company still need to educate consumers about the brand when it opens a new territory? "They don't necessarily know about us. We arrive and sometimes they think we have something to do with an underground train. So it does take some education.

In some markets, we have to train people or educate people on the benefits of eating sandwiches, why they're tasty, why they're healthy, why they're fresh, why we have them on fresh-baked bread. It's kind of starting from the ground up to provide the idea of putting meat between two pieces of bread and making a meal out of it.

In other countries they're already eating sandwiches, but maybe in France, for example, they're eating a baguette with a little bit of meat that they get at a stand on the street corner, they're all pre-made and they're there ready to go and you can grab them and they're cheap and the bread is hard. People are used to that, but then we have to educate them that when they look at a Subway sub it's very different. It's got more meat, it's made to their order, they can have lettuce, they have those veggies, they can have it with or without veggies, as many veggie assortments as they want. It's a whole new eating experience."

Are international consumers comfortable with making demands about what should be on their sandwiches? "Sometimes people are almost afraid to ask. We've come across that in some cultures and there we have to teach more suggestive selling on the part of the sandwich artist. But sometimes that's difficult because the sandwich artists are also shy about offering the products."

For readers who are interested in taking their brands beyond US borders, what would be your best advice for starting that process? "The first piece of advice I would give is take a look at the quick-service landscape in that market, and see what kind of growth is occurring there. Are the folks even familiar with quick-service restaurants and franchising?

The next thing would be don't be too quick to second guess the consumer and make immediate assumptions as to what to change. Ultimately, you'd be surprised how many folks are looking for the original experience. Sometimes you can be way too speedy in saying, 'We see a lot of people who are eating rice and beans, so we better have a rice and bean sandwich'."

Source: www2.qsrmagazine.com/articles/interview/138/don_fertman-4.phtml

The last word

The quote below on global marketing summarizes a number of the issues that have been embedded in this unit. It links international marketing to globalization and the impact on practices and strategies.

> *Global marketing is not a revolutionary shift, it is an evolutionary process. While the following does not apply to all companies, it does apply to most companies that begin as domestic-only companies. International marketing has intensified and is evident for approximately nearly all aspects of a consumer's daily life.*
>
> *Local regions or national boundaries are no longer restricted to the competitive forces. To be successful in today's globalized economy, it is a must for the companies to simultaneously be responsive to local as well as global market conditions and varying aspects related to the international marketing process. Hence, international marketing skills are an important ingredient for every company, whether or not it is currently involved in exporting the activities for the endorsement of the brand or the company.*
>
> *The internationalized marketplace has been transformed very quickly in recent years by shifts in trading techniques, standards and practices. These changes have been reinforced and retained by new technologies and evolving economic relationships between the companies and the organizations which are working for the trade across the globe.*
>
> Source: Wikipedia, 2014

Setting the scene

We shall begin our investigation into e-commerce (or the buying and selling of goods using the Internet) by considering a quotation from one the world's most successful and wealthiest investors, Warren Buffet.

I pay for only three things on the Internet: the Wall Street Journal, online Bridge and books from Amazon. They must be doing something right.

Amazon rightly takes its place as one of the great e-commerce success stories of recent times. We shall be looking at Amazon's business model to see how e-commerce can benefit consumers.

Features of e-commerce (A01)

There is generally broad agreement that the following are broad features or characteristics of e-commerce:

- E-commerce effectively has **no geographical limits** in terms of new markets given the possibility of global reach.

- E-commerce has **ubiquity**. It is possible to buy consumer goods and services from home, at work and while travelling, across a number of time zones.

- E-commerce **reduces the time and cost** of buying goods especially given **ubiquity**.

- E-commerce has reduced the supply chain for a number of organizations and developed richer experiences for customers through video, audio and social media.

- E-commerce has reduced entry costs into a number of global markets.

- E-commerce has allowed greater "**personalization**" of the marketing message and allowed greater targeting of goods once an initial transaction has been made.

Of course, as technology and Internet bandwidth develops, new features of e-commerce will be added or existing features modified.

Now consider the following case study.

RARE RETRO

Rare Retro is a specialist music store owned by 55-year-old former jazz guitarist, Lee Carlton, known as "Bluey".

Rare Retro sells hard-to-find blues, jazz and world music CDs and vinyl records. The store is located in Toronto, Canada.

Bluey and his 10 staff travel all over the country to purchase CDs and vinyl music and listen to live concerts from unknown bands. They enjoy a friendly relationship with customers who are encouraged to browse, chat and discuss the latest CD or vinyl releases over a coffee or to listen to live music. This loyalty to Rare Retro allows the company to charge above market prices. Rare Retro rarely needs to use above-the-line promotion and relies on positive word-of-mouth recommendations in the community.

However, recent ill health has forced Bluey to spend less time in the store. Control has passed to his son, Jaco, a change that has not been popular with the other staff. Jaco had been working as a management consultant. He feels that Rare Retro needs to adapt to a changing technology and embrace e-commerce.

Jaco has researched B2C (business-to-consumer) relationships in other competing stores. He thinks that Rare Retro should have a website, an online ordering service, a customer loyalty scheme and a greater exposure to social media. Jaco has recommended an e-commerce focus.

Jaco has also conducted a quota survey of customers and friends. His results revealed that many customers use the Internet to search for and purchase music. A trip to Rare Retro is now viewed more as a social visit and less as a purchasing experience. However, there is a group of very loyal customers who would welcome more information on possible new releases and recommendations but do not have the time to travel to Rare Retro every week.

From this brief case study, we can speculate on the type of marketing mix that existed at Rare Retro in the past and speculate on what it could look like if Jaco's ideas on introducing a greater e-commerce focus are implemented.

Marketing mix before Jaco's decision	Marketing mix after Rare Retro decides to adopt a greater e-commerce focus
Product – niche market selling blues and jazz CDs and vinyl	Product – is there an opportunity to stock a wider range of CDs and vinyl by linking to other websites?
Price – higher than market price. To a certain degree, Rare Retro may be skimming (see unit 4.5, page 100)	Price – given the transparency of the Internet, will Rare Retro have to adopt going rate or market pricing or some other form of pricing method?
Promotion – minimal apart from some below-the-line promotion	Promotion – does Rare Retro need online and social media to accompany word-of-mouth recommendations? Rare Retro may need to create a Twitter, Facebook page and/or an instant messaging service such as WhatsApp
Place – music is distributed from one store only. (It is a very short channel)	Place – the store will remain but Rare Retro will need to consider supply chain management and overseas distribution channels. Channels are likely to get longer if the firm expands
People – Bluey's staff are loyal and knowledgeable about the products they are selling. The emphasis is on customer service	People – some customers may look for online recommendations rather than travel to the store to discuss purchases. Will Rare Retro be able to support the current level of staffing given greater social marketing?
Process – CDs are sold in store over the counter	Process – online security payment systems will need to be set up and Rare Retro will need to ensure that customer orders are dispatched on time and received
Physical evidence – we are told that the store encourages browsing and discussing music. Is this like a coffee-lounge experience?	Physical evidence – does Rare Retro need a physical and a virtual store; will Rare Retro have to create two separate presences? Some have called this a "bricks **and** clicks" strategy

Effects of changing technology and e-commerce on the marketing mix (AO2)

Rare Retro is a fictitious company name but it represents a real-life organization looking to introduce e-commerce. The Rare Retro case study provides an example of how the development of an online presence can have an impact on the marketing mix of a firm.

The analysis included in the Rare Retro case study demonstrates that simply opting to develop a business online through e-commerce will have significant implications for all elements of the marketing mix. Key issues for an organization looking to adopt a greater e-commerce focus are how to manage human resources and operations. Will the move also have an impact on the organization's objectives in the short and long run? Setting up an e-commerce presence will require some capital. How will this be sourced?

The benefits and costs of e-commerce to consumers (AO2)

Amazon has responded successfully to changes in the external environment by launching its own music download service and a host of other related service developments. Amazon, in common with Google, has been one of the e-commerce success stories of the last decade. Amazon's survival and growth is testament to the success of its respective e-commerce models which have prospered despite the shattering events of the dot.com boom and bust which occurred at the beginning of this century.

Amazon has managed to maximize the benefits to consumers and minimized the threats of conducting business over the Internet so successfully that, during the 2013 Christmas period, online sales reached record levels in a number of countries. Such has been the threat of the e-commerce revolution that many "high street" retailers have been put out of business. Ironically, one of the founding retail music units – HMV – has had to scale back its operations considerably. In 2012, it looked likely that the whole global chain could collapse outside of strong markets in Hong Kong and Japan. Even in the UK – its original retail market – the number of HMV stores has been dramatically reduced.

Benefits

The benefits to consumers of e-commerce include the following:

- Consumers benefit from significant cost savings by ordering online.

- There is an incredible range of choice for many products, not just books and CDs, which established Amazon's core business. We have made reference in this study guide to "long tail" marketing and the Internet has created a model for nearly infinite wants to be satisfied.

- Direct customer feedback from previous customers allows consumers to gauge product performance.

- In countries where Amazon operates, delivery can be on the same day as the order is placed. There can be substantial discounts for big orders.

- Amazon can customize web pages tailored to customer purchases or searches from previous transactions, allowing greater consumer targeting.

- Amazon and e-commerce in general have fostered a much greater degree of price transparency and consequently this has made the market-place much more competitive, to the benefit of all consumers.

Drawbacks

The great drawbacks of the online model of e-commerce still exist. However, to an extent they have been minimized, as outlined below.

Concerns expressed by stakeholders about the transmitting of personal data such as address and credit card information over the Internet have been addressed. Secure payment sites such as PayPal have eased fears. Security issues are being monitored. Some consumers felt uneasy about paying hundreds of dollars for a product that they could not physically touch or test before committing to purchase, but this issue is being addressed. For example, Amazon's return and satisfaction policy has reassured customers that they can "try before they buy" for clothing items. Many online retailers such as Asos, the online fashion retailer, have been able to convince customers that their online experience can match their retail one.

Conclusion

It would be correct to say that Amazon has managed to allay the fears of the majority of consumers. However, we should note that with the proliferation of e-commerce activity there has been an increase in email "spamming" and "phishing".

The trust and brand loyalty that Amazon has managed to create has had enormous impact through the online community. The number of "me too" imitators has been considerable. Perhaps, though, it would be fair to say that Amazon has earned the marketing attribute of "online retailing". One key question for the management of the company is, given its presence and ubiquity in global markets, how much more growth can it achieve?

The growth of business-to-business (B2B) trade over the Internet (AO2)

We have already noted the tremendous impact of the Internet and its important implications for businesses in terms of communication and the spread of globalization. B2B activity measured by the number of online transactions between organizations now outnumbers the number made via B2C (business-to-consumer) transactions such as those conducted through Amazon.

This growth can be explained further by reference to the section on supply chain management in unit 5.5. Linking the whole process of supplier–producer–consumer has become an integral part of defining a new competitive strategic direction for many companies ("red ocean" – see concept 5: Strategy). The Internet has provided the ideal conduit to allow these links to develop with little regard for time zones or geographical isolation. Perhaps in terms of the growth of B2B, the world is now truly flat!

Customer to customer (C2C)

In 1995 eBay was founded by Pierre Odiymar. Operating in over 30 countries, it is perhaps the best known example of an online C2C platform, allowing individuals to list a spectacular array of products. It is tempting to state that if an individual cannot find a product on eBay, then it probably has not been invented yet. eBay is a global online phenomenon.

However, in keeping with some of themes developed in unit 4.6 on the prospects of a local shop and service provider (Granada Books) trying to compete with a much bigger global competitor, (Amazon) we have an example from New Zealand.

It would be remiss of the author not too mention this "local hero" based in New Zealand – the author's own country – which has created its own C2C platform (see the brief case study that follows).

TRADE ME

New Zealand is one of the few countries to have its own local equivalent of eBay – a company called Trade Me.

Now New Zealand's largest retailer, Trade Me was created by a young social entrepreneur, Sam Morgan, in his bedroom which apparently at the time was an old caravan. (Innovation can take place anywhere.)

Trade Me acts in a socially responsible manner providing transparency in online transactions at a low cost. Consumers are blacklisted and banned from trading if they do not supply goods as described and/or give false or misleading information.

Trade Me has ubiquity in New Zealand and has now extended its range of services to house purchases and job searches. New Zealand is a small country with a thinly spread population outside the main centres of Auckland, Christchurch and Wellington. Trade Me provides a vital service to connect customers online.

Setting the scene

To quote from the *IB Business Management Guide*, with respect to operations management:

students return to the fundamental rationale of the subject. Without efficient operations, leading to products and services customers are satisfied with, success in the other business functions is unsustainable.

Given this importance of operations management, it is sometimes surprising to note that students often find the study of the topic difficult or fail to appreciate its significance fully. This point is reflected in the lack of internal assessments or extended essays that are centered on operations management. Marketing and HR management internal assessments are common but forward-looking projects focused on operations management problem-solving are rare. This is the case despite the ease of finding suitable cost data and the many potential business tools and techniques available to students to analyse and evaluate these problems.

From the author's experience of moderating internal assessments at HL, forward-looking projects based on operations management consistently satisfy the marking criteria more accurately than HR management and marketing assignments. As a result, projects centred on operations management gain significantly higher final marks.

For business decision-making, the importance of operations management cannot be overstated. Faced with maturing markets and an explosion of choice, organizations are revisiting lean production, the creation of cost and profit centres, outsourcing, total quality and supply chain management as new cornerstones of creating a new strategic direction.

With revenue growth under threat, the shift towards operations is to ensure cost reduction to boost profits and satisfy the growing demands of shareholders for increasing returns. Operations management in an era of globalization, change and innovation is critical for an organization's economic sustainability.

Relationship of operations with other functions (AO1)

As indicated above, operations management could clearly lie at the centre of an organization's *raison d'être*. Without the process of transforming factor inputs into outputs for the market, a business would not exist. (Readers are advised to review section 1.1 again in this guide to remind themselves of the relationship between different departments in an organization especially those between operations management, marketing, finance and human resources.)

Figure 5.1.1 illustrates the operations management process of transforming inputs into outputs.

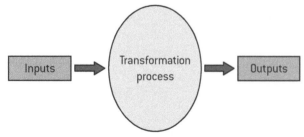

Figure 5.1.1 Transforming inputs into outputs

Operations management – goods and services (AO2)

How an organization chooses to produce goods and services via this transformation process will depend on two key factors which will be developed through this section. In keeping with the conceptual theme of this study guide, these factors will be linked to concept 3: Innovation and concept 1: Globalization.

A business could choose to create and manage the means of production itself through the purchase of capital and revenue items, as identified in unit 3.1. The key advantage of this would be that the business would have complete control over the operations management process. However, it would of course be costly to set up the system and would take time to establish procedures before final goods and services could be produced.

Alternatively, a business could choose to take advantage of the opportunities made available by improved technology and globalization and decide to allow an outside party to produce goods and possibly services on its behalf. This is the process of outsourcing. We should not forget that new innovations could be available in another region or country if a business decides to outsource.

The risks of offshoring or outsourcing are a potential lack of quality control and disadvantages arising from the interdependence of relying on a stakeholder to provide resources for a production process. We shall cover this aspect in greater detail when we consider the role of just-in-time production. However, the benefits of a reduction in costs and the adoption of the most up-to-date technology leading to further gains in productivity cannot be denied.

For the production of services, the options for operations management are narrower given that services are usually consumed at the point of delivery and so options for offshoring and outsourcing are limited. This aspect was looked at in greater detail when we considered the seven Ps marketing mix in unit 4.6.

Operations management – ecological, social and economic sustainability (AO3)

Increasingly, with growing scrutiny from stakeholders such as pressure groups via the world wide web and/or social media, organizations' transparency in their operations has become critical. External stakeholder concerns about the exploitation of both human and natural resources, in addition to substantially large profits earned by some corporations, have led to calls for an additional line of financial reporting to monitor the operations especially of large organizations. This has been termed as "the triple bottom line"' and is shown in Figure 5.1.2.

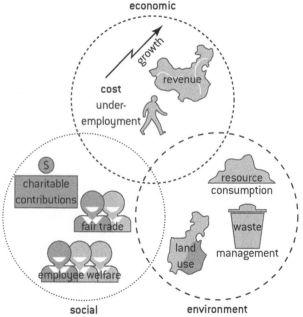

Figure 5.1.2 The triple bottom line

Source: Wikipedia

The intention behind the triple bottom line is neatly defined by noting that organizations have a responsibility to people, planet **and** profit. The operations management connection is that given the scarcity of resources and the need for environmental sustainability, organizations need to ensure that in addition to profit, they consider the "wider" picture of their economic activity, as Figure 5.1.2 shows.

Not all organizations are required to report their triple bottom line given the existence of a wide range of global accounting and reporting conventions. However, it is argued that there are compelling financial and social marketing reasons for reporting an organization's wider commitment to the community in which it operates.

Consider the following corporate information provided by one US organization – Novo Nordisk.

OUR TRIPLE BOTTOM LINE

We believe our commitment to the Triple Bottom Line – social responsibility, environmental soundness, and economic viability – makes good business sense, so we have made it a top strategic priority. We take this philosophy one step further by producing an annual environmental and social report that accounts for the ways in which these values are put into practice within the Novo Group.

At Novo Nordisk, we take all our commitments very seriously, especially our commitment to people. We also take particular interest in the preservation and restoration of the global environment. We want to minimize the ecological impact of our operations by developing more processes that reduce emissions and the consumption of energy and raw materials.

Social: We will work to continuously improve our social performance by setting high objectives and integrating social, human rights and health and safety considerations into our daily business. We will maintain an open dialogue with our stakeholders and report annually on our social performance.

Novo Nordisk supports the United Nations Universal Declaration of Human Rights.

We offer a patient assistance program to help people who do not have private health insurance and who do not qualify for private, local, state, or federal prescription reimbursement. Individuals who fall into these categories can contact Novo Nordisk directly about the program.

Environmental: We will work to continuously improve our environmental performance by setting high objectives and integrating environmental and bioethical considerations into our daily business. We will maintain an open dialogue with our stakeholders and report annually on our environmental performance.

We will subscribe to the International Chamber of Commerce's Business Charter for Sustainable Development.

Novo Nordisk supports the United Nations Convention on biological diversity.

Financial: We will work to continuously improve our financial performance by setting high objectives for growth and value creation, and deliver competitive performance in these areas. We will maintain an open dialogue with our stakeholders and comply with international reporting standards.

Source: For more information go to: www.novonordisk.com

Criticisms of the triple bottom line

The criticisms of the triple bottom line are quite technical and TOK in nature. In essence, some writers argue that reporting the triple bottom line can lead to vague, imprecise declarations of commitment and there is concern about how these commitments will be accurately measured. For example, you may be surprised to know that Novo Nordisk's main product or service relates to the treatment of diabetes. It would be difficult to tell this from the triple bottom line statement quoted. This raises an important question: Should an organization that treats one of the world's most pressing health problems in the developed world need to report its impact on people and planet as part of the triple bottom line? Surely it should be doing this already.

The debate over the triple bottom line is really only beginning. However, as mentioned in unit 1.3, some writers are now beginning to talk of the need for a quadruple bottom line to assess the operations management performance of an organization. The additional line of reporting is a commitment to cultural sustainability.

Setting the scene

From the analysis conducted on the triple bottom line in unit 5.1, determining *how* we produce a good or service could be considered as important as *what* we produce. In this new era of hyper-competition, globalization, change and the need for innovation, large organizations are constantly looking for ways to improve product quality and enhance product value in the eyes of consumers – all, of course, at a reduced unit cost.

However, for smaller organizations producing products in other niche markets, which cannot take advantage of such economies of scale, the decision of how to produce becomes crucial. Factors influencing the decision of which production method to choose will be varied, as the following analysis will illustrate.

Different methods of production (AO2)

Table 5.2.1 compares the features and applications of different methods of production.

Using an appropriate method of production (AO3)

From Table 5.2.1 we can draw some conclusions:

- Job production lends itself appropriately to niche markets, as production runs are very small. Producers may find it demanding to service niche markets as customers may require specific requirements not catered for by batch or flow production.

- Batch production allows a greater degree of flexibility of the consignment perhaps to cater and customize for larger production runs. This means that batch production can avoid the problems of standardization, which is a feature of flow production. Batches can also be "made to order" for customers in reasonable quantities, allowing some economies of scale not available when using job production. This will have an impact on the final price charged to customers.

- For mass markets with large and mostly predictable sales through repeat purchases, flow and mass production provide the most cost-effective methods of production. Significant economies of scale can be obtained. In order to achieve these economies of scale, investment in large-scale capital items such as machinery is required. Moreover, financial, HR management and technological issues can be considerable in a flow production environment. Coordinating and organizing these aspects will need careful planning in order to avoid diseconomies of scale.

A summary diagram, which analyses the different types of production, is called the product-process matrix (see Figure 5.2.1). It is a useful tool to compare appropriate methods of production as discussed above.

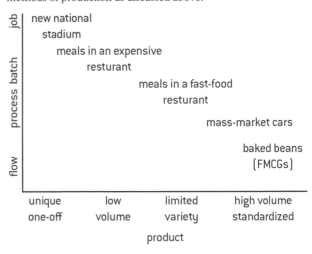

Figure 5.2.1 The product-process matrix

IB Learner Profile

Inquiry ?

In global organizations is job and batch production, in a flow production world, looking to become more local and specialized? As a competitive weapon or marketing tactic, some producers now offer complete customization or some modification of a product even though it may be produced in a flow environment. This has been enthusiastically embraced by the fast-food and computing industries. For example:

- Burger King and Subway allow consumers to customize their burger or sandwich to suit their own tastes. (Is this batch production instead of flow?)

- Dell computers allow purchasers to upgrade RAM or add other features per specific customer requirement before delivery. (Is this job production instead of flow?)

- Apple allow individual engraving for customers to personalize an iPhone or iPad if they are going to give it to someone as a gift. (Is this job production instead of batch?)

Production method	Description	Examples
Job	This is the production of a one-off project built to specific customer or industry specifications	The building of a ship or production of a film, or a house which is built specifically to customer requirements
Batch	Items are produced in consignments and undergo a part of the production process together. The whole consignment is then moved on to the next stage and another task is performed	Carefully planned groups of products with slight modifications allowed to customize batches. The best examples are bread making and beer brewing. Batch production allows for product variation such as wholegrain or brown bread or low-alcohol beer
Flow/process	This is a continuous production process. It is similar to batch production but the consignment moves from one stage of the process to the next without stopping	The car industry with its mass-market car production. Note that luxury cars such as those made by Ferrari are usually produced by the job method
Mass	This is large-scale production based on flow production with production quantities in the millions	Large-scale food processing. FMCGs such as food items in a supermarket are usually mass produced

Table 5.2.1 Features and examples of different methods of production

Perhaps the undisputed champion of a globalized organization looking to allow local customization is McDonald's. The following excerpt is taken from its website.

CATERING TO LOCAL TASTES
McDONALD'S MENU ITEMS AROUND THE WORLD

Quiche, red bean pie, and cabbage soup ... not exactly what you'd expect from a quick-service restaurant company, right?

But those are actual menu items at McDonald's restaurants around the world. You can order up a Quiche de Queijo (cheese quiche) in Brazil, Red Bean Pie in Hong Kong (where red beans are commonly used in desserts), and traditional Caldo Verde soup (made with cabbage, kale, onion, potato, and chorizo) in Portugal.

Fear not, Big Mac lovers – you can still walk into almost any McDonald's and get those two all-beef patties with special sauce, lettuce, cheese, pickles, and onions on a sesame-seed bun that you've come to know and love. (After all, we didn't get to be a global company by losing sight of what made us successful in the first place.)

But we also understand that tastes vary around the globe. That's why, in many markets, we supplement our iconic menu items with distinctive offerings that embrace local tastes. But instead of simply duplicating local favourites, we take what's familiar and put a McDonald's twist on it.

In France, for example, our popular M Burger features tangy, natural Emmenthal cheese and a Ciabatta-style roll baked in a stone oven. In India, where much of the population doesn't eat beef, we offer options like the potato-patty McAloo Tikki burger and the Chicken Maharaja Mac.

We work with local suppliers to produce many of these specialty menu items. For example, when we introduced the 280gr Parmigiano Reggiano burger in Italy, we formed an alliance with the official Consortium of Parmigiano-Reggiano, made up of 650 small, artisanal cheese producers in Northern Italy.

When you walk into a McDonald's restaurant in a different country, you may be surprised to see what we're cooking up. But whether it's a Big Mac or a Big Rostï (available in Germany), you can be sure it's affordable, portable, great tasting, and distinctly McDonald's.

Source: www.aboutmcdonalds.com/mcd/our_company/
amazing_stories/food/catering_to_local_tastes.html

QUESTIONS FOR REFLECTION

- Do you think that this excerpt from McDonald's website describes a genuine attempt by a globalized company to be more localized?

- In your IB class, ask students to reflect on their McDonald's experiences in their own countries. Are these experiences "the same" as the excerpt suggests they should be?

- How should we perceive McDonald's? Is it a global organization or a local fast-food outlet?

- Can an organization be perceived as both globalized and localized?

Cell production or cellular manufacturing (AO2)

Cell production has been described as splitting a flow production line into self-contained units. Each cell (or group of individuals) will produce a significant part of the finished product, giving the cell responsibility to complete a unit of work. Herzberg argued that this was a strong driver for firms to incorporate job enrichment programmes in their operations. The cell may also be responsible for setting the job descriptions, covering staff absence due to sickness and offering advice to senior managers on issues such as quality improvements and recruitment of workers. In some instances, the cell used in Japanese management systems may be allowed to decide on discipline and grievance procedures in cases of conflict.

Not surprisingly, cell production has been given high status in Handy's "Athenian culture" (see unit 2.5) and organizations where problem-solving and teamwork are viewed as powerful motivational forces. Cell production also has links to quality circles, which is an important aspect of total quality management (TQM), to be analysed in unit 5.3 for HL only.

Setting the scene

With the attention of many organizations now focused on reducing costs and saving time in the production process, an important strategic goal is to develop an operations management function in which efficiency can be achieved **without** compromising product quality. It can be possible for an organization to reduce costs, but what if the final product fails to live up to consumers' expectations in terms of quality? A sale will not occur and resources will have been wasted.

Moreover, in the drive for greater efficiency, how can an organization ensure that during the production process mistakes are being minimized? How is quality being monitored? Can waste be eliminated and can we be confident that in the drive for efficiency the organization is meeting national and international standards? These are just some issues that will be analysed in this unit.

Features of lean production (AO1)

Based on an entry that appeared on Wikipedia, the key features of lean production can be summarized as follows:

- Lean production is about doing more with less: using less time, inventory, space, labour and money.
- Lean manufacturing is shorthand for a commitment to eliminating waste, simplifying procedures and speeding up production.
- The aim of lean production is to be as efficient as possible in the production process.

Five areas drive lean production or lean manufacturing. These are shown in Figure 5.3.1.

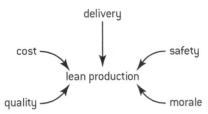

Figure 5.3.1 The five areas that drive lean production

Wikipedia has proclaimed:

Just as mass production is recognized as the production system of the 20th century, lean production is viewed as the production system of the 21st century.

IB Learner Profile

Inquirers and knowledgeable

LEAN PRODUCTION

An engaging way to learn more about lean production is to watch the YouTube clip "30-storey building built in 15 days (time lapse)". It shows how Broad Group in China built an environmentally sustainable skyscraper in just 360 hours.

Apart from showing this incredible feat, the YouTube clip will have implications for topics featured later in this unit such as just-in-time (JIT) production, cradle-to-cradle design and national quality standards.

Lean production and total quality management – TQM (AO2)

This section looks at methods of lean production and the impact of lean production and TQM on an organization. Lean production should be regarded as a "philosophy of operations management" that incorporates a number of developments from the Japanese company Toyota. Working with US statistician W Edwards Deming, Toyota created the founding ideology behind lean production. We will return to Deming's work later when we explore quality assurance.

First, we consider the roles of kaizen, JIT production, and kanbon and andon.

Kaizen

Kaizen is a Japanese word for the concept of **continuous improvement** that forms the basis of the TQM and lean production ideologies. Kaizen incorporates a number of important elements.

Kaizen is based on the idea that it should be the goal of the organization to introduce small incremental changes to operations in order to improve quality. **Quality circles** should be introduced for subordinates and managers to work together to identify causes of poor quality, perhaps through use of a discussion prompted by a fishbone diagram (see unit 1.7, page 31). Hierarchical barriers **should be removed** to allow discussions to take place to solve problems and not to apportion blame. These quality circle discussions can also take place in cells created by the organization to avoid duplication and this empowerment will lead to improved motivation and increased productivity.

In some quality circles, groups agree to work on solving problems during their lunch breaks. It is that important to these groups to be involved in the decision-making process. As we saw in unit 2.4, Daniel Pink believes that autonomy is a powerful motivating factor in cognitive or higher-order thinking tasks.

Kaizen should be extended to include continuous improvements in maintaining customer satisfaction as well. The objective is to produce products that have zero defects. "Zero defects" is a term that is often misunderstood. Kaizen does not assume that mistakes will not happen; however, it is assumed from the start of the production process that there will be no failure rate.

Kaizen is not without its critics. First, in order to monitor and implement continuous improvement successfully, statistical control and data collection need to be rigorous. This will take time and use up scarce resources, especially if the intention is to achieve zero defects. Second, when successfully applied, a kaizen philosophy requires that managers and **employees will be willing to change**. Quality circles will involve changing the **culture** of the organization and the nature of the relationship between subordinates and managers. There may be some resistance from both sides.

For kaizen to be implemented effectively constant training is required. The costs of disruption will need to be considered given that the training is likely to be both on and off the job.

JIT production

As part of a commitment to lean production, JIT production (or JIT delivery) allows organizations to minimize the costs of holding stock. Goods are made by a third party – but not always – to order. The third party firm will hold stocks of components and materials subject to the prevailing level of demand, and only the absolute minimum is held.

In our example from the YouTube clip, before constructing the building shown, Broad Group calculated exactly the moment that a particular component was required. Each item was delivered to the construction site in real time.

However, JIT requires excellent communication and strong committed supplier relationships. In the car manufacturing industry, for example, component parts are delivered to the factory in real time (that is, just as they are about to enter the production process). Suppliers in JIT environments are consequently responsible for ensuring quality and zero defects and this may be a concern for some organizations looking to broaden their JIT possibilities: they may be concerned about delegating the responsibility of quality to a third party.

Kanban and andon

www.leanproduction.com states that kanban and andon contribute to lean production in the following ways:

- **Kanban** is a method of regulating the flow of goods both within the factory and with outside suppliers and customers. This system is based on automatic replenishment through signal cards that indicate when more goods are needed. The idea of kanban is to reduce the need to over-supply and over-process and through this reduce the possibility of waste.

- **Andon** is a visual feedback system for the plant floor that indicates production status alerts when assistance is needed and empowers operators to stop the production process. Clearly, the intention here is to try to be proactive and reduce errors or problems before they become significant and costly.

Cradle-to-cradle design and manufacture (A02)

In an era of increasing scarcity of resources and the race to fulfil unlimited wants, concerns have been raised about the over-supply of products that are now taking up space in landfill sites in countries around the world. Linked to the ideas mentioned in unit 5.2 about the triple bottom line and the responsibility of an organization to people, planet and profit, cradle-to-cradle design and manufacture takes the ecological angle to a much deeper level and reminds us that the ever-growing waste that corporations produce needs to be incorporated into operations management decision-making.

IB Learner Profile

Inquiry ❓

To learn more about cradle-to cradle design refer to the following resources.

In 2002 Michael Braungart and William McDonough published a book called *Cradle to Cradle: Remaking the way we make things* – a manifesto for cradle-to-cradle design that gives specific details of how to achieve the model. The model has been implemented by a number of companies, organizations and governments around the world, predominantly in the European Union, China and the United States (source: Wikipedia).

Cradle-to-cradle design has also been the subject of many documentary films, including the critically acclaimed "Waste = Food" (available on both YouTube and Vimeo video sharing platforms).

Quality control and quality assurance (A01)

The difference between quality control and quality assurance can be described as follows:

- Quality control is a process that focuses on the inspection of a product and attempts to identify defects.

- Quality assurance is a process created to prevent defects from occurring in the first place.

Introduction to quality assurance

Although the Japanese have been rightly applauded for achieving outstanding levels of quality in the production of consumer goods, the original idea for adopting a TQM philosophy, which was at the forefront of a major change in thinking

about approaches to quality, came from the US statistician W Edwards Deming. Deming rejected mass inspection (the more traditional method of quality control) by one individual department assigned to this task.

Quality was to be built into each stage of the production process to allow quality assurance to be present. This was to be analysed carefully by use of statistical methods.

Training was to be continuous and available to all workers to allow them to undertake quality inspections. Quality circles were set up to allow an additional check on this process.

Hierarchical barriers between departments and senior managers were to be removed, with quality becoming everyone's responsibility. This was the very essence of TQM.

Deming called for a PDCA cycle of continuous improvement:

1 **P**lan (find the right data, analyse the problem, plan the solution)

2 **D**o

3 **C**heck

4 **A**ct (modify the process as necessary).

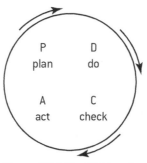

Figure 5.3.2 The PDCA cycle

Deming's ideas, incorporated with those of Kaoru Ishikawa (whose fishbone diagram we covered in unit 1.7) began the TQM movement.

Benchmarking (A02)

A second approach to quality management or quality assurance is through the process known as benchmarking. The idea behind this is that companies will try to benchmark or measure either their operations, customer service, marketing or HR management against what is considered to be the market leader in their industry. Then they will try to model their own behaviour on what could be considered to be industry best practice.

Examples of benchmarking

Examples of benchmarking can be found in the airline industry. Many airlines in South East Asia have tried to benchmark customer service on economy flights against that of the market leader, Singapore Airlines. Southwest Airlines in the United States has long been considered to be the benchmark provider which all "no-frills" or budget airlines should try to emulate.

Arguments against benchmarking

Benchmarking has a number of critics. On a straightforward level, one argument put forward is that benchmarking represents a poor use of senior managers' time. Why would they spend time thinking about their competitors when they should be focusing on the strengths of their own company?

Next, there is a philosophical criticism that all benchmarking can do is make all companies look the same, leading to similar strategic positions and therefore a distinct lack of differentiation. Not surprisingly, on this point Trout and Rivkin (2008) are unequivocal:

Benchmarking doesn't work because regardless of a product's quality, people perceive the first brand to enter their mind as superior. When you opt to benchmark a product and become a me-too, you are a second-class citizen.

Benchmarking can also have significant legal implications. At the time of writing, Apple and Samsung are yet again involved in a legal dispute over "copying" design features. Apple is suing Samsung for $2 billion. The following excerpt from www.cnet.com outlines the case.

Almost two years after Apple and Samsung faced off in a messy patent dispute, the smartphone and tablet rivals have returned to the same courtroom in San José, California to argue once again over patents. Apple wants Samsung to pay it about $2 billion for infringing five patents, while Samsung wants about $7 million from Apple for infringing two of its patents.

Apple and Samsung have accused each other of copying features used in their popular smartphones and tablets, and the jury will have to decide who actually infringed and how much money is due. This trial involves different patents and newer devices than the ones disputed at trial in August 2012 and in a damages retrial in November 2013.

For instance, the new trial involves the iPhone 5, released in September 2012, and Samsung's Galaxy S3, which also debuted in 2012.

Source: Taken from an article entitled "Apple: Samsung made 'false statements' during opening argument", by Shara Tibken, posted on www.cnet.com, 2 April 2014

The importance of national and international quality standards (AO2)

We have looked at two sources of quality assurance: TQM and benchmarking. A third source is to demonstrate a commitment to an internationally recognized standard of quality such as ISO 9001. For example, child car seat manufacturers complying to such a standard are able to reassure customers that their product has satisfied a number of internationally agreed standards on safety.

Unfortunately, ISO certification highlights the fact that a company is following accepted manufacturing processes only, which could be considered to lead consumers to view a product as a safe product. Certification in itself unfortunately does not guarantee the product's "quality". Given this point, some commentators have argued that ISO recognition is simply a marketing tool designed to convince customers that the product has the quality stamp of approval from an independent body.

Think back to the YouTube clip on the Chinese building which was created in 15 days. At various intervals, Broad Group (the company that constructed the building) is at pains to point out that safety standards around earthquake reinforcements and quality thresholds, and environmental processes surrounding air purification, are strictly applied. The building may have been constructed in 360 hours but the contractors ensured that above-minimum quality standards were applied.

Assessing the impact of TQM and kaizen (AO2)

This unit has been dominated by the philosophy of lean production and TQM. It would appear obvious that the detection and prevention of defects before they occur, with quality during the production process becoming every individual's responsibility (TQM), will save considerable time and resources. This approach will clearly be preferable to waiting until the final product is produced in order to discover defects. Once the detection process begins as advocated by more traditional methods, it is already too late. What happens and who is responsible if one defective item slips through and enters the market-place?

Deming's work was initially overlooked in his own country. Only when the Japanese rate of productivity soared, coupled with significant reductions in waste as part of the new competitive framework of lean production, did the US car manufacturers take notice. Unfortunately, for some it was too late and Toyota, Nissan and Mazda began to eat into US market share. They continue to do so.

TQM and kaizen implementation have important links to and consequences for organizational culture and hierarchy, management style and non-financial motivation. Herein lies one major issue for senior managers. Traditional styles of management are not appropriate to implement TQM. Are senior managers willing to change and give up some of their power and authority?

Setting the scene

This unit explores the dilemma for traditional location theory in an era of rapid change, innovation and globalization. We have already discussed many of the factors affecting the location of a firm, without a direct reference to location theory. These factors include:

- the growth of multinational activity (concept 1: Globalization and unit 1)

- the impact of ICT on the ability of firms to communicate across many countries and time zones with the increased possibilities of a firm structuring itself by geographic function (unit 2.1)

- the growing appetite for firms to engage in offshoring and outsourcing parts of their customer service and HR management functions (unit 2.2).

The final point in this list illustrates the fact that parts of traditional location theory are being challenged. For example, firms now do not have to locate in an area of high unemployment to find pools of labour. They can effectively transfer the responsibility to a geographic region offshore. In addition, in the new global environment, the locations of key functions of a firm are not constrained by having to be in the same country as the head office.

Summary

We have seen that with the growth of global branding and international marketing, firms can now market their products successfully across the planet. Companies can now market regionally and allow a degree of decentralization, especially in marketing, to suit local tastes (as we saw in the excerpt from McDonald's website on page 115).

The growth of offshoring has now enabled firms to concentrate their production in countries with lower labour costs. For example, the growth of call centres and ICT services, especially in Malaysia and the Philippines, has allowed firms to relocate their customer service programmes at greatly reduced costs.

Finally, as we saw in unit 3.1, the globalization of modern finance and the growth of venture capital have enabled firms to raise finance from all parts of the globe. This has led to a vital transfer of funds from the developed to the developing world, as facilitated by organizations such as Kiva.org and crowdfunding sites such as Kickstarter.

The reasons for a specific location of production (AO2)

Before we completely leave location theory out of our thinking we should consider that not all organizations are large enough or have a big enough market to take advantage of the opportunities globalization may bring.

Location can be influenced by the following factors:

- Accessibility to the market will be a consideration. Easy access will limit transport costs, which is especially important for firms where the production process involves weight gaining. This argument is strongly applied in "heavy goods" industries (such as the car industry) and "white goods" production (manufacturing goods such as fridges and washing machines).

- Location may be influenced by access to government grants and allowances and tax considerations. Ireland has seen a surge in firms wishing to locate there due to favourable government incentives and tax environments.

- Availability of land will be an important factor for firms involved in large-scale production or perhaps looking to build a distribution network around large warehouse space. This is becoming very important in e-commerce firms such as Amazon or retailers such as Tesco and Wal-Mart that are looking to the Internet to provide extensive product ranges.

- The existence of reliable infrastructure such as energy generation and transport links is important. Traffic congestion and delays can significantly add to firms' costs and in the case of retailers such as IKEA lead to considerable stakeholder frustration.

- Location will be influenced by a company's ability to develop good reliable working relationships with suppliers. This is crucial if a firm wishes to employ JIT stock control methods and kaizen, as described in unit 5.3.

- A firm will need to consider the availability and suitability of local labour to satisfy its manpower requirements. This can be a powerful motivating factor although increasingly, with globalization, firms are able to offshore and outsource more and more of their labour input.

Outsourcing, subcontracting and offshoring (AO3)

Outsourcing differs from offshoring in that it can be achieved without the need to subcontract or move production overseas.

Outsourcing is the process by which firms will subcontract to (or use) independent suppliers rather than undertake the activities themselves. Offshoring is carrying out these activities in another country.

However, given the growing transparency around global labour costs, the two terms have become synonymous with each other. For brevity, they will be discussed together in this section under the single term "outsourcing".

Outsourcing allows firms to concentrate on their core activities and benefit from the experience and knowledge of specialists. Examples of commonly subcontracted activities include catering, call centre and other customer service activities, security, office cleaning, market research and, in some industries, design.

Benefits of outsourcing

Outsourcing has been most commonly proposed as a strategic decision for organizations looking to remain competitive in an increasingly connected and transparent external environment.

ICT functions remain the most outsourced function, with India being the main beneficiary. The growth in the number of Indian university graduates has been noted by multinational firms in particular and has allowed firms to outsource administrative and call centre functions with no noticeable drop in the quality of service provided.

Disadvantages of outsourcing

Outsourcing will transfer final responsibility regarding quality to the outsourced company, especially if the outsourced company is working under the regime of JIT in the global supply chain. The quality process will need monitoring and senior managers from the host company may have to visit the outsourced company regularly to enforce the host company's expected standards of performance.

Concerns have been raised about the security of information, as host companies have to share intellectual property with the outsourced company.

Russell-Walling (2007) has argued that the cost savings from outsourcing are not as dramatic as one might think once "cultural alignment activities have been completed". Despite training and cultural awareness activities, there will be transitional costs in outsourcing.

There may also be PR issues for the firm outsourcing operations in the host country. Outsourcing organizations may be regarded as unethical if they transfer work to other subcontractors overseas while the rate of unemployment increases in the host country in which the outsourcing organization is based.

This last point has considerable political impact, as we saw earlier in the report of the UK Prime Minister setting up a working group to encourage the reshoring of human resources and other activities linked to operations management (see unit 2.1, page 38). Two weeks after Mr Cameron's announcement, the following UK newspaper article appeared.

Conclusion

As domestic economies recover after the shocks of the global financial crisis, we are seeing evidence of a shift in thinking around outsourcing. We are witnessing growth in many of the G8 countries and organizations centrally based in these countries are rethinking their operations management decisions given some of the concerns raised in the article. However, care is required as this trend is only starting to emerge. The movement of goods, labour and capital around the globe is still a key driver in the relentless spread of globalization.

However, in the next unit when considering topics such as the supply chain in greater detail, we will view evidence to back up Russell-Walling's claims that the gains from offshoring may be disappearing given the significant wage growth in China, South Korea and Singapore. The labour cost advantage, which once existed in these countries, is rapidly shrinking.

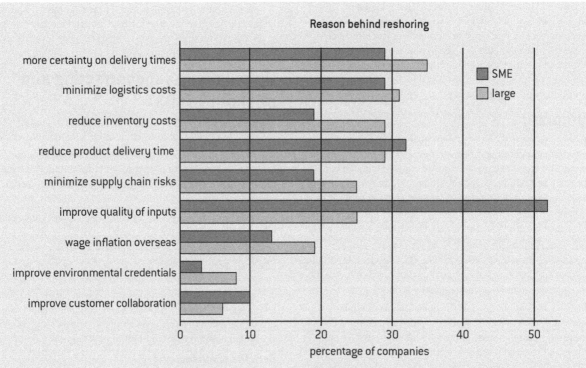

Source: EEF/GfK Make it in Britain survey

Why are UK firms bringing manufacturing back home?

The number of British companies "reshoring" production is on the rise.

The ebb and flow of global economic tides is increasingly turning in favour of the UK with a growing number of our manufacturing businesses bringing back work to British shores.

A major new report released today from manufacturers' association EEF found that one in six companies has "reshored" production in the past three years, up from one in seven when a similar study was carried out in 2009.

Having once looked to cut costs by moving production to low-cost emerging nations, more and more businesses are heeding Prime Minister David Cameron's call in his World Economic Forum speech to come home as these countries'

economies mature and labour costs rise, according to the report "Backing Britain – a manufacturing base for the future". But cost isn't the only reason. Other factors include capitalizing on Britain's reputation for excellence, the ability to create shorter, more responsive supply chains and ease of communication with customers.

"The trend may be gradual but it is highly encouraging to see more reshoring," said Terry Scuoler, chief executive of EEF. "While it will always be two-way traffic, the need to be closer to customers, to have ever greater control of quality and the continued erosion of low labour costs in some competitor countries mean that in many cases it makes increasingly sound business sense."

But reshoring is not without its problems – common issues cited were disruption to production, taking up management time and finding suppliers.

Source: Taken from an article by Alan Tovey, posted on www.telegraph.co.uk, 3 March 2014

Setting the scene

Russell-Walling (2007) defines a supply chain as:

a chain that is made up of physical and information links between suppliers and the company on one side and the company and its customers on the other.

Figure 5.5.1 shows a basic version of a supply chain.

The supply chain process (AO2)

Figure 5.5.2 illustrates the supply chain process for Amazon, as we saw in unit 4.8 on e-commerce, a very successful online retailer. It should be clear from Figure 5.5.2 that this process involves not only the physical movement of goods but also information flows between consumers and the organization. The benefits of this e-commerce process were explained in greater detail in unit 4.8. The supply chain can also include production planning, purchasing, materials handling, transport and storage.

Supply chain

Links to unit 5.4 and concept 1: Globalization

Given our previous comments surrounding the impact of globalization and the growth of outsourcing, supply chain management has taken on a whole new competitive focus. There is urgency for large firms to trim costs and improve efficiency. As Kevin O'Connell from IBM remarked in 2005:

The supply chain is no longer a back-office activity. It has become the competitive weapon in the boardroom.

We must note that a trend towards long supply chains is not without difficulty. For example, when a Finnish mobile phone producer manufactures a mobile phone in China to ship to a retailer in Australia, the supply chain is potentially stretched to breaking point. The more links in the chain over a greater distance, the more likely that mistakes will occur.

However, Russell-Walling (2007) concludes that:

It is not surprising that many companies feel that, in order to draw every last cost saving, outsourcing in the new millennium has become the mantra for proponents of the global supply chain. A number of manufacturers have outsourced every link in the logistics process.

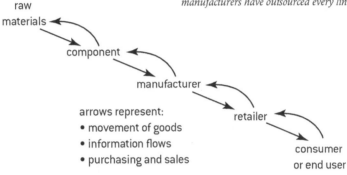

Figure 5.5.1 A basic supply chain

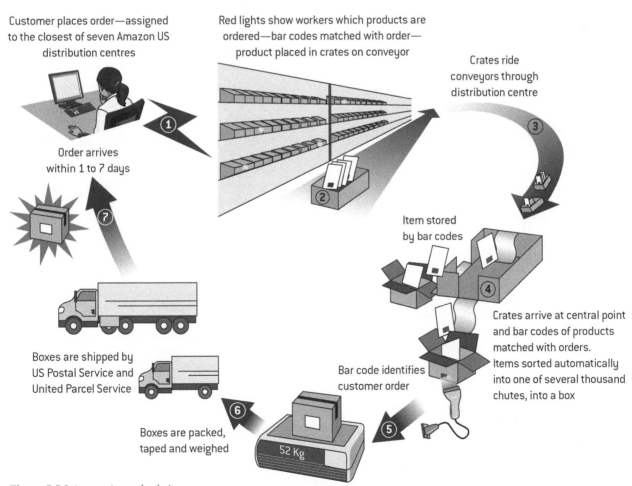

Figure 5.5.2 Amazon's supply chain

Source: http://files.myopera.com/CHIEMKIMNGAN/blog/amazon.JPG

IB Learner Profile

Inquiry and balance ? ⚖

We must be careful before we jump to the conclusion that all supply chain management and outsourcing is being directed at the developing world. As we saw in unit 5.4, a number of organizations are currently rethinking their operations management models, especially the notion of reshoring instead of offshoring and outsourcing. The article above provides an interesting counter point to conventional thinking about the supply chain.

Questions for reflection

- "With the wage gap between the UK and China narrowing" what are the implications of this for outsourcing and offshoring to the Far East?

- Given the rapid technological changes and evolving markets, is it sensible to reduce the length of supply chains?

Just in time compared to just in case (AO2)

We noted in unit 5.3 that when using just-in-time (JIT) systems, firms try to minimize the costs of holding stock. Goods are made to order. The firm will hold stocks of components and materials subject to the prevailing level of demand, and only the absolute minimum is held.

JIT requires excellent communication and strong supplier relationships.

In just-in-case (JIC) systems, additional stock is held in order to provide a contingency against unexpected events. These might include a sudden increase in demand, or a breakdown in the production process or supply chain.

JIC is considered to be an expensive way of holding stock. However, it does reduce the risk of pauses or major stoppages in the production process, which could be even more costly to the organization.

IB Learner Profile

Reflection Я|R

From our analysis so far, would you consider Amazon to be a JIT or JIC retailer? Read on to see whether your answer is correct.

Stock control charts (AO2)

Stock control

The purpose of stock control is to be able to hold sufficient quantities of raw materials, work in progress and finished goods in order to enable production and sales to continue uninterrupted. A number of different ways have been suggested to try to achieve this. The two methods of stock control, which we have already considered, are JIC and JIT.

Figure 5.5.3 (on the next page) is a traditional stock control graph identifying lead times, buffer stocks and reorder levels and quantities.

The costs of holding stock and link to JIT and JIC

The costs of holding stock can be considerable. They include:

- costs of storage (e.g. refrigeration) and, if necessary, warehousing

- insurance and security costs

- (if stock levels begin to increase beyond the buffer stock) opportunity costs of tying up money which could have been used elsewhere in the business.

JIT demands that there is a very strong and reliable relationship between supplier and final manufacturer. For example, until recently, Nissan's production plant in Sunderland, UK, demanded that suppliers of components sign contracts guaranteeing that components for its assembly line would be on-call (ready to deliver) 24 hours a day, 7 days a week.

Although JIC is expensive, some online retailers, such as Amazon and Wal-Mart, have built their business infrastructure around huge warehouses stocked full of products to satisfy incoming online orders from customers. JIC is appropriate for Amazon given the organization's enormous influence in the e-commerce environment. Small business start-ups may not be able to use JIC stock control and may have to service customer requirements by the use of JIT, usually at higher prices to the final end user.

What about economies of scale? By using JIC, Amazon is able to take advantage of bulk-buying economies of scale that firms using JIT will not obtain.

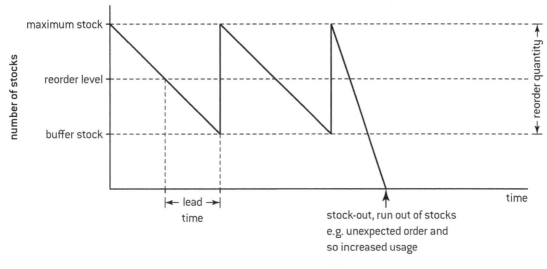

Reorder level: level of stocks at which new supplies are ordered

Reorder quantity: amount reordered

Buffer stock: safety stock in case of sudden increase in demand or supply failure

Lead time: time taken from ordering supplies to supplies arriving

Figure 5.5.3 Stock control

Capacity utilization and productivity rates (AO2, AO4)

The formulae to calculate these rates are given below.

$$\text{Capacity utilization rate} = \frac{\text{actual output}}{\text{productive capacity}} \times 100$$

$$\text{Productivity rate} = \frac{\text{total output}}{\text{total input}} \times 100$$

Capacity utilization

The capacity utilization rate for an organization refers to the degree of actual capacity being used. A rate of 100% implies that an organization is using every available resource at its disposal and producing at a maximum amount. Rates of below 70% will be a concern for an organization and questions will need to be asked whether the current rate of production is sustainable.

Working at maximum capacity may have its drawbacks: employees may feel stressed and fatigued; and working capital is being used up in such a manner that **overtrading** may occur and liquidity issues may arise. Some organizational slack is accepted in many cases, as this will allow the organization time to ensure that aims and objectives are being met, or that reviews of performance (e.g. appraisal and opportunities for 360-degree feedback) are being carried out effectively.

Productivity

As an organization approaches 100% capacity utilization, it would be fair to assume that "high productivity" across all departments in that organization is occurring. In economics, we define productivity as output per factor produced. "High productivity" is a term often used to describe a situation where output per worker is increasing. Productivity has its strongest links to human resources where, in some industries, output per worker can be easily measured. Improvements in training, the introduction of new reward systems or a change in senior management may be some of the reasons why productivity can grow.

In common with capacity utilization, productivity growth must be checked carefully. Increases in individual output per worker are welcome, but if it is at the expense of product quality or has an impact on relationships between and within departments, then some unwelcome side effects could arise. This will depend on the organizational culture present. From our understanding of the Enron culture, increases in productivity at this organization were welcomed whether they were legal or unethical. The author is confident that this is a pathway that few organizations, if any, would wish to follow.

Cost to make and cost to buy (AO2)

Link to outsourcing decisions

The following brief analysis provides an example to illustrate some of the considerations an organization needs to consider when looking at the possibility to outsource a particular part of a production process. You may wish to refer back to some of the contribution material, which was considered in unit 3.3.

There are compelling reasons, relating to capacity and productivity, why an organization may decide to produce an item "in-house" at a slightly higher cost than it would cost to outsource. These reasons include considerations of quality control and transportation costs. When considering make-or-buy decisions, managers choose whether to buy in components or make them in-house in their organization.

We have already discussed several factors behind the decision for firms to outsource production. However, we can also consider some figures.

For example, if a certain component will cost firm X either $12 to produce in its own factory or $10 by outsourcing production to company Y, then company X will have to consider the following issues:

- Is the $2 saving significant, given quality control concerns that will arise when another firm produces the component?

- The $2 per component saving could be used as a contribution to overhead costs for company X.

- Will company Y be able to guarantee delivery and sufficient batch size?

- What are company X's core activities and should it be producing this component?

- Given time, larger batches and economies of scale, will company Y be able to charge a price lower than $10 in the future?

- Does company X have sufficient capacity to produce this component? If the company is running close to full capacity, what are the implications for HR management and quality control?

- By producing this component will productivity be affected? Will additional training be required to maintain current productivity levels?

Setting the scene

Link with concepts 1: Globalization, 2: Change, 3: Innovation, 6: Culture

Gary Hamel's assertion that "to earn one's place in the market given hyper competition, organizations now have to innovate" is a compelling one (Hamel quoted in Robertson and Breen, 2013 – see concept 3: Innovation). With "knowledge advantages" quickly disappearing, the need to innovate in a global market-place is never more apparent.

One important question remains. If knowledge, as Hamel puts it, "is a commodity" and organizations can clearly see what other organizations are creating by benchmarking against each other, then why are some businesses so much better at innovating than others? Surely, these advantages would be eradicated as new products enter the market?

Given change and globalization, perhaps the answer lies in the cultural make-up of the organization, which perhaps is difficult to replicate in others. As Steve Jobs famously stated:

Innovation has nothing to do with how many R&D dollars you have. When Apple came up with the Mac, IBM was spending at least 100 times more on R&D. It's not about money. It's about the people you have, how you're led, and how much you get it.

However, we first must discuss the process by which businesses may arrive at solutions to the issue of endlessly having to be creative in the 21st century market-place.

Importance and benefits of research and development (AO3)

Research and development (R&D) for an organization is commonly defined as the ability to create and develop new products. We identified this process when we looked at the product life cycle in unit 4.5.

Successful R&D brings a number of benefits to an organization. It will result in increased revenue and market share, especially if the new product forms the basis of a new "blue ocean" strategy (see concept 5). Lego's return to profitability in 2007 was achieved by a much greater focus on R&D through looking at what customers could do with Lego products rather than what the company wanted them to do. This led to a much more market-oriented approach to R&D at Lego than was previously experienced.

Given the "tyranny of choice", if a new product created by R&D becomes "first in the mind", innovation can be a very powerful differentiating factor. As we shall see with Apple's iPad, this is a critical reason for engaging in effective R&D even if this takes longer than expected and when the product appears in the market-place consumers are not exactly sure what it is for.

R&D, however, should not be restricted to the creation of new products. It is perfectly reasonable for a firm to investigate and develop non-tangible products such as new production methods, or customer service programmes, or innovative ways of advertising or marketing. R&D can also be applied to achieving new levels of quality assurance. Organizations will hope that further opportunities for cost reduction and/or productivity gains can be realized through innovative approaches to operations management.

Finally, one of our conclusions from unit 4.5 is that product life cycles are becoming shorter. The process of change is rapid. As Lego discovered, R&D must have a strong commercial focus and not be locked away in a "laboratory", because a firm's survival in some competitive markets may depend on its capacity to bring an innovative product to market quickly.

Costs of R&D

R&D will take considerable time and involve human, non-human and financial resources. As Lego discovered when the company attempted to innovate its way out of its financial crisis in 2004, the demands placed on an organization which may be creating everything and selling nothing can threaten economic sustainability.

In the pharmaceutical industry, figures from the United States indicate that businesses looking to invest in R&D for new medicines or life-saving drugs may spend up to 50% of their annual revenue in the process. This investment is not guaranteed to repay itself quickly, if ever, leading us to some understanding of why the gross profit margins on some successfully tested and implemented pharmaceutical products reach over 90%. The recouping of this investment also allows for future R&D to take place.

Finally, we must acknowledge that if successful R&D leads to innovation then a business will need to apply for a patent and will also need to finance intellectual property protection methods in order to stop existing or potential competitors from 'copying' the new idea. Both of these measures will incur further costs to the business. Patents and intellectual copyright protection are also necessary to encourage a business to undertake future R&D activities.

Goods and services that address unmet needs (AO2)

Now we turn to the importance of developing goods and services that address customers' unmet needs – needs of which they may or may not be aware (AO2).

Of course, the ultimate goal of R&D would be to create a product that is currently not on the market, and that satisfies a need which it is yet to be recognized. This would be the very essence of a "blue ocean" strategy (see concept 5, where we considered the success of Cirque du Soleil and its creation of a "blue ocean" within the entertainment industry).

The iPad: what is it good for?

It goes on sale on Friday, but it's one of the most keenly anticipated technology launches in recent years. So why has the iPad become such a focus of attention, what is it really for and, oh yes, is it any good?

Critics have said it's nothing more than an oversized iPhone, though frankly, that doesn't sound too shabby. It certainly has a display and interface which are instantly recognizable to iPod touch and iPhone users – all the iPhone's 200 000+ apps work on the big screen, too, and around 5 000 iPad specific apps are also available.

So the range of things you can use it for is pretty wide. This is both the iPad's strength and weakness: it does so much it can be hard to get an idea of what it is.

Apple recognizes this, saying that the iPad is a whole new category of gadget, that people didn't know what to make of it, ranging from curious to skeptical – at least until they tried it for themselves.

But, whatever you say, it's still not paper. You can't read it outside on a summer's afternoon (though those sunny days are nearly over now, right?) and although the iPad has exceptional battery life, you'll curse it if it runs out just before the murderer's identity is revealed. Paper, after all, doesn't need batteries. And you quickly miss the special elements of a physical book – the sense of how much further the story will last that is evident from the way it sits in your hand, the cracked spine, even the coffee stain.

And although you can carry hundreds of books in a package weighing less than one Dan Brown blockbuster, do you need to?

The iPad is the perfect storm, a coming together of three things: appealing, high-end hardware, the ingenuity of designers creating apps exploiting large-screen real estate and the versatility offered only by touchscreens. Need an extra button for that app to work? No problem: regular buttons have to wait for new hardware so they can be built in, but with touch-sensitive displays you can have as many as you want, now.

Apple execs freely admit they're addicted to the iPad. They pick it up first thing in the morning (to check email, see the weather forecast, catch up on news) and put it down last thing at night.

Even so, is it worth it, for a machine that doesn't even have a USB socket (though there is a cable accessory which allows you to transfer photos from your digital camera to the iPad to display your shots)?

Apple's biggest problem is the people who haven't used it who, for now, is nearly everyone. Last week, a survey in the US claimed sky-high satisfaction levels among iPad users. And it's true, once it's in your hands, skepticism evaporates. Sure there's no camera on board and no onscreen keyboard with feedback to make it easier to type.

But the more you play with it, the more uses occur so that within days it's insinuated its way into your life. What started out as a whimsical luxury, a gorgeous piece of kit, becomes a necessity. Maybe you don't yet know what it's for, but the iPad's great trick is that, before long, you will.

Source: Article from the UK newspaper, *The Independent*, 26 May 2010

Now we focus on another "blue ocean" candidate. When the iPad was first released in 2010, many stakeholders (including the author) actually asked the same question as the one introducing the article below.

Having wondered what the iPad was good for in 2010, four years later it is ingrained in our lives. Schools are using iPads to allow students to research in class and to assist students with learning difficulties relating to reading and speech. Restaurants, hotels, airlines and hospitals are now using iPads in a variety of capacities. We have finally discovered what the iPad is for!

Types of innovation (AO2)

Reread concept 3: Innovation to remind yourself of some of the ideas discussed there. Below we explore different types of innovation:

- **Product innovation** is defined as the creation of a new product or service or a modification to an existing product that improves performance or adds value in the eyes of the stakeholder to an original idea.

- **Process innovation** has links to supply chain or distribution systems where there is innovation in the production or delivery of a product or service to the end user. Moore's law has driven process innovation in the computer industry especially. The PlayStation 4 is a significantly improved version of its predecessor the PlayStation 3 given the increase in the amount of RAM now available.

- **Positioning innovation** refers to the process by which an existing product in marketing could take on a new "perception" in the minds of a consumer. The innovation aspect is the process of creating a new "use" for a product or to change its target market completely. One of the most famous examples of positioning innovation occurred when the famous glucose drink Lucozade was re-branded into an energy drink:

Lucozade was sold in a glass bottle with a yellow Cellophane wrap until 1983, when Lucozade was rebranded as an energy drink to shift the brand's associations away from illness. The slogan "Lucozade aids recovery" was replaced by "Lucozade replaces lost energy". A plastic one replaced the glass bottle. After the rebranding, between 1984 and 1989 UK sales tripled to almost £75 million.

Source: Wikipedia

Paradigm innovation is the hardest to achieve but can be the most successful commercially. Launching the iPad is an example of a paradigm or disruptive innovation. The iPad has changed stakeholder behaviour towards mobile computing devices and created a market on its own which could be termed "tablet" or recently "phablet". There are many imitations of the iPad but the original idea and disruptive breakthrough belongs to Apple.

In Figure 5.6.1 further categories of innovation are shown:

- "Fundamental" innovation in the figure is what we describe as paradigm innovation above.

- "Variations" equate to product innovation.

- "Derivatives" refers to a type of product innovation. Derivative innovation involves slight modifications to the main product.

- "Platform" innovations are innovations that lead to the practical application of fundamental innovations, sometimes launching new industries.

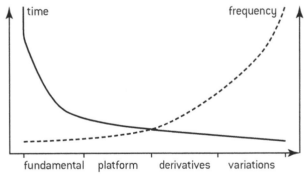

Figure 5.6.1 Types of innovation

Figure 5.6.1 clearly shows that fundamental (paradigm) innovation occurs less frequently and with a much greater time commitment than, say, variations (product innovation).

Difference between adaptive creativity and innovative creativity (AO2)

Adaptive creativity is adapting something that exists and innovative creativity is creating something new. Below we look at the difference between these two types of creativity.

For a list of reasons, such as capital that needs to be invested, the time taken to develop products and services, the rapid social and technological changes which are upon us, many organizations will continue to try and innovate creatively. If successful in this, they can create a paradigm shift in consumer behaviour. Many of the companies used as examples in this study guide have created paradigm-breaking innovative products and services. Here are a few examples:

- Apple – computers, smartphones, mobile devices (e.g. the iPad)
- Pixar – animation
- Google – research, communication, cloud services
- Lego – toys.

We have listed Pixar, but we could also argue that the movie industry in general has tried to be innovative and creative. However, as we have argued, this industry continues to adapt existing ideas, giving them the odd twist to make them appear fresh. The new "Avengers" movie, the new Adam Sandler comedy and the new British romantic comedy will no doubt be in movie theatres by the time you read this sentence. Remember William Goldman's famous phrase about what makes a movie successful: "Nobody (in Hollywood) knows anything".

Finally, let's return to the case of Lego, which we investigated in concept 3: Innovation. Lego is an organization that has looked into the financial abyss of bankruptcy in 2006–07. By 2014 Lego was the most successful toy company in the world with a growth rate that far exceeded that of Apple and Google.

Robertson and Breen (2013) examine some of the lessons learned from Lego's unsuccessful attempt to innovate its way out of its financial crisis in 2004. Their book focuses on a number of product areas but one section concerns Lego's decision to create an online platform for using Lego on the Internet with the creation of Lego Universe.

Lego Universe was an attempt to allow users effectively to create their Lego experience online. The Lego Universe project leader, Mark Hansen, stated:

Lego Universe is the largest and most complex project that Lego has ever undertaken. It touches every part of the company.

Lego Universe costs millions of dollars to create. It was launched in 2010 and was shut down in 2012. What lessons for innovation can we learn from this? Here are some suggestions:

- Do not jump into a new business before you understand it.
- Do not demand that a new or young technology deliver a near-perfect experience.
- Insulate innovation projects away from the demands of other parts of the organization during the development stage.
- Make the product for customers, not managers.
- Price the product to meet what the market will bear, not to recoup your investment.

POSTSCRIPT 2014

Lego was very wise to shut down Lego Universe in 2012. In 2009 a Swedish video game programmer and designer named Markus Persson posted a rough version of a 3D world (game) he had created called Minecraft. It featured textured building blocks and its popularity soon spread through the global gaming community. By 2012 Minecraft had 36 million registered users with over 7 million who had purchased the game, raising over $100 million dollars. At the same time, Lego Universe had only 38 000 subscribers.

CRISIS MANAGEMENT AND CONTINGENCY PLANNING (HL ONLY)

In this unit we "flip the learning" of crisis management and contingency planning. What is a crisis in business management? Perhaps the article below can give us an answer. It is written from the perspective of the expatriate community in Canada.

IB Learner Profile

Inquiry and reflection ? Я|R

Questions for reflection

- Does banning these products count as a crisis?
- Who is this crisis actually affecting – the organization that makes these products or the retail owner?
- To what extent is it possible to plan for a crisis such as this?

Setting the scene

The media overuses the term "crisis". When the term is applied to business, it may be perceived to have lost its true value. At the time of writing, there is a "crisis" at one of the world's most popular and financially successful soccer teams – Manchester United – because they will not win the English Premiership. They hold the record for most titles ever but this year they lost to their local rivals Manchester City in one, albeit important, game.

However, the impact on an organization of a PR embarrassment arising from a "crisis" cannot be underestimated. Consider:

- the Fonterra "crisis" in China over contaminated milk powder (which proved false)
- a product recall due to safety concerns (e.g. as faced by Toyota)
- examples of companies found guilty of false and misleading advertising (e.g. GlaxoSmithKline).

Interested students are invited to research the case given last in the list above. Two young New Zealand students, Anna Devathasan and Jenny Suo, found, in their own classroom experiments – similar to a group 4 project – at school, that claims by GlaxoSmithKline that Ribena contained four times the vitamin C of orange were false. GlaxoSmithKline had been running a misleading campaign for many years and had to retract its advertisements, offer apologies to customers and pay a substantial fine. This was most certainly a crisis.

Given these potentially damaging consequences, a number of organizations have generated contingency plans to try to pre-empt or plan for potential "crisis" events, which may not actually happen. There is debate as to whether firms should divert resources (including financial resources and the cost of managers' time) to a situation that might not occur.

Crisis management and contingency planning (AO2)

The difference between crisis management and contingency planning can be explained as follows.

"Crisis management" is a term believed to have been coined by US Secretary of Defence, Robert McNamara, after the Cuban Missile Crisis of 1962, to describe a way of dealing with crises as they arise in real time, without having undertaken any long-term strategic planning. Crisis management assumes that because the actions of others cannot always be predicted or planned for, crises have to be dealt with when they happen.

Contingency planning can be illustrated by the experiences of two well-known organizations (Wrigley's and Kellogg's). In 2009 both companies experienced a PR crisis when celebrities associated with them tarnished the companies' image through inappropriate behaviour. Both organizations were quick to disassociate themselves from these individuals. One is tempted to suggest that, given the unpredictable nature of some celebrities who are

---

Marmite, Irn-Bru and Bovril banned in Canada after they fall foul of food additive rules

In Canada it is perfectly legal to acquire a firearm and bullets. But Marmite and Irn-Bru are apparently a threat to the nation's health after the Canadian food watchdog banned some of Britain's most popular exports from supermarket shelves.

A British food store in Saskatoon faces closure after the Canadian authorities declared that the essential supplies it provides for Bovril- and Marmite-loving English expatriates are illegal in the country.

Marmite, Irn-Bru, Penguin bars, Lucozade, Bovril and Ovaltine have all fallen foul of the Canadian Food Inspection Agency (CFIA), which objected to food-colorings, vitamins and minerals contained in products from the United Kingdom.

Tony Badger, owner of Brit Foods, a convenience store in the Saskatchewan city, warned that his livelihood was under threat after officials pulled products from his shelves and impounded goods which had been imported via Montreal.

Mr. Badger, who has supplied British foods for 15 years, warned: "Unfortunately, as time goes by, I'm not importing. As the shelves start to empty … if it takes too long we'll have no option but to close."

Irn-Bru, the sugary orange caffeinated brew, described as "Scotland's other national drink", contains Ponceau 4R, a synthetic red food colorant which is not permitted in Canada.

Marmite is fortified with vitamins and minerals including Vitamin B12 and Riboflavin (Vit B2), a combination which previously saw the savory spread fall foul of Danish food regulators.

According to the CFIA's letter to the shop-owner, Marmite, Ovaltine, Lucozade, Penguin bars and Bovril "are enriched with vitamins and minerals" and therefore illegal.

"We've been bringing Irn-Bru in since the very beginning. I haven't heard of anyone dying from consuming Irn-Bru in Scotland or Britain," Mr. Badger protested.

Source: www.independent.co.uk, 23 January 2014

---

paid to sponsor or promote a product, thus generating media coverage, firms should have an action plan in place to deal with any potential crises **before they occur**. This process is known as contingency planning. Acting before a problem occurs is the key difference between contingency planning and crisis management.

Possible threats to effective crisis management (AO2)

Time

Rapid technological change and social media have increased the **speed** of communication of a crisis and reduced the **time** organizations have to deal with that crisis. Lee Iacocca, one of the most successful CEOs in US business history, had this to say:

When you are in a crisis, there is no time to run a study. The prospect of dying has a way of focusing your attention in a big hurry. (Lee Iacocca, quoted in Trout and Rivkin, 2010)

A PR expert on the European rail industry commented:

When there was a crisis, we used to have 20 minutes before the news broke, during which time we could get a "handle" on the situation and what to do next; today we have 20 seconds. (European rail industry expert quoted in McInnes, 2012)

Transparency

Change, social media and the world wide web have now forced organizations to be as transparent as possible. They must demonstrate transparency even if the crisis does not affect them directly.

In 2012 it was reported that assembly line workers working for Foxconn – a subcontractor used by Apple and other technology companies to assemble iPads, mobile devices, etc. – were being mistreated through poor working conditions. Some of these workers were threatening suicide. When the allegations were reported, Apple launched a PR campaign to indicate that it was taking these media claims very seriously and would take action.

Apple was not the owner of Foxconn – there was a B2B relationship between the two firms – but given Apple's global success the organization felt that it had to be open and transparent and consider the wider picture of its operations. The crisis abated much more quickly than if Apple had decided that it had no responsibility and would not admit that there were issues. Soon after, the notoriously publicity-shy CEO of Apple, Tim Cook, visited Foxconn's factory to indicate that Apple took these issues very seriously and to see what action was required to remedy the situation.

Control

By acting quickly and decisively, Apple was able to exert some control in tackling the media allegations to create an appropriate media response. Perhaps surprisingly, some organizations have outsourced this PR function of dealing with crises to third parties. These third parties may have previous experience in this area though. The issue comes down to how much control the organization wishes to have. It is tempting to quote the cliché "you only get one chance to make a first impression".

The tragic events surrounding the disappearance of Malaysia Airlines flight MH370 highlight the issues surrounding the reporting of a crisis. A number of stakeholders have criticized the airline's handling of this.

Advantages and disadvantages of contingency plans (AO2)

Contingency plans can be drawn up in a number of different areas of an organization including finance, HR management and operations. This is especially important for potential liquidity or staffing problems influenced by external factors that can change very quickly.

As we saw through the eyes of Trout and Rivkin (2010), the perception and positioning of the company or product is a defining factor in determining the success of the marketing effort. Contingency plans can be used to try and protect brand image in the eyes of stakeholders especially if a crisis does occur.

To return to our example of the allegations that GlaxoSmithKline's advertising of the vitamin C content of Ribena was misleading, the company's response to the accusations was swift. It began with an apology and the intention to redress any false claims. It is certain that this organization will have plans in place in case similar accusations are made in future.

In large-scale organizations contingency plans can "save lives" and ensure that a project stays on course. This is particularly true if there are many thousands of different subcontractors or third parties involved in the operations process.

Disadvantages of contingency plans

Clearly the most obvious disadvantage of contingency plans is that **working capital** funds, **time** and **human resources** are tied up in a project or planning group to solve a problem which may not occur. What are the **initial (fixed)**, **ongoing (variable)** and, importantly, **opportunity costs** of this process? How will they be accurately measured?

Second, how does an organization accurately measure the **risks** of a crisis occurring, thereby having an impact on the validity of the contingency plan? Do the organization's leaders use a scientific approach involving complex algorithms or computer programs or do they use "gut feeling" or experience? This scientific versus intuitive decision-making conflict lies at the heart of the analysis of the value of contingency planning. Furthermore, one could argue that this conflict lies at the heart of all business management decision-making.

Setting the scene

As part of this study guide, in order to deepen your understanding of some important business content, contexts and concepts and to align your study of business management to the IB learner profile, a number of inquiry activities are provided. Some are designed to stimulate your thinking, others to challenge.

This section will try to prompt, suggest and/or create some new lines of inquiry. These could be followed in class if this guide is being used as part of your regular teaching classes or at home as part of your individual study.

Preparation for the final exams is given in the next section. This section is to provide stimulation of your teaching and learning of business management. The idea is to encourage you to adopt an inquiry approach to your learning of the subject. Put simply, an inquiry approach to learning demands that you develop your learning of a topic or issue by being able to **ask the right questions to seek an answer** which may not be perfect but is the "best" answer given the available evidence. This contrasts with the more traditional or what the author calls the "impatient approach" which is where the student responds without due consideration of the appropriate context; or, at worst, the student relies solely on the teacher to give a "model" answer, which of course in business rarely exists.

The temptation to provide "model" answers in the following discussion points is resisted. In part this is because of the author's and the IBO's intention that this guide is perceived as a learning guide or toolkit and not positioned as a revision crammer.

Moreover, an inquiry approach to your study of business or even life will be required long after you will have finished your IB Diploma or tertiary study. It is also to fulfil the author's commitment to an old proverb, which has underpinned much of his teaching practice in this subject and the IB mission – the need for students to become life-long learners:

Give a man a fish and he can eat for a day,
Teach a man to fish and he can eat for a lifetime.

The need for an inquiry approach

The intention behind an inquiry approach is to build the capacity for students to apply their knowledge and understanding of the subject across a range of different business contexts. Being able to ask probing questions in response to a business situation or issue is a key skill in developing understanding of an appropriate solution to the issue. Considered balanced solutions to a business problem inevitably lead to good decisions being made and, of course, in final exams to higher marks.

The author has used the following example with his own business classes to demonstrate how effective asking the right questions can be, rather than shouting out random answers. It is adapted from a question that appeared in a magazine called *The Eagle*, published in 1951.

> A young person walks into a large store and purchases a number of items. The items can be held in a hand easily.
>
> The person buys:
>
> 1 for $1
> 10 for $2
> 100 for $3
>
> What is the person buying?

This question has been asked a number of times and rarely have any students achieved the answer on their first attempt. It should be added that the questioner (teacher) waits for responses and encourages students to **ask questions rather than give speculative answers**. However, without fail, students rarely ask questions.

There is usually the reward of a chocolate bar for the first correct answer and in their "excitement" to gain the reward, students give the following brief answers:

- small items such beads or nails (anything that could be held in the hand)
- small items of food such as rice or pasta.

After 10 minutes of answers the classroom will go quiet. It is likely that not one single student will have asked a question.

Then one brave soul might ask: What can I buy for $4?

The answer from the teacher could be 1 000 or 2 000 or 2 004.

At this point some students are trying to see a pattern between 1, 10, 100 and 1 000 (if this is the answer given) and may offer some answers similar to beads, nails or other small items.

The **key is to ask another question** such as: What can I buy for $5?

It would be even better to ask: What does it cost to buy 2 or 20?

The answer to the first question could be 10 000 or 20 000 but the answer to the second question is $1 for 2 and $2 for 20.

Armed with this information, students may now start to ask **good probing questions** such as: What does it cost to buy 99? Soon they may have an appropriate answer.

> The person is buying numbers, such as door numbers.

An inquiry approach by asking deeper and/or probing questions based on the right context can be a very successful way to unlock further understanding. Your study of TOK, for example, will be successful if you adopt an inquiry approach rather than just waiting for someone close to you to come up with an answer to a question raised in class.

Note

Not all of the inquiry activities have been included in this section and the following ideas should be treated as suggestions only. It is worth repeating that there are no model answers in business management and these suggestions could easily be challenged – which is why they are included.

1 Business organization and environment

1.1 Introduction to business management

IB Learner Profile

Inquirers and managing risk (page 11) ?

This activity is included for students to discuss the need for entrepreneurs to manage risk. Bill Gates, who at the time of writing is the richest business man in the world, has famously stated that his greatest lesson in business was learned when he took a risk and failed. Of course, it is anticipated that learning from failure will occur so that the same mistakes are not repeated but of course in business there are no guarantees.

Steve Jobs, Sir Richard Branson and many other successful global entrepreneurs have made business "mistakes" but obviously have been able to "bounce back". In addition to saying that entrepreneurs must calculate and manage risk, we should add that they must show resilience and determination.

1.2 Types of organization
IB Learner Profile
Thinkers and knowledgeable (page 14)

The "free-rider" problem is not on the IB Business Management syllabus but it has some excellent application to the idea that public sector organizations should produce goods and services for free in contrast to the private sector. Goods such as streetlights and signs, and services such as those provided by police officers, are very difficult to consume without other unrelated stakeholders receiving the benefits for free. They are also very difficult goods and services to price accurately.

It is assumed that through taxation collected from citizens, governments should be able to finance these goods and services in such a manner so that they are provided at no charge at the point of use. The private sector would be unable (or more likely unwilling) to do so.

Flipped learning activity (page 16)

The YouTube clip clearly spells out some of the advantages of the public-private partnership when applied to large infrastructure projects. The public-private partnership combines the government's ability to set the rules and framework of the agreement and the initial financing, with the private sector's expertise in managing large projects and attracting additional capital to ensure the project is completed on time and within budget. The analogy of a public-private partnership being like a football match is a clever and insightful one. The challenge is to find out and discuss how a public-private partnership could look in your country of study.

1.3 Organizational objectives
The Lego context (page 18)

In the exam practice question section (page 145), there is a question on brand loyalty which you could use to test some of your knowledge from this case study. The question is from May 2011 HL paper 2 and it is out of date given our recent understanding but remember that for the new HL and SL exams in 2016 you will have to be able to apply your knowledge of business content and concepts to a real-life business context in section C of paper 2. It is likely that given the enormous success of the first Lego movie – the sequel will be released on 26 May 2017 according to Wikipedia – the Lego brand and company will remain very much in the public consciousness for some time to come. Whichever real-life business you choose when answering section C, it is clearly important to choose a context which engages you and is easy to update.

1.6 Growth and evolution
IB Learner Profile
Inquiry (page 28) ❓

Either through the website or by directly contacting the organization, you should be able to find out a great deal of information about the franchising agreements of large multinational organizations in your country. Many organizations will send out "franchise packages" to prospective investors, which will include some very valuable insight into the terms and conditions of the agreement. A great idea could be to invite two franchisors into your school, such as Subway and McDonald's, to compare and contrast the different franchise models.

2 HR management
2.1 Functions and evolution of HR management
IB Learner Profile
Risk-taking (page 35) ⚠️

The notes below relate to the two interview questions asked of candidates applying to Google.

Question 1: The numbers 10, 9, 60, 90, 70, 66 follow a possible pattern based on the number of letters they have when written as words: three letters for ("ten") then four letters ("nine") and so on until eight letters ("sixty-six"), so the next number should have nine letters. There are ten letters in 100 so the next number in the sequence could be 96, which has nine letters. This is just one possible answer.

An alternative could be "one google" or "ten google", both with nine letters. Both are acceptable. Notice the use of the term "acceptable" rather than correct.

Question 2: Vince Vaughan gives an answer to this interview question from the movie but it is not the answer Google liked. The company's preferred answer is:

Jump out!

The key to this question is that your density is the same if you are shrunk. Most humans can jump the height of a blender and you would be able to do so, even if you were shrunk to the size of a penny or boosted to the size of a skyscraper. In all three scenarios, the height jumped would be the same.

2.2 Organizational structure
IB Learner Profile
Balanced (page 41) ⚖️

The Sports Direct case study highlights some of the issues facing both employers and employees in the new 24/7 economy. These include increasing online competition and changes in consumer behaviour due to new and improved technology such as mobile commerce (m-commerce). This activity also has links to the topics of workplace patterns and flexible working covered in unit 2.1.

The argument from the employer would seem to be that if consumer behaviour is being influenced by the "new economy" then organizations need to structure themselves differently to take advantage of opportunities. A zero-hours contract for part-time workers is one such response. To quote from the case study:

The contracts, handed to 90% of the company's 23 000 employees, leave staff not knowing how many hours they will work from one week to the next, with no sick pay or holiday pay, and no guarantee of regular work.

One is tempted to ask whether this is an inevitable process. Will all work in the retail industry become part-time? Are there short-term cost advantages to a firm but longer-term disadvantages such as additional recruitment and retraining costs? Are we entering a new "paradigm" of what is considered the working week?

There are undeniable links to motivation theory which are discussed below.

IB Learner Profile
Balanced and reflective (page 42) ⚖️ ЯⱤ

From the author's and teachers' perspective it would be hard to argue with the sentiment expressed by Einstein in "The day that Albert Einstein feared has arrived!" (which can be found online). The IB learner profile demands that students be reflective learners and the questions on page 42 which form the basis for the discussion illustrate one view that even with all the available technology, communication challenges remain across all cultures.

Here are some interesting TOK questions applied to business management, which arise from further consideration:

- How culturally significant is the idea that technology has become or is becoming a substitute for real human intervention?

- Are some cultures more likely to use technological communication rather than communicating face to face?

- What are the implications given the rapid changes in technology for business operations across a range of international global markets?

2.4 Motivation
IB Learner Profile
Open-minded and principled (page 47)

In the Sports Direct case study in unit 2.2 (page 41) the issue of the introduction of zero-hour contracts was discussed. The case study extends on page 47 to include the bonus scheme, which is paid to full-time employees but not those on a zero-hour contract. While a restructuring of an organization due to changes in the external environment could be justified – "unless the organization changes all jobs could be under threat" – it would seem more challenging to pay a bonus to some employees but not all, especially if the payments are financed through **overall** company profits.

Another example is found in the financial sector. The issue of bonus payments to senior bank officials has been raised a number of times since the global financial crisis. Financial institutions who were "bailed out" by national governments under the threat of bankruptcy are now using taxpayers' money to reward managers for "improved performance".

It is interesting to note from the extended case study that other retail organizations such as John Lewis adopt a different philosophy to the remuneration of employees, and also that Sports Direct declined to comment. A theme developed throughout this guide has been transparency and clearly some stakeholders may be influenced in their financial relationships with Sports Direct and John Lewis by the two stands taken.

It would be useful to discuss whether more "up-to-date" motivational theories such as those proposed by Daniel Pink are more appropriate for the retail environment in the 21st century, rather than those proposed by Taylor and Maslow in the 20th century.

2.5 Organizational culture
Questions for reflection (page 51)

The Pixar case study illustrates how difficult it can be to be completely objective about the success of an organization. Even with Pixar's success to date, the critics' reception of the most recent Pixar Film "Brave" was "lukewarm at best" with some writers asking if Pixar was losing its way. This criticism was made despite Pixar's amazing track record of success from movies spanning nearly 20 years.

Pixar's problems were compounded by the fact that the studio's most recent production "The Good Dinosaur" was pushed back to 2015 due to production delays and the sacking of the director. In 2014, there will be no new Pixar movie in theatres. This could damage the company given the success of competitors' movies such as Disney's "Frozen" and the Lego movie, which was produced principally by Warner Brothers.

Students interested in seeing the Pixar process and culture at work are advised to view any number of the Pixar movies on DVD and search for the extra features on how the films were produced. "The Incredibles" is a particularly good starting point.

The Pixar culture should not be regarded as Utopian. Clearly, though, it seems to be appropriate for this organization and its objectives.

3 Finance and accounting; 4 Marketing
3.3 Break-even analysis and 4.3 Marketing planning
IB Learner Profile

Inquirers (pages 60 and 81)

The David Beckham example in unit 3.3 and the example of "The Lone Ranger" in unit 4.2 illustrate that in business management, organizations can take nothing for granted. There is no guarantee of success even with a significant famous celebrity attached to a football match or movie. Under these circumstances, the break-even calculations should always be treated with a degree of caution.

Businesses should use the break-even point as the start of their investigations into whether a particular course of action is financially desirable. They will have to consider further analysis and non-financial information before making a considered final decision.

Unfortunately for Johnny Depp at the time of writing, his most recent film –"Transcendence" – has been met with a poor critical response and low "box-office take" (a revenue term used for movies). Some writers have even begun to question whether Depp can now be considered a "star" given the poor performance of this most recent film as well as that of "The Lone Ranger". This would seem unduly harsh given that Depp has up until now had a very successful movie career spanning nearly 25 years. As it has been said elsewhere in this guide, the movie industry is a tough and unforgiving one.

www.boxofficemojo.com and www.imdb.com are two excellent sources of information for those looking to develop their understanding of the movie industry, including topics such as marketing and sales forecasting.

3.4 Final accounts and 3.6 Efficiency analysis
IB Learner Profile

Inquirers and knowledgeable (pages 63 and 68)

Even though 12 years have passed since the Enron financial scandal, this example of mismanagement and unethical behaviour is still shocking. How did Enron's financiers think they were ever going to get away with their deception? Fortunately, there are so many of our business management concepts and content wrapped around the enticing story of greed that the study of Enron makes for fascinating if slightly morbid viewing.

In one respect, though, we must acknowledge that Enron was an innovative organization especially in the creation of new energy markets and services. However, given the need for publicly traded organizations to be transparent in their financial reporting, it is alarming how easily investors were lied to and how other financial institutions disavowed any knowledge of wrong-doing and were accomplices in the deception – as long as the profits kept tumbling in.

The case of Enron is not the only corporate scandal but, given the scale and size of the fraud and the characters involved, it may be one of the most compelling corporate cover-ups.

However, along with all the scandal and intrigue, Bethany Mclean – one of the authors of the book from which the film is derived – shows us that the Enron catastrophe had enormous impact on people. As a student of business management and with respect to accounting and finance in particular, you should try never to lose sight of the stories behind the numbers. These stories have an impact on a range of human stakeholders. Accounting profits may be made but at what cost?

4 Marketing
Setting the scene

The advice given here is that students of marketing should be critical. All students are stakeholders in the marketing process and, consequently, should have a view or position to take when discussing marketing strategies. The inquiry activity on page 77 is just one way to build an inquiry approach to the understanding of marketing from the student's perspective.

Throughout this unit there is extensive reference to the work of marketing commentator Jack Trout. Trout's work is just one voice. There are many others and students are encouraged to find their own sources of information.

What is compelling about Trout's writing is that he has worked for a large number of US companies as a marketing consultant over a 30-year period. His thinking on marketing strategy for organizations is clear and unambiguous, "differentiate or die".

The problem for organizations is that the market-place is becoming increasingly crowded. Competition can come from a number of different sources. These include regional, national and global sources.

The Internet and social media have both changed the marketing landscape forever, as every stakeholder can use them to register a view or an opinion. As Gary Hamel states: "Knowledge advantages can quickly dissipate" (disappear). Competitors will know what a business is doing and that business will know what its competitors are doing in a time frame which would have been unthinkable before the era of the Internet.

Second, given our discussion of Einstein's thinking around the ever-present technology and our reaction to it, how easy is it for an organization to get its marketing message across? During the course of a typical day, as a student you may be "bombarded" with over 1 000 marketing messages through your smartphone, your tablet and your computer – not including your TV.

How can a new business with a new product ever hope to match the marketing power of established global brands?

Marketing is much more challenging than many students think.

4.1 The role of marketing

The illusion of choice figure (which can be found on the following web page: http://elitedaily.com/news/world/illusion-choice-10-companies-responsible-virtually-every-product-market/) should make sober reading for those who are in favour of the role and influence of trans-national corporations. Given the ubiquity and presence of these corporations' brands across a range of global markets, how can local or even national brands compete?

4.2 Marketing planning

By the time this study guide is published, the new iPhone will be upon us. It will be interesting to see how the device is received. Rumours are already circulating that Apple will release two new versions. The existence of Moore's Law will ensure that the new iPhone will be "able to do more". However, will the new device be any cheaper given the experience of the iPhone 5c (see page 83)?

Students who are interested can research what happened to the Porsche Company – famous for its luxury sports cars such as the 944 – when it released a cheaper version of this iconic product. The author is confident that you can make an educated guess at the consequences for Porsche based on the experiences of Apple.

IB Learner Profile

Inquiry (page 84) ❓

The implications of excessive segmentation should not be hard to ascertain. If we take, for example, jazz music we discover over 19 different categories of jazz such as abstract, fusion, smooth, traditional. Marketing each segment will require a different marketing mix. Unless this is clearly articulated, customers will become confused.

For example, take an album by jazz superstar Michael Bublé:

- Is it traditional?
- If so, what is the target market?
- What much will this target market be prepared to pay?
- How will the album be promoted?
- What if some consumers view this new album as pop or pop jazz?

4.4 Market research

IB Learner Profile

Reflection (page 92) Я|R

Most if not all students will probably have covered in their mathematics or statistics courses the reasons behind the selection of an appropriate method of presentation for a particular set of data. These methods include the use of bar charts or graphs, line graphs, pie charts, histograms and pictograms.

Suggestions to answers in the inquiry exercise are given from question (e) onwards as they have a much stronger link to business management than the other questions.

(e) (i) Sales figures for an organization are usually represented by line graphs. In common with other **time series data** where a variable such as sales or sales forecasts are measured over time, a line graph can easily shown trends either upward (rising) or downward (falling). Careful consideration must be given to the scale used for the sales data on the graph. If an inappropriate scale is used the line graph may appear too flat (its scale is too wide) or too steep (its scale is too narrow). The latter presentation may give a more dramatic look to the data and could easily lead to misinterpretations by the user of the information. Statisticians sometimes refer to this distortion effect by inappropriate scaling of the axes as the "gee-whiz effect".

A good presentation with some clear ideas about how statistics may not reveal the whole truth is given at:

http://www.mshuynh.com/statistics/notes/ch5.pdf

(ii) If the intention is to highlight the fact that the number of industrial accidents is too high, then a pictogram with an image of an injured person may be more emotive and effective in communicating the message.

(iii) The male/female ratio could be represented with a pie chart, bar graph or pictogram.

(iv) The number of different nationalities in your IB World School may be over 50. A pie chart would be too confusing given that there would be over 50 segments and the need for a good deal of labelling. Consider using a simple table instead.

(v) The income levels of 10 different occupations would best be presented by a series of bar graphs or charts with an appropriate scale. The height of each bar would clearly show the differences between the occupations, although of course some clever logarithmic scaling would be required if the intention is to compare the income of a UK Premier League soccer player with that of, say, an IB Business Management teacher.

(f) This inquiry into "who is doing the best" has been used by the author in his own business classes to try and ascertain the degree to which students can analyse data, draw conclusions and make judgments based only on the information present. It looks deceptively straightforward on paper and in keeping with the inquiry example given on page 129, students who have attempted this have generally blurted out answers based purely on the size of the numbers present without really engaging in deep thinking.

A great start to this exercise is to challenge the question. What does the question mean by "doing the best"? Or, perhaps more perceptively, what could "doing the best" actually mean?

It is possible using alternative criteria, given the data, that each department, is doing the best:

- **In absolute terms** the jazz department has the biggest overall increase in sales. This means the biggest increase in sales – from 1.2 to 2.0 = 0.8 million.
- **In relative terms**, the alternative department has achieved the biggest percentage increase in sales – from 0.2 to 0.8 = 300% increase.
- **In terms of contribution to overall sales**, however, rock still contributes the biggest share (2/3.4) and (2.1/4.9) to total sales.

Hence by using alternative criteria, absolute change, relative change and contribution to overall sales, each department manager could claim that his or her department is "doing the best". We can combine this knowledge with the approach taken in the inquiry exercise relating to who is the greatest sportsperson of all time (see unit 3.5, page 67).

It is difficult to make outright objective judgments as to who is the greatest sportsperson ever. If we extend this to organizations, how we can decide which is the best organization in the world? It is worth noting that Enron rather optimistically tried to proclaim this.

Even on a more personal level, how would any individual know if he or she were "doing the best"? Are you?

Note

Note that in Table 4.5.5 (page 100), there is a reference to price elasticity of demand in the section on price discrimination (market-based). Price elasticity of demand has been removed from the IB Business Management syllabus for the exam in 2016. However, it is a vital term for students to understand if they are to be able to grasp the motivation behind an organization's decision to separate a market into different parts to take advantage of price discrimination.

Price elasticity of demand measures how responsive the demand of a product is (that is, how willing and able consumers are to purchase a product) to a change in price. Highly responsive demand is termed "elastic" and not very responsive is termed "inelastic".

Briefly, an organization practising price discrimination which can successfully separate a market or groups of customers into price elastic and inelastic categories will enjoy higher revenues. It will offer a lower price (than market expectations) to elastic consumers and use the reverse pricing method for price inelastic customers.

4.6 The extended marketing mix of seven Ps
Questions for reflection (page 104)

Granada Books is only one of a number of book stores that are trying to fight back against the online giant Amazon by offering a more personal direct service incorporating the additional three Ps of people, process and physical evidence. The article states that the American Booksellers Association reported a 7% increase in the growth of independent bookstores for the year to 2012.

Providing coffee, armchairs, free wi-fi, and enabling people to spend time with friends and staff discussing books are all ways of building a community focus around physical evidence and people in the marketing mix.

Interestingly, a global chain of bookstores – Borders – tried a similar approach by forming joint ventures with Starbucks and Gloria Jeans coffee outlets. It wanted to increase customer satisfaction and create a sense of community by offering coffee, armchairs and free wi-fi. Unfortunately, Borders' recent financial difficulties and closures internationally reveal that this joint venture may have failed.

An interesting question is raised: why did a large book retailer such as Borders fail yet a smaller more locally driven book business (Granada Books) continues to thrive?

Introduction

This unit is designed to provide some additional advice and guidance on some of the new external and internal assessment challenges faced by students when completing the IB Business Management course. Some of the ideas here will be obvious and each IB World School will have its own approach to preparing students. However, the author has a number of years experience as an examiner in paper 2 HL and as a moderator and examiner in internal HL assessments and extended essays in business management.

The guidance covered in this section focuses on:

- the pre-issued case study to assess material for paper 1 for HL and SL
- the new section C for HL paper 1
- the IB Business Management course extended essay approaches to the HL internal assessment and the SL written commentary

We shall consider each in turn.

The pre-issued case study (paper 1)

Introduced in 2002, the pre-issued case study as an assessment tool was a significant step forward for the IB Business Management course. It has allowed students to prepare material before the exam. In addition, importantly, it has allowed ESOL students a great opportunity to save time in the final exam and focus on displaying their knowledge of business management.

Preparing for the pre-issued case study

Since 2002, it is assumed that IB Diploma centres will have developed their own way to help students prepare for the final pre-issued case study. The analysis below is offered as a guide to help you navigate through the material and should not be considered exhaustive.

One very positive development is that changes in technology, especially the availability of new Web 2.0 tools, have allowed schools and students to connect with each other and share ideas. If these ideas could be shared across different cultures, then students' knowledge base and cultural understanding could increase dramatically. Students could apply this increased knowledge and understanding to the problems and issues presented in the case study, in order to find solutions. Consider asking your teacher to find out whether you could connect with students from different IB World Schools to do this.

The pre-issued case study provides an excellent opportunity for students to exercise their IB learner profile muscles. Not only is this a great learning opportunity, but those students moving onto further education after completing the IB Business Management course will find that the approaches used in the IB learner profile will prepare them for the challenges of studying for a higher degree.

IB Learner Profile

Here are suggestions with some aspects of the IB learner profile attached.

Inquiry ?

When you read the case study, you will identify and investigate a number of issues or problems arising from it. Ideas could be then shared with a fellow student (perhaps from another IB World School, as mentioned above).

By adopting an inquiring approach and asking questions rather than just seeking the first answers, it is likely that your understanding of the case study material will deepen as the following two examples illustrate.

Knowledgeable

You are encouraged to develop understanding of how the six concepts could be applied to the case study, for example asking questions such as these:

- How could the onset of **globalization** have an impact on this business and its decision-making processes?
- What are the key factors driving **change** either inside or outside the organization?
- What are the important **ethical considerations** concerning this case study? Can they be resolved?

Balanced ⚖

Examination of the key stakeholders in the case study will lead to questions such as these:

- What are the broad areas of agreement and conflict?
- Can we understand why this conflict exists?

By creating a palate or range of skills to be used, you prepare yourself for any particular concept, content or even context question that the examiner may choose to ask. This flexibility, shown in the ability to adapt your knowledge to the demands of the case study, often scores very highly.

Care over use of pre-prepared packages

A trend that has developed over the last few years is the production of pre-prepared case study packages. Commercial organizations and individuals have prepared "ready-made" packs with attractive sounding promises such as "100 possible questions for the IB Business Management HL and SL case study paper with 100 possible answers". It should be obvious why these packs are popular with students and teachers alike.

However, apart from running against the philosophy of the IB learner profile, using pre-prepared packs leads to students coming into the exam room with "rote" or prepared answers. Feedback from senior examiners indicates that this "one size fits all" approach rarely allows students to achieve the top marks in exams.

Note that students preparing material for section C paper 2, for both HL and SL, where they have to apply their knowledge of business concepts and content to a real-life organization, **cannot use** the pre-issued case study in paper 1.

Additional guidance for the pre-issued case study

The following could act as a checklist of ideas to help you recognize, dissect, analyse and ultimately evaluate key issues emanating from the pre-issued HL or SL case study:

- Identify the current position of status of the firm. A great starting point is to draw up a SWOT analysis from the information given in the case.
- Sketch out the main characters in the case study. Who are they? What are their roles? If there are leaders, what are their qualities or styles? (Some schools assign students to act out the mannerisms and qualities of the key players. This is a great idea if there is time.)
- Identify and define the key business terms in the case study. Make sure you have exact definitions and explanations that have direct relevance to the case study. This is known in examiner jargon as context. (Your answers to questions must be in context: they must refer to the organization in the case study and not just any other similar organization.)
- Identify a mission or vision if one is not given. What are the organization's main aims and objectives?
- Identify which market the organization is currently operating in. Is it a niche or a mass market? Who are the key current and potential competitors?

- Linked to this point, try to determine who the key internal and external stakeholders are.
- Consider the external environment. A good idea might be to undertake a PEST or STEEPLE analysis from the stimulus material.
- Identify any areas of concern in the organization that immediately present themselves. You may wish to consider motivation, communication, leadership and management issues.
- Note the organization's current financial position. Are there any immediate liquidity and profitability concerns?

HL paper 1 section C

New extended response question (HL only)

From 2016, the section C questions for the HL paper 1 will change. (SL students do not have a section C in their paper 1.) Previously for the section C question, HL students were given new additional stimulus material on the day of the exam – having also prepared material from the pre-issued case study – and asked to define, explain, analyse and then evaluate a new strategic decision facing the organization. The question was normally broken down into four parts.

For the new exam, additional stimulus will be given but there will only be **one** compulsory extended response question in this section and it will not be broken down into parts. Students will be expected to structure their answer and provide a response that has an introduction, a body of analysis and a conclusion. The structure of the response will be awarded up to 4 marks.

Within the extended response the examiner seeks the following evidence to award marks:

- knowledge and understanding of business management theories, tools and techniques (up to 4 marks)
- application of these tools to the case study that is relevant (up to 4 marks)
- reasoned arguments – which means that analysis is balanced with different arguments considered, with their strengths and weaknesses noted as well as the implications for the question (up to 4 marks)
- a recognition that consideration is given to at least two different points of view or perspectives arising from the question (final 4 marks).

Each extended response is therefore worth a maximum of 20 marks.

With this question being compulsory and with the relevant AO being AO3, students preparing to answer this question will have to ensure that they look at the *IB Business Management Guide* and make a note of which business theories, tools and techniques are assessed at AO3. These are possible topic areas for section C HL paper 1.

For example, financial rewards in unit 2.4 are assessed at AO2, while motivation theories in the same unit are assessed in AO3. Hence a possible question could be:

- Using a motivational theory of your choice, discuss how company B could improve motivation and teamwork given the new merger (where company B is the organization that features in the pre-issued case study and additional material).

HL/SL paper 2

Paper 2 HL and SL section C requires the application of and evaluation of business concepts to a real-life organization of the student's own choosing. This will be covered in greater detail in a future assessment guidance unit. The organization chosen cannot be the same one which has been analysed in the pre-seen case study for paper 1. This applies to both HL and SL.

The extended essay

From the author's experience, IB Business Management extended essays are popular with students for a number of reasons:

- An extended essay in the IB Business Management course allows students to pursue and develop knowledge of and insight into a topic, such as HR management or marketing, which has engaged them.
- Anecdotal evidence from a number of students who have applied to tertiary institutions in the United States, Australia, New Zealand and Europe suggests that university admissions tutors regard the preparation of an extended essay in business as a valuable higher-order learning skill which will allow students to flourish on a degree or equivalent course.
- We also now have a very positive reason to take an extended essay in IB Business Management as explained in the material on preparing for section C paper 2. The extended essay research process can easily provide an excellent way to apply business content and concepts to a real-life organization. This effectively allows students – given the nature of the research and the research question – an opportunity to achieve economies of scale in learning and diploma completion.
- If a student is a stakeholder in an organization such as a family-run business, the extended essay can provide an opportunity to examine a current or future issue objectively with the possibility of suggesting feasible solutions. (This is also true for the IB Business Management internal assessment, which we will come to later.)

The distinction between the extended essay and internal assessment

New assessment (or marking) criteria for the extended essay that came into operation in 2009 make a much clearer distinction than previously between the extended essay and the HL internal assessment.

With its "positioning" firmly established, the extended essay has taken a major step forward to be regarded as an opportunity to practise and develop tertiary academic research skills because of the importance of collecting predominantly secondary data sources. The internal assessment for HL requires much greater use of primary data (with some secondary, of course).

A common pitfall relating to the extended essay
Failing to narrow the research focus

One of the most common problems that consistently emanates from the annual examiner reports on extended essay performance in IB Business Management is that, given the 4 000-word limit, students try to cover too broad an area of a particular topic.

To illustrate this point, here is an extended essay title that is too broad for effective treatment:

- An evaluation into company X's new marketing strategy designed to launch a new product into a new international market-place.

This type of essay, focusing on evaluating a new marketing strategy for a new product into a new market, appears quite often. It is the author's view that the submission of an extended essay based on marketing strategy needs to be handled carefully. Close scrutiny of the research topic needs to be carried out before the student begins.

More appropriately focused research questions would be:

- Should company X release product Y into country Z?
- Given the changing economic environment, to what extent should company X attempt to change its marketing mix for product Y?

These questions may not be perfect titles: both require further fine-tuning and negotiation between the student and supervisor. However, completing each is more realistic within the word limit, as these questions are significantly narrower in focus than the first example.

Here are some questions for students and supervisors to consider:

1 Should company Z remove product X from its current portfolio?

2 Will company Y be able to survive the significant downturn in economic activity in its host country?

3 Will the release of product Z save company Y from insolvency?

4 To what extent should company X attempt to reposition product Z to increase market share?

Justification

All of the above research questions (essay titles) have been written to convey how narrow a good research question for the extended essay should be. They leave little room for doubt as to the scope of the investigation and may provide a clue into the possible theoretical framework that will be employed:

- In title 1, product portfolio analysis and contribution may be important theoretical concepts.

- In title 2, the external environment is clearly going to be an important theoretical framework on which to build an argument around whether company Y will survive.

- In title 3, cash flow, liquidity and marketing may be important theoretical topics.

You are invited to discuss the merits (and demerits) of title 4.

Other pitfalls relating to the extended essay
Challenging business paradigms

In their extended essay students sometimes try to "reinvent the wheel". In other words, the extended essay attempts to answer a knowledge question that might be more appropriate for a TOK environment.

Here are some examples for discussion:

- Is all marketing unethical?

- Given the growth of e-commerce, is the seven Ps marketing mix now redundant?

- Is there an accurate way for a firm to calculate probabilities on a decision tree to make the expected monetary values more useful for decision-making?

These attempts are very laudable but, without wishing to dampen students' enthusiasm, these topics are too vast for effective treatment within the extended essay's word limit. They may lend themselves more appropriately to a class TOK discussion, especially the first question on marketing and ethics.

Focusing on subject-specific criteria, neglecting general criteria

The extended essay is marked according to a set of prescribed criteria. Students need to be issued with both the subject-specific criteria and the general criteria early in the process of selecting possible topics for investigation.

A crucial part of the relationship between the supervisor and the student in determining success is to make sure that they carefully check that the essay satisfies the general criteria as well as the subject-specific criteria. This check should be made when you submit the penultimate draft of your extended essay.

Impact on final marks

In the race to finish, attention to detail can sometimes be overlooked and important marks lost. This is frustrating for the student, the supervisor and the final assessor. The marking process for the extended essay gives greater weight to the general

criteria than the subject-specific criteria. You can avoid needlessly losing marks by asking yourself the following questions in the final draft stage:

- Is the research question clearly stated in the introduction?

- Is the reason for the extended essay clearly stated and why the topic is worthy of consideration?

- Are the arguments presented reasoned and balanced? (That is, do they attempt to show both sides?)

- Has sufficient analysis has been carried out, including the use of numerical data?

- Have sources been referenced according to the IB guidelines?

- Has the abstract been included and does it conform to the expectations of the marking criteria?

In common with the word limit, these aspects of the extended essay are within the control of the student and are not related to business content *per se*. Students must observe the general criteria first before considering the subject-specific criteria.

What makes a great business extended essay? The answer is: an essay that could be picked up by a non-specialist business stakeholder with limited knowledge of the subject and be readily understood; an essay that is presented following accepted research practices.

Internal assessment
HL internal assessment

From the author's experience as a senior examiner and moderator, the HL internal assessment (also referred to as the business report) provides many students with a challenging but very rewarding experience.

Over the last 12 years the author has moderated a number of superb, professional-looking business reports which would have been of significant practical value to the senior managers of an organization. Each of these reports could have been used as a forward-looking document to aid decision-making.

There are clear guidelines about the assessment criteria for the HL internal assessment in the *IB Business Management Guide* and online advice and guidance is available in the senior examiner reports which are published after each exam session in May and November. Despite this, a significant number of students are not producing business reports that satisfy the assessment criteria.

One consistent area of weakness in this latter group is that an increasing number of projects do not include financial information or costs of any kind. This point is important for two reasons:

- First, without cost information incorporated into the analysis, the scope for discussion and evaluation is limited and therefore the number of marks available is limited too.

- Second, the report must have practical value to management. Without a single cost or sales forecast included, for example, senior managers could not seriously consider changes to a marketing mix.

Suggestions for improvement
Access to data and confidentiality issues

A number of candidates continue to ignore the following advice from the IB online support materials.

Students must ensure that the organizations selected for the project are willing and able to provide the necessary data. It is not uncommon for organizations to fail to provide this. This will seriously undermine the quality of the final written report. If students have not gathered sufficient material, they may have to give up the project and start another.

Each year, HL students have claimed in their research proposals and conclusions that a potential difficulty or limitation of the report has been either the presence of confidentiality issues or simply that the owner of the business was unwilling or unable to submit the relevant primary data. These projects are unlikely to score highly. Students and their supervisors need to decide early on in the investigation whether data collection is going to be a significant issue, and find a different project if necessary.

Primary data collection: interviews and questionnaires

Primary data should be collected from a large enough sample, or enough sources, to be seen as useful in making a reasoned judgment about a course of action. It is unlikely that any business would undertake a significant strategic or tactical change based either on the opinions of 20 or even 50 customers from a single questionnaire (even if the responses were 100% accurate and complete) or from one interview conducted with the senior management team or CEO.

Showing critical thinking in the HL internal assessment

Students are generally successful in defining concepts such as primary and secondary data. However, issues surrounding the analysis and evaluation of market research methods are not well understood and this can translate into low marks in the final report.

A common issue for the HL internal assessment is not drawing on enough data during the research process. In the internal assessment assignments for both levels, students tend to assume that using a single questionnaire or a single article from a journal or the Internet provides sufficient depth when being asked to research an issue. Neither method constitutes thorough research, with the result that students will not gain access the top mark bands for data collection and analysis. Despite this, a number of reports submitted in recent examination sessions have placed their entire justification for a particular course of action on the responses to a single questionnaire given by 25 individuals or fewer.

Rarely has a questionnaire itself been evaluated. This is one way in which a **student can demonstrate critical thinking**. Choose a sample of, say, five students and ask them to complete the questionnaire and also to critique it. Here are some suggestions for the critique:

- Were some of the questions included not clear or difficult to interpret? If so, which ones?

- Did some of the questions allow you to give a clear response? Which questions were they?

- How would you improve this questionnaire? Would you reduce or increase the number of questions?

Having taken into consideration the responses of this small sample, a revised questionnaire is designed and this time the sample size is increased to over 30 respondents. This evaluation of the questionnaire is **just one possible method** of showing critical thinking in an internal assessment but it is rarely carried out.

Before you begin a project you must ask yourself this important question:

- Will I be able to collect significant primary data to allow me to make reasoned judgments on the suitability of a particular course of action?

Length and marking criteria

In 2016, the word limit of 2 000 words for the final report remains. The research proposal will be 500 words maximum. Teachers and moderators have been advised that after 2 000 words for the project and 500 words for the research proposal, any excess will not be marked.

Students are advised to check carefully the marking criteria at the end of the assignment. This is available in the *IB Business Management Guid*e. A key difference in this new syllabus is

that the marking criteria have been extended to include nine different criteria:

- Research proposal
- Sources and data
- Use of tools, techniques and theories
- Analysis and evaluation
- Conclusions
- Recommendations
- Structure
- Presentation
- Reflective (or critical) thinking.

The suitability of family businesses

There are a number of compelling arguments why students may wish to undertake an investigation of their family firm for the business report. They include but are not limited to:

- perceived speed and readily available access to primary data

- prior knowledge of the workings of the organization through connections.

However, as a basis for internal assessment projects the choice of a family business can suffer from one vital flaw. The decision in the business report needs to be one that has not yet been previously considered or undertaken, i.e. the project needs to be forward-looking, not reflect backwards on something that has already happened. It is the objective of the business report to try and ascertain through good analysis and evaluation that a business should either accept or reject a particular future course of action. A number of recent reports submitted which featured a family business gave the impression that the student was already aware of the final decision and was in a sense working backwards from the conclusion to the introduction to justify this. This type of project is effectively a descriptive essay and will score lower than expected marks.

If two students have two separate family businesses that they wish to use as models for their business report, it may be useful to ask them to swap businesses for the duration of the project. This will help to increase objectivity.

Appropriate research questions for the HL internal assessment

Here are some examples of appropriate research questions:

1 Should company X purchase a new combined fax, printer and scanner?

2 Should company X lease or purchase laptop computers for its senior managers?

3 Should company X advertise its products on the outside of buses?

These questions share common factors – they **are narrow in focus and are proposing tactical changes** to an organization's operations that lend themselves to effective treatment within the word limit. Another important justification is that these research questions will require students to include numerical data in their project:

- In question 1, the student will have to look at the purchase cost and the depreciation on a new fax machine and estimate future cost savings.

- In question 2, the student will have to compare leasing costs and purchase costs of laptop computers directly and will have to consider depreciation.

- In question 3, to see whether advertising on buses is cost-effective and would achieve sufficient audience reach, alternative methods of promotion will have to be considered, with their costs presented.

SL internal assessment

From May 2009 the internal assessment for the IB Business Management course for SL students takes the form of a written commentary. The intention is that **students will use mostly secondary data sources** (some primary data is, of course, allowed) to analyse and discuss a real issue or problem facing an organization.

The title of the SL internal assessment must be phrased as a question. Three to five supporting documents must be given as evidence and students must highlight sections of the documents that have been used as research material in their commentary. A range of different points of view is encouraged. For example, the *IB Business Management Guide* notes that:

the selection of three to five documents published by a single company, or three to five surveys of similar populations, would not provide balance or objectivity.

The documents must be as recent as possible and published not more than three years earlier than the submission of the commentary. For example, for students submitting written commentaries for the examination in November 2016, the documents presented must be dated no earlier than November 2013.

One of the supporting materials submitted may be a video or podcast but this must be transcribed. Clear referencing should be given so that the source material can be easily traced and verified by the teacher.

Marking criteria

The marking criteria for the SL written commentary have changed to include seven different aspects. The commentary will be assessed against:

- Supporting documents
- Choice and application of business tools, techniques and theories
- Choice and analysis of data and integration and theories
- Conclusions
- Evaluation
- Structure
- Presentation.

Possible topics

It is important that the aim of the commentary is written in the form of a question. Here are some examples:

- Should company X develop change its promotional mix to enter market Y?
- Should company A outsource its customer service function to country B?

Further details of each element of the marking criteria can be found in the *IB Business Management Guide*.

IB BUSINESS MANAGEMENT PRACTICE QUESTIONS WITH SUGGESTED ANSWERS

HL/SL paper 2 sections A and B

Setting the scene

Any study guide that aims to prepare students for both the teaching and learning of a new subject will inevitably include past exam questions with example answers to guide revision and give students an insight into the final exam process. With this guide being prepared in May 2014 and the first exams in this new IB Business Management course not due until May 2016, you should be aware that guidance on past paper questions will be tentative. The approach taken in this section has been to adapt previous section B questions from past exams to illustrate what these questions could look like.

The assessment for paper 1 for both HL and SL, as we saw in unit 6, is based on a fictitious case study that changes every year and is issued to schools six months before the final exam. Each IB World School will have its own approach to prepare students for this paper. In unit 6 we also considered section C of paper 1 (an HL requirement only). This is an extended response where students have to apply their business knowledge to a compulsory question.

The suggested answers in the following pages **should not be treated as model or perfect answers.** In business management when students are trying to justify one course of action with another, for example, there is no such thing as a perfect answer. In keeping with the objectives of this guide and the IB learner profile, suggested answers are given for selected questions only. In some cases, hints and tips on how to satisfy the command word through the assessment objective (AO) are given.

Reflections on students' performance from the author's experiences as a marker of HL paper 2 scripts over the last 11 years are included. New teachers to the IB Business Management course may find these comments particularly useful but they represent only one examiner's view.

Particular attention and guidance will be given to command words in the question. Failure to follow command words such as "examine", "analyse" and "evaluate" is one of the most critical reasons why many candidates fail to achieve high marks in final exams despite the fact that their knowledge of theoretical concepts may be sound.

In many cases below, only part of the question is covered in order to allow greater focus on technique rather than knowledge. More detailed answers are given to numerate questions from units 3 and 5 to allow students to gain confidence in tackling these types of question, since – for both HL and SL – a compulsory quantitative question in the exam cannot be avoided.

The material covered in these questions is suitable for both HL and SL students, unless designated HL only.

1 Business organization and environment

1.4 Stakeholders

> With reference to the Walt Disney Company, analyse the potential effects on stakeholder groups of a global conglomerate investing in China. (November 2007)

The important command in this question is "analyse the potential effects on stakeholder groups". "Analyse" is at AO2 level.

Students will need to analyse the potential positive and negative effects of a large global conglomerate investing in China. Specific knowledge of the Walt Disney Company (or Disney) and China is not required in the answer, although information given in the question could be quoted to highlight a potential stakeholder concern. However, this quotation alone would not be considered

as good analysis; additional depth and detail and explanation would be required.

We could identify the following **positive effects** on stakeholders. There will be increased capital and new technology transfers to the host country (China). There will be improved infrastructure, employment opportunities and thus an increase in the standard of living for local Chinese residents. In addition, consumers will gain greater choice in the media markets in which the Disney Company operates such as TV and movies.

However, some stakeholder groups could feel **negative impacts** from an investment by Disney. There will be increased competition for local media businesses. This could lead to redundancies for some workers in those businesses.

Possible government financial incentives given to Disney to encourage it to locate in China may increase local and national tensions if the same assistance is not offered to other Chinese firms. This is particularly pertinent given the bail-out packages being awarded to some but not all firms in many countries.

Given time constraints and mark allocation of possibly 4 marks, students would be expected to come up with a brief 2 + 2 answer. However, a simple list of concerns should be avoided. Analysis requires that there will need to be some development of each point.

> Analyse why BP might find it difficult to satisfy all its stakeholders. (May 2004)

Although this question is over 10 years old, an understanding of the nature of conflict between stakeholders of a business remains central to the study of business management. Put simply, large high-profile organizations such as BP can find it very difficult to reconcile all stakeholder demands and avoid conflict. This is especially true for BP given the critical markets it operates in.

Oil companies have enormous influence in our daily and business lives. There are growing concerns about environmental sustainability and pressure groups are able to exert influence via improved ICT and demand greater transparency. Companies such as BP have to tread a very careful line between these stakeholder concerns.

When answering a question that has the command word "analyse" many students only give one side of the argument. In this example, they might focus on giving the reasons why BP might find it difficult to satisfy all of its stakeholders. For true balance in the analysis, reasons should also be given as to why BP might **not** find it difficult.

> Examine the potential problems that Subway may face as a result of its planned rapid expansion. (May 2006)

1.6 Growth and evolution

Links to contexts, concepts and other business content

Given our discussions in concept 1: Globalization and some of the issues identified in unit 4.7 on international marketing, this question neatly links a context (Subway) to content (business expansion) and, of course, the concept of globalization.

The command word "examine" in the new *IB Business Management Guide* is an AO3. It requires that students provide a number of potential problems and then, for balance, state why these problems may not be an issue. Finally, an **overall judgment is expected for all AO3 questions.**

In order to achieve high marks on AO3 questions, high-scoring exam candidates link other aspects of their learning of business content to the question. As you will see below, the suggested answers include reference to unit 2 (HR management) and unit 3 (finance and accounting).

Suggested answer

The following are examples of potential problems for Subway as a result of its planned rapid expansion.

Liquidity problems can occur where working capital is "squeezed to the limit" in order to sustain rapid rates of growth. This will jeopardize a firm's ability to meet its short-term liabilities.

Coordination of human resources may become too complex as spans of control widen. Managers may not be able to keep up with the pace of change and productivity could start to suffer. Diseconomies of scale will result. Linked to this point are **the problems of maintaining consistent and effective communication across operations** leading to further diseconomies of scale.

However, the planned rapid expansion will provide opportunities for Subway (as we saw in concept 1: Globalization). Subway is currently the largest franchised organization in the world and further expansion would bring considerable opportunities in **global marketing** and **economies of scale (financial and risk bearing)**. The interview with the CEO of Operations in unit 4.7 indicates that Subway would be able **to take advantage of local entrepreneurial spirit** and motivation (especially in potentially very large markets such as India).

Judgment

Even as Subway grows and sales revenues rise inevitably, the impact of the first three points combined is that direct costs could rise and ultimately the increased sales activity may not be translated into increasing profitability. With rapid expansion, it is important to keep a close eye on the key financial ratios (outlined in units 3.5 and 3.6) to detect potential diseconomies of scale. However, it would appear that, given Subway's significant growth to date, it has been able to manage this change successfully.

HL Goal plc is a South American football club. Although the players are highly motivated and united as a team, they have won very few games. Loyal supporters and shareholders are worried about relegation to a lower league and a significant fall in revenue and potential cash flow problems as a result. The management team is considering three possible options to improve the team's performance and attract more spectators.

The expected returns from each option depend on the prevailing economic conditions. These economic conditions and the probability of each occurring are shown in the table below.

	Expected return ($)		
	Improved	**Unchanged**	**Worsened**
	20%	**50%**	**30%**
Option 1. Buy new players from top European teams. Cost $2m	5m	4m	1m
Option 2. Build a new modern stadium on a nearby underdeveloped site. Cost $3m	6m	5m	(-1m)
Option 3. Renovate the stadium and the training facilities. Cost $1m	3m	2m	1m

Construct a fully labelled decision tree. (Show all your working.) (November 2007)

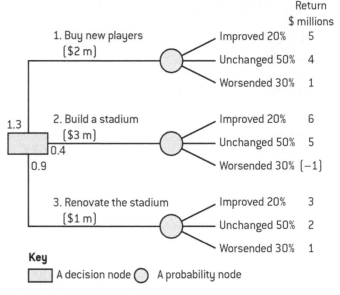

Key

▭ A decision node ◯ A probability node

2 HR management

2.2 Organizational structure

> Explain two advantages and one disadvantage of moving from an existing tall hierarchy to a matrix structure. (May 2008, AO2)

Regularly each year in the senior examiner's report there are comments that students do not answer questions containing "analyse" or "evaluate" in enough detail and depth. The reverse is true for questions asking students to "explain": many students **write too much.**

The question set is worth 6 marks. Assuming that 80 marks were available for the whole paper completed over 2 hours and 15 minutes, a student should take about 10.125 minutes to explain two advantages and one disadvantage, or one point roughly every 3.3 minutes.

Good explanations are not excessively detailed but define terms or concepts clearly. Wherever possible they provide a concise example to illustrate a point being made.

Suggested answer

Moving from an existing tall hierarchy to a matrix structure

Possible advantages: Experts can be brought together from different departments increasing the knowledge pool available to find a solution to the task. If the intention is to find causes to a particular problem in the manner of a fishbone analysis then a matrix structure will allow for a wider range of views than functional departments would put forward.

Increased motivational possibilities can be created by job enrichment and enlargement opportunities and through teamwork. In addition, there will be greater cooperation between departments with longer-term intangible benefits for the organization.

Possible disadvantages: This change will be costly to implement in terms of time and resourcing. There will be disruption to departments with key workers removed in order to take part in the matrix project.

A new leader will need to be appointed to run the project or matrix team. There could be loyalty issues and tensions if the whole team does not value an appointed "temporary" leader.

There could be potential "cultural" clashes between workers from different departments.

2.4 Motivation

> Evaluate the financial rewards and methods of payment that will enable firms to recruit and retain skilled workers. (May 2008, AO3)

Examiner's hints and tips

Motivation was a very popular area of the IB Business and Management course, given the large number of students who chose to answer this question.

Financial rewards and payment systems, tied into theories such as Taylor's "economic man" approach, are well understood. It is always good practice to include a theoretical model in an answer wherever possible, if time allows.

However, issues identified earlier, such as a lack of balanced discussion and appropriate context not identified, will undermine the final marks available for this type of question. Many answers were too one-sided and did not include analysis as to why financial rewards **may not enable firms to recruit and retain** skilled workers. Some students listed endless theories as to why workers are motivated by financial rewards; in a sense repeating information gleaned from their textbook. This second point is crucial as the context of recruiting and retaining skilled workers was often ignored.

Students could have argued that skilled workers may value opportunity, respect and self-actualization as much as their financial reward, given the job enrichment opportunities proposed by writers such as Herzberg as a mechanism to recruit and retain workers in an organization. Pink's ideas on motivation could also be used in the analysis to provide a counter argument.

It is likely that, as skilled workers, these employees may have already met a number of the lower-order needs as specified by Maslow's hierarchy of needs. Answers including balanced discussion with specific reference to skilled workers were rare.

Examiner's hints and tips

A good tip is to take a highlighter pen after the 5-minute reading time **has finished** and **mark out the key command words** or contexts of a particular question. This will remind you that you must try to answer the question presented on the exam paper, rather than one you had expected and prepared for.

> Explain two disadvantages and one advantage of introducing a piece-rate system at Fish Packaging Limited. (May 2008, SL AO2)

Suggested answer

A piece-rate system is a way of rewarding labour by paying workers for each unit produced. In the example of Fish Packaging Limited, it would be appropriate that workers are paid for each kilogram of fish "landed" or caught.

Even though a definition has not been asked for, it is always good practice to define key terms, especially in an explanation question. Second, it is even better to define the term "in context" and apply it to the company in question. As you can see above it is possible to do both in four lines and not use up unnecessary minutes in the final exam.

Disadvantages and advantages will depend on whose point of view we are considering. For the workers a key advantage is that the weekly or monthly wage will be directly influenced by the amount they produce. The harder somebody works and catches more fish, the higher the wage. This type of advantage would suit employees who are influenced by Taylor's "economic man" approach.

Two disadvantages for the workers could be that, in the fishing industry, it would be assumed that external factors such as

weather are crucial. Wages being directly linked to output will be lower if the boat cannot sail. If a negative situation due to external factors is prolonged, workers may have to move to other occupations. This would then lead to labour shortages for Fish Packaging Limited when the external factors turn in its favour.

For Fish Packaging Limited, increased productivity is possible if wages are tied to production. However, the firm will need to monitor the use of a piece-rate system especially if workers are driven to work harder but neglect quality control in a race to satisfy higher production targets.

Second, making the firm's output level a function of the workers' motivation instead of customer demand runs the risk that waste may occur. Losses may be incurred if Fish Packaging Limited can only sell additional fish at deeply discounted prices.

The second part of this answer overcooks the explanation a little. The question does not specifically ask for advantages or disadvantages from the point of view of the firm or workers. However, the intention was to raise points which had not been covered in the text and to show that if the question does not explicitly state which stakeholder group is being affected, then appropriate answers in context will still be rewarded.

3 Finance and accounting

3.1 Sources of finance

> Evaluate the potential sources of finance for a small business like Gemel Ltd to fund the purchase of the following:
>
> i   stocks of finished goods for resale
>
> ii delivery vans
>
> iii land and buildings. (November 2007)

Examiner's hints and tips

As a general rule, if the purpose or objective to be financed is considered to be long term – over a number of years – then the most appropriate method of finance will also be long term. If the purpose is short term, then a short-term funding solution should be found.

In too many cases, students did not apply this rule in their answer. In some exam scripts, students asserted that stocks of finished goods for resale were to be financed by loans, or delivery vans were to be paid for by issuing shares.

One could argue under certain conditions that issuing shares if no other method of finance were available could finance delivery vans. However, depreciation needs to be taken into account. Also, the shares might not be purchased if the intention is to finance delivery vans – potential purchasers of shares may wish for the company to finance longer-term strategic plans – and a longer-term financing solution to a medium-term tactic is not appropriate.

In common with many other evaluation questions, many students did not provide a balanced discussion of the financing methods. It is accepted by all examiners that this balance only needs to be brief given time constraints. However, the costs or difficulties of sourcing finance for each of these assets needs to be mentioned for the answer to receive marks in the top marking band.

> Construct a cash flow forecast for Coffee-Cool for each month from July 2006 to December 2006 assuming a loan is taken for renovation. (Based on May 2006, AO4)

Coffee-Cool has provided the following cost and revenue information for July to December 2006.

Revenue	4 000
	Costs and revenue ($)
Cost of buying and holding stock (coffee beans)	700 per month from July until October 400 per month in November and December
Cost of ordering stock (coffee beans)	100 per month from July until October 200 per month in November and December
Own drawings	1 200 per month
Opening balance for July	400
Promotion	200 per month
Electricity	800 per year to be paid in equal instalments every January and July
Rates	600 to be paid in January every year
Finance charge (interest paid)	100 per month for three years
Repayment of loan	2 500 per payment to be paid in September and February for two years

	July	August	September	October	November	December
Inflow ($)						
Sales	4 000	4 000	4 000	4 000	4 000	4 000
Outflow ($)						
Costs of buying and holding stock	700	700	700	700	400	400
Costs of ordering stock	100	100	100	100	200	200
Promotion	200	200	200	200	200	200
Electricity	400	–	–	–	–	–
Drawings	2 400	2 400	2 400	2 400	2 400	2 400
Finance charge	100	100	100	100	100	100
Repayment of loan	–	–	2 500	–	–	–
Total outflow	(3 900)	(3 500)	(6 000)	(3 500)	(3 300)	(3 300)
Net cash flow	100	500	(2 000)	500	700	700
Opening balance	400	500	1 000	(1 000)	(500)	200
Closing balance	500	1 000	(1 000)	(500)	200	900

Mark allocation for this question would have been as follows.

5–6 marks: The cash flow forecast is entirely accurate and well presented. An appropriate format is used. For 5 marks there may be one error.

3–4 marks: The cash flow forecast is largely accurate. Allow up to two mistakes. The format used may not be entirely accurate or well presented.

1–2 marks: The cash flow forecast is simplistic, lacks detail and incorporates more than two mistakes. The format used is not appropriate.

> Comment on Coffee-Cool's liquidity position. (May 2006, AO2)

In September and October the company will be short of cash due to the first repayment of the loan. This liquidity deterioration, however, will be eased by December and thus should not be viewed as significant. If the owners can for a short time reduce their own generous drawings from the business, this will improve the liquidity situation considerably. Overall, Coffee-Cool's liquidity position is good and is expected to improve.

Coffee-Cool is selling coffee beans and the cash flow forecast is written for a perishable product. Some of the outflows of cash are assumed to be constant. There may be changes in external factors so the firm may wish to redraw and update the forecast in a few months, for example as new cost information becomes available.

Note that the command word "comment" implies that the student should try to add a little more detail to the answer

rather than just repeating the information in the table. This is at AO2 level and not AO1 where only a very brief description would be required.

> Evaluate the potential sources of finance available to developers of innovative products such as the Segway (a hi-tech environmentally friendly scooter). (Adapted from May 2005, AO3)

This question covers elements of unit 3.1 on sources of finance and unit 5.6 and concept 3 on innovation. Some possible discussion points are explored below.

In a previous question, we looked at evaluating the potential sources of finance available to a small engineering firm – Gemel Ltd – and how it could finance stock of finished goods for resale, delivery vans or land and buildings. For this question **the context is innovative products**.

Given that innovative products may not have been brought to the market-place in large quantities or be fully positioned in the minds of consumers, the developers of these products face a number of different challenges in trying to raise finance. Obtaining "**traditional**" **bank loans** and other "traditional" sources of finance may be problematic as they may be offered by risk-averse institutions or lenders who are unwilling to finance untried products. This could be frustrating even though the maker of the Segway will, we assume, have provided a detailed business plan on how it intends to use the funds effectively to ensure that the risk of failure is minimized.

For innovative products different sources of finance may be required. **Venture capitalists** may sense that the Segway represents a significant leap forward in personal mobility without having too much impact on the environment. They may be tempted to fund the launch of large production runs of the Segway in the hope that the scooter is exploiting a market gap.

If social responsibility issues are involved, the Segway's developers could apply for funding from philanthropic investors or institutions such as the **Grameen Bank** or the **Acumen Fund**. The growth of e-finance has been considerable, especially in socially responsible projects. A financial partnership with a non-governmental organization may also be possible.

There is no definitive answer here and original thinking would be well rewarded in context as long as the discussion is balanced. To achieve a mark in the top band for an AO3 question, remember that you must apply some overall form of judgment to the analysis.

4 Marketing
4.4 Market research

Discuss the types of market research that the Walt Disney Company should carry out before deciding whether to build a new theme park. (November 2007, AO3)

Examiner's hints and tips

Note: These comments are based on the fact that we know that a new theme park is soon to be completed.

The context of the case study needs to be given. The Walt Disney Company (or Disney) was looking to build a new theme park in China to extend the Disney brand in this leading emerging economy. A theme park already exists in Hong Kong and the company was looking to take advantage of the growing affluence of the young Chinese professional worker and Disney's increasing desire to be considered as a global entertainment organization.

Many students when attempting this question were able to write down a number of market research methods from both primary and secondary sources. **Textbook treatments** (implying generic methods and **not specific** to the issues facing Disney) and thus long lists were common.

The issue of discussion was rarely tackled and many students felt that if Disney effectively "did its homework and researched the market" success was inevitable. An area of weakness in students' knowledge has been in the understanding of the problems or carrying out market research and sampling in particular.

The following are some inquiry ideas relating to the market research methodology for Disney:

- Secondary data collection would be low cost and easy to obtain but how relevant would it be to a new theme park in China?
- Could Disney easily compare costs of the Disney theme park in Hong Kong and the one to be built in China?
- Would this secondary data from Hong Kong be already out of date?
- How relevant would primary data be to Disney if it were to ask Chinese people about their understanding of a company which may not yet have a significant influence in this growing economy?
- Would questionnaires or interviews be effective?
- Should Disney consider the potential **cultural** and linguistic problems from opening a theme park in China?
- Should Disney employ a specialist organization to carry out its market research to increase objectivity? (Disadvantages of this are that it would increase costs significantly and would take considerable time to report back to Disney before a final decision could be made.)

Evaluate two methods available to the Fair Trade movement to select a sample for its market research. (May 2003, AO3)

This is a tough question but one which adds business content to a context in business ethics.

Suggested answer

The Fair Trade movement has been a key stakeholder in the drive to promote a "fairer deal" for producers or growers of commodities such as coffee beans. The intention is to give producers, who are predominantly in the developing world, a much larger share of the value added – which is similar to, but not exactly the same as, profit – which the processed coffee gives to the final retailer.

The current share of this value added received by the growers is very low as a percentage of the final purchase price. It is argued that the retailer enjoys a significantly higher share of the value added and this has been considered to be unethical.

A company which is essentially trying to promote itself as ethical and socially responsible under the Fair Trade Agreement will need to conduct its market research carefully, given that many consumers may be unaware of the values of the movement and may feel embarrassed when questioned if they show a certain degree of "ethical ignorance". For this reason, **a random sample of a chosen population may be inappropriate.** A quota survey may also prove to be ineffective if the group selected is unaware of the mission and vision of the Fair Trade movement.

To increase accuracy of the data collected the firm may have to pre-select its market research respondents. It could perhaps choose a **cluster group** or a **stratified sample** with tightly defined criteria such as monthly spending on ethically traded goods and services. These groups may be small and unrepresentative of a general population but the issues being discussed here are unlikely to appeal to the mass market.

Finally, a few well-chosen "ambassadors" may be selected to go out in to the market-place with the specific task of "spreading the message" of the Fair Trade movement through "**snowballing**". This would not be as costly as the other two methods. However, the Fair Trade movement will need to ensure the ambassador is giving a consistent message. Word-of-mouth recommendations could also be difficult to measure objectively for research purposes.

Judgment

Even if the Fair Trade movement is able to penetrate local and global markets, significant issues remain for non-governmental organizations when collecting market research data. The collection of random samples of consumers may lead to unbiased results but will be costly. Clustering may lead to more precise data around local niche markets and, in the short term, this may be the optimal route to take before the Fair Trade movement launches a more mass-market campaign.

5 Operations management
Break-even question with solution
Paolo's Pasta

Paolo sells his pasta for a price of $7 per kilogram

Full capacity is 12 000 kg pasta per year

Current output is 10 000 kg per year

Paolo's expenses:

Lease costs	$200 per week
Mortgage payment	$500 per month
Paolo's salary	$300 per week
Raw materials	$1.25 per kilogram (kg) of pasta produced
Wages	$1.60 per kilogram (kg) of pasta produced
Electricity/Gas/Water	$0.15 per kilogram (kg) of pasta produced

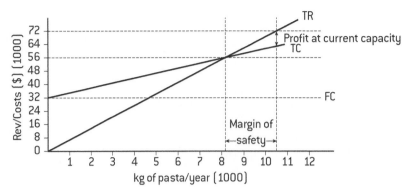

kg of pasta/year (1000)

Construct a break-even graph showing the break-even level of output, the margin of safety and the amount of profit at current output level. (Show any relevant workings.) (Adapted from May 2007)

Contribution:

Variable costs	$1.25 + $1.60 + $0.15 = $3 per kg of pasta
Selling price	$7 per kg of pasta
Contribution	$7 - $3 = $4 per kg of pasta

Break-even level of output:

Fixed costs	($500 × 52) + ($500 × 12 = $6 000) = $32 000
Contribution	$4 per kg of pasta
Break-even quantity	$\frac{$32\,000}{4}$ = 8 000 kg of pasta per year

Margin of safety:

Current output level - break-even level

10 000 kg - 8 000 kg = 2 000 kg

Profit at current capacity:

Margin of safety × contribution: 2 000 kg × $4 = $8 000

Evaluate the methods for achieving a TQM culture in a large organization such as Jaguar – a luxury car maker. (Adapted from May 2005, AO3)

Examiner's hints and tips

A number of writers have dismissed TQM as a new management fad or tool. Jack Trout is particularly scathing:

"I was startled to find out that 81 per cent of the 5,600 executives I surveyed said that management tools (including TQM) promised more than they delivered. That is a polite way of saying that 'we wasted a great deal of money'" (Trout, 2001:151).

We have already stated the case for TQM, kaizen and quality circles in the analysis in unit 5.3. Here we shall concern ourselves more with the difficulties of introducing a TQM culture in order to fulfil the requirements of the command word "evaluate".

Suggested answer

There are substantial costs of training workers to be able to take the required responsibility TQM demands. These costs are ongoing as the firm recruits and inducts more labour into the workforce. Appraisal systems within Jaguar will also need to be carefully monitored to ensure employees are able to give feedback to the organization if concerns or issues are raised.

TQM increases the degree of bureaucracy and record keeping in ensuring objectives are being met and that the new working environment is being maintained. Jaguar's line managers in particular could be put under significant pressure to ensure TQM is being followed and will have to record significant amounts of data to be able to justify that a TQM culture is having the desired effect.

Judgment

Introducing any new management philosophy is not without risks. It can be simpler in small organizations with a flatter hierarchy and smaller spans of control. In large organizations, such as Jaguar, small incremental improvements in quality may have to be accepted as changing a workforce with many thousands of workers to a TQM culture will take considerable time and capital.

HL You are given information about Coffee-Cool's stock control system which is presented in the following graph. Coffee-Cool roasts and distributes coffee beans to cafés and retailers.

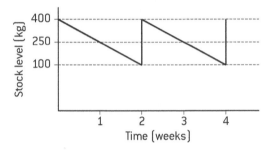

Time (weeks)

Identify the following for Coffee-Cool:

i lead time

ii buffer stock

iii reorder quantity. (May 2006)

Here are the answers:

i lead time = 1 week

ii buffer stock = 100 kg

iii reorder quantity = 300 kg.

Explain the advantages and disadvantages of Jaguar of using just-in-time (JIT) production rather than the more traditional just-in-case (JIC) systems. (Adapted from May 2005, AO3)

Students are advised to look back at unit 5.3 and unit 5.5 (for HL) on stock control methods to check their understanding of the generic differences between JIT and JIC. The differences will not be repeated here.

Questions such as this can sometimes lead students to list every single point they have revised. Descriptive lists of advantages or disadvantages with no detail or depth and no context are unlikely to score above the lowest possible mark band.

Bullet-point answers in the final IB Business Management exam are generally to be avoided. However, if the bullet point is detailed and does try to explain the advantage being presented, it is acceptable to offer this style of answer.

Suggested answer

Advantages of using JIT production at Jaguar:

- JIT as part of kaizen demands an approach where TQM is at the centre of the philosophy of operation. Quality becomes the responsibility of a number of stakeholders and so Jaguar should benefit from a reduction in waste, and improved quality of its finished products, to name only two of the benefits.

- JIT demands minimal level of stocks; for example, it is estimated that the Nissan car plant in Sunderland had managed to keep stocks to only one day's worth of production. This means that working capital is not tied up unnecessarily. Some opportunity costs of holding too much working capital can be avoided.

- Linked to the above point is the reduction in storage costs, including power, electricity and security, which are not needed as warehouse space to house stocks of components and semi-finished vehicles is not required.

Disadvantages of using JIT production at Jaguar:

- JIT requires a complete change in organizational culture and a thorough review of the supply chain. The adjustment and transitional costs of these processes can be significant.

- Economies of scale through ordering bulk quantities of components in the assembly process of vehicles are not experienced with JIT production but they could be with a JIC system.

- Some aspects of quality assurance for the final vehicle coming off the production line are taken out of the hands of Jaguar. There are potential short-term difficulties as suppliers come to terms with the new working culture. For example, Nissan had its suppliers on call for components 24 hours a day when it was running production through the day and night.

HL/SL paper 2 section B

The questions given above were selected from different exam papers and have been adapted to meet the demands of the new AO1–AO3. The following is a sample of additional new specimen questions prepared by the author to guide you as to what the 2106 exam questions in paper 2 section B could look like.

Remember that for the HL paper 2, students are expected to answer two of the three questions given in section B. SL students only have to answer one question. The following questions can be applied to HL and SL unless stated.

AO1

AO1 command words such as "define", "describe" and "identify" have not been covered extensively in this assessment section. They are usually worth up to a maximum of 2 marks and focus on defining an aspect of some business content. However, it is likely there will be a number of AO1 questions in your exam and they are designed to try and give you some confidence around the start of the question.

Look at the example questions below. Note the mark scheme for these questions if the command word is to "define":

1 mark for a basic definition that conveys partial knowledge and understanding

2 marks for a full, clear definition that conveys knowledge and understanding

1 mark for only a relevant example or application to the stimulus.

> Define the following terms: "profit", "takeover", "working capital", "economies of scale".

Suggested answer

Profit is defined as the reward to an entrepreneur for taking a risk in combining factors of production such as land, labour and capital into the creation of a business idea. Profit can be calculated by subtracting fixed and variable costs (also known as total costs) from total revenue.

Takeover – a takeover occurs when one organization decides to "absorb" the business operations of another by purchasing a majority shareholding of 50.1% or more of the acquired company.

A takeover is usually described as involuntary given that the acquired company may not wish to be absorbed, as opposed to a merger where all parties agree to the financial union.

Working capital, defined as the difference between current assets and current liabilities, is sometimes regarded as circulating or day-to-day capital. A business will use working capital to purchase raw materials to be processed into finished goods or services for sale either by using cash or by agreeing credit transactions.

Economies of scale are the long-run cost advantages achieved by an organization when it embarks on large production runs reducing the unit (or average) costs of production. Economies of scale can be internal – earned by the individual firm through growth – or external, when a whole industry expands.

> State two causes of a liquidity problem.

Suggested answer

Two causes of a liquidity problem could be:

- insufficient cash balances flowing into an organization to meet daily cash outflows
- rising cash outflows due to unexpected changes in the external environment such as a rapid increase in the price of oil or other essential raw materials.

Comment

It is hoped that these examples give an indication of the depth of information required for an AO1 answer. It could be argued that the first sentence in the definition is the partial answer for 1 mark. Consequently, note that for definitions which could be answered by just stating a formula, such as definitions of profit or working capital, it is unlikely that full marks will be awarded. The second sentence of development is critical.

AO2

The command words such as "explain" and "analyse" will appear in AO2 questions and it is likely that the number of marks available will be up to a maximum of 4. Allocating the correct amount of time for these questions is critical. It would not be sensible to spend excessive time on these AO2 questions at the expense of, say, AO3 questions, which have a considerably higher mark tariff.

> Explain two benefits of brand loyalty to Lego. (May 2011)

Brand loyalty can allow an organization to develop a closer relationship with its customers. Clearly, in the toy market in which Lego competes with a number of competitors this will allow Lego to maintain market share.

Maintaining market share through brand loyalty could allow Lego to charge higher than market prices for its products. It might also allow the organization an opportunity to reduce risk when launching new products as potential consumers will be already familiar with Lego's brand core values.

> Explain two disadvantages of a physical bookstore from having too much working capital in unsold second-hand books.

Suggested answer

Having too much working capital in unsold second-hand books may tie up funds in stock purchased that could have been used elsewhere in the organization. A liquidity problem may occur if unexpectedly short-term cash outflows increase due to an unforeseen event.

In a physical bookstore, too much stock may put the store layout under pressure and have an impact on the physical evidence of the marketing mix. Customers may become irritated by the store layout having an impact on customer service and also putting additional pressure on existing staff trying to satisfy customer requests. The bookstore may have to continually update its databases if too much stock is held and this will take up valuable time and resources.

> Analyse two possible reasons why Mattel would have tried to take over Lego given that Lego reported a significant loss. (May 2011)

Suggested answer

Lego's significant losses highlighted the fact that the organization was struggling financially. Mattel, a key competitor of Lego, could take advantage of a horizontal takeover by absorbing Lego, not only to reduce existing competition but also to capture Lego's brand loyalty. This would have been perceived as a very valuable intangible asset. There would also have been a number of potential economies of scale in finance and marketing.

Second, given the significant losses present at Lego, Mattel could have considered the possibility of purchasing Lego – a private limited company – at a much cheaper market valuation than if Lego had reported a significant profit.

> Analyse two possible impacts of multinational companies such as McDonald's on the host country.

Suggested answer

It is likely that a multinational organization will bring fresh thinking, managerial expertise, employment opportunities and new knowledge into a new overseas market. The host country could benefit from a whole new range of innovation technology ideas leading to external economy of scale benefits to the fast-food industry.

Culturally, there could be some concerns that multinational corporations may have a negative impact on the host country and that local businesses may be forced to compete with a much larger and financially well-resourced rival. Local fast-food organizations may find that their own economic sustainability is under threat. Recent media reports that some large multinational companies are able to transfer their tax liabilities to low-tax environments away from the host country may mean that any tax revenue benefits available to the host country from multinational activity may be limited.

Comment

Note that for full marks a clear explanation is required which will extend beyond one sentence per point made. Second, for an "analyse" question, both sides of the argument should be developed but do remember that time is limited.

Some examiners would argue that it is always worth spending, say, an additional 5–10 minutes in an exam on a question worth 8–10 marks, rather than trying to obtain an additional mark by spending the same amount of time on a new question.

AO3

Guidance and suggested answer

In the new exam for paper 2 for both SL and HL students, the AO3 assessment questions will be marked out of 10. Therefore, successfully answering these demanding evaluative questions will have a significant impact on the final grade award on this paper.

> To what extent will the introduction of a $4 shop change perception of the $2 shop in New Zealand? (May 2012)

Guidance

"To what extent…?" is a difficult command phrase to define and explain briefly. The intention of this question is to measure how far a change such as the creation of a new $4 retail outlet will alter the perception of older $2 outlets in the context of New Zealand. In many countries, the $2 (or equivalent) shop has become the epitome of the "cheaper outlet" in the high street of many developed countries. In the UK, the national chain called Poundland has become very popular with low-income families trying to manage their household budgets.

When trying to satisfy the command word "to what extent" it may be useful to consider a number of factors:

* the cost in resources required to make the change
* the key stakeholders who will be affected by the change
* the time frame, which will need to be considered in order to decide whether the change of perception has occurred.

The challenge now is to weave these ideas into a coherent answer in roughly 20 minutes of exam time. The actual answer to the question would normally appear in the judgment section and the analysis should be balanced. Consider the example below.

> Evaluate the decision of a telecommunications company to outsource its customer service and complaints department.

Suggested answer

Increasingly as a competitive strategic move, larger organizations are looking to outsource aspects of their operations to lower wage-cost economies. The cost savings in terms of HR management can be considerable. Training via improved technologies can be undertaken on the job and quality assurance processes can be introduced so that consumers looking for service may in fact be unaware that they are being directed offshore away from the main head office of the telecommunications company.

Communication technologies have been improving and cultural intelligence is such that customer service and complaints programmes have been moving offshore. The Philippines and Malaysia are just two of the countries which have benefited from the outsourcing of the customer service function.

However, recent media reports have highlighted that many large organizations have begun to consider that perhaps reshoring the HR function may be preferable. Controlling and monitoring the supply chain has been seen as integral to ensuring and maintaining a strong competitive position.

Second, the move to offshoring has lead to significant increases in local labour costs. It is argued that these increases may eliminate any productivity gains obtained from using local offshored labour services.

Finally, with unemployment – especially youth unemployment – increasing in many developed countries, there has been significant political pressure from governments on large organizations to "bring jobs home".

However, the degree of reshoring remains small. It is too early to tell whether this trend will sustain itself. Given the rapid changes in technology and growth of global market opportunities, but with revenue growth stalling due to increased competition, many large organizations such as telecommunications companies feel compelled to continue to outsource as many of their operations as possible. This will be the case as long as stakeholders such as customers continue to give positive feedback and competitors continue to outsource operations.

Introduction

This unit links content from units 2, 4 and 5 to a conceptual understanding to be applied to a real-life organization. The aim is to help students prepare for HL and SL paper 2 section C.

Setting the scene

We began this study guide with concept 1: Globalization to introduce the six concepts that underpin our understanding of business management. Our aim was to connect the learning of business management with other parts of the Diploma course including TOK. Then we defined, explained, analysed and discussed through the IB learner profile the business theories, tools and techniques that make up the content of the new IB Business Management course.

The task now is for you to tie the six concepts to business content and provide a context or case study, linked to the your own experiences of studying business. This is the challenge of paper 2 section C for both HL and SL.

From 2016, in section C, you will be presented with three questions and you will have to answer one. Each question will be evaluative in nature (AO3) where an understanding of one or two of the concepts studied throughout the course will be assessed. The question is marked out of 20 and follows a similar process to the marking criteria given in our discussion of section C for HL paper 1.

At the time of writing, the first exam is over two years away, so the following suggestions on how to prepare for this section of paper 2 should be treated as not definitive.

Choice of organization is important

Clearly, the choice of organization to be studied is critical in this process of linking content to concepts. It may be prudent for you to follow and record information based around the concepts for two businesses throughout the duration of the course. They could be in the same market or industry or alternatively they could be in completely different sectors. Your own interests should drive this choice.

Throughout this study guide, contexts as diverse as Apple, Lego, Google, Disney and Pixar have been used. These reflect the nature of the author's own interests but they are also organizations which regularly appear in the media. It is not too difficult to find examples, articles or features that illustrate business content and – in the case of Lego, Apple and Google especially – business concepts such as innovation and change.

The company you chose should be one which you as a stakeholder "identify" with. By this, it is implied that you may be a consumer of the organization's products or services or you could have a family connection or some other association. (See also the key learning point in unit 1.3, page 21).

Balanced view and structure of the answer (AO3)

The need for a balanced view and structure of the answer is important given the assessment objective (AO3).

You will need to consider a range of views about the organization you are studying, as the assessment objective is AO3. The command words that are classified by this include "evaluate", "discuss" and the demanding "to what extent...?"

To satisfy the demands of the question, you will need to provide a balanced analysis before reaching a justified conclusion. For this reason, students who choose a business due to a close family tie or association are advised that it may be difficult to achieve objectivity. This does not mean that choosing a family business is not appropriate but students who make this choice should bear in mind that one-sided views of, for example, innovation in an organization are unlikely to score highly.

Paper 2 section C HL/SL answer

The structure of the answer in paper 2 section C for HL or SL is important. The marking criteria for this piece of work, which are given below, include marks awarded for structure. A full copy of the marking criteria for both internal and external assessment is given in the *IB Business Management Guide*.

Criterion D: Structure

This criterion assesses the extent to which the student organizes his or her ideas with clarity, and presents a structured piece of writing comprising:

- an introduction
- a body
- a conclusion
- fit-for-purpose paragraphs.

Marks	Level descriptor
0	The work does not reach a standard described by the descriptors below.
1	Two or fewer of the structural elements are present, and few ideas are clearly organized.
2	Three of the structural elements are present, or most ideas are clearly organized.
3	Three or four of the structural elements are present, and most ideas are clearly organized.
4	All of the structural elements are present, and ideas are clearly organized.

Given this point, it may be sensible to practise discussing concepts linked to an organization in advance under timed conditions. An example of a tutor's answer under timed conditions is given below.

Benefits of shadowing an organization

Shadowing a real-life organization brings benefits ("economies of scale") to other internal assessment parts of your IB Business Management course. In addition to growing your knowledge base about a real-life organization, the paper 2 section C requirement will also have some positive spillover effects to your study of business management.

For SL students

As part of their internal assessment SL students prepare a written commentary analysing and evaluating an issue affecting a business based on a collection of articles. Inevitably, by collecting articles over the two-year course, students will find information relating to the organization they are studying, perhaps linking innovation with strategy or globalization with ethical considerations. In essence, some of the time in and out of class that students are using to prepare for the SL written commentary could be used to develop conceptual understanding and links to business content.

For HL students

For HL students, working on the internal assessment report, which is based on a real-life organization trying to solve a forward-looking problem, provides a learning opportunity to develop conceptual understanding at the same time. Although the internal assessment for HL is not prepared extensively over the two-year course, there is no reason why students who are collecting primary and secondary data for an organization could not also use this information to aid their conceptual understanding of concepts such as change, cultural influences and ethical behavior.

For HL and SL students – link to the extended essay

Of course, both HL and SL students could use research material as a basis to frame a question (which could be conceptual but not necessarily so) which considers deeper treatment of a context that the word limits of the HL internal assessment and SL written commentary do not allow. As with all extended essays, the nature of the question and the reason for the investigation need to be carefully considered but there is no reason why this knowledge and understanding developed from a considered study should not be put to good use in this external assessment opportunity.

How to collect information

Web 2.0 tools, which could help in this process, include creating a business blog or sharing ideas through a business class wiki. For those who are familiar with RSS feeds, a system could be set up which allows a student to automatically track an organization if new developments occur via websites or blogs or wikis (if this feature is available).

Even just emailing a business may yield surprising results. Today on most organization websites there are invitations such as "Contact us" or "Find out more". What are you waiting for?

Learning outcomes

Learning outcomes from the guide could form the basis of a question in paper 2, section C HL/SL. At the end of each unit from units 2, 4, and 5 from the IB Business Management syllabus there are a number of learning outcomes that require students to discuss and evaluate:

- from unit 2.1: how **innovation**, **ethical** considerations and **cultural** differences may influence HR practices and strategies in an organization

- from unit 2.3: how **ethical considerations** and **cultural differences** may influence leadership and management styles in an organization

- from unit 2.6 (HL only): how **innovation**, **ethical considerations** and **cultural differences** may influence employee–employer relations in an organization

- from unit 4.1: how **innovation**, **ethical considerations** and **cultural differences** may influence marketing practices and strategies in an organization

- from unit 5.6 (HL only): how pace of **change** in an industry, **organizational culture** and **ethical considerations** may influence research and development practices and strategies in an organization.

From these learning outcomes we see the predominance of the key concepts of:

- innovation
- culture
- ethics.

The business management content to link is:

- HR management, leadership, employee–employer relations
- the role of marketing
- research and development.

It is also important to develop an understanding of different stakeholder perspectives in your final answer.

Example

The following is an example written by the author in 30 minutes to demonstrate one possible approach to answering a popular topic. It is not designed to be a model answer and for this reason the company is anonymous and fictitious.

This is just one approach to answering this question. Given that you will only need to answer one question out of a choice of three, time can be saved by focusing attention on perhaps three of the concepts in detail and how these apply to a real-life organization. However, you are warned, against "question spotting" and are encouraged to ensure that all six concepts are embedded in your learning of business management.

A discussion as to how ethical considerations and cultural differences may influence marketing practices and strategies in an organization.

Alpha is a provider of coffee beans, ground coffee and espresso-making machines which operates in a number of markets especially the United States and the Asia-Pacific region. Alpha sources its raw materials (green coffee beans) from developing countries and then processes them in its country of origin before they are shipped back to its markets. The **supply chain** of Alpha is complex and the company has been looking at ways to reduce costs by allowing coffee roasters in its overseas markets to process the beans but sell them under the Alpha **brand** name.

The growing consumer awareness campaign of the Fair Trade movement has strongly influenced the ethical practices of Alpha. Prices paid to its suppliers are above the world price for raw coffee beans although some pressure groups have argued that Alpha could do more to help local farmers as part of its Fair Trade commitments. The decision to allow local producers to process their own coffee beans and sell under the Alpha brand is part of this process to become more ethical.

The Fair Trade connection has valuable marketing benefits to Alpha as the company's packaging and promotional activities are built around social responsibility. However, these benefits are slowly being eroded away with growing competition and other coffee producers who are **benchmarking** their marketing practices against Alpha. Consumers are now overwhelmed with other coffee roasters who are also showing a commitment to social responsibility and ethical objectives and creating a point of difference is proving to be challenging for Alpha. A new project team has been created and given the task to develop a new marketing strategy.

As part of this marketing strategy, Alpha has been looking to develop a presence in a new market such as the UK where coffee consumption, although increasing, is still well below the European average of cups consumed per individual per day. Although it is one of the oldest countries in the world, a coffee culture has yet to fully take hold in the UK outside the many city centres. Many respondents' replies to a recent market research survey indicated a preference for tea. It has also been argued that the weather in the UK is also not conducive to a "coffee culture" as seen in France or Italy, where consuming espresso outside on the pavement of a café is seen as the norm.

In order to penetrate this market, Alpha has used new **viral marketing** methods and promotions that position espresso drinks – which Alpha sells – as a vital energy drink to start the day. The company has created a range of caffeine-flavoured drinks to be sold in supermarkets. Some media commentators have described this approach as socially irresponsible as children could consume these drinks before school. Alpha has launched a social marketing campaign to try and convince customers that an espresso shot is not as harmful as a full cup of coffee but it is too early to say whether this approach has been successful.

Even with its track record of ethical marketing practices, Alpha has found the conservative culture of the UK market difficult and challenging. The company has carried out a number of cultural intelligence surveys into UK attitudes towards coffee. These surveys have shown that consumers' liking for coffee and sophisticated tastes are growing, but there is still some way to go in raising the awareness of espresso as a morning drink. It may be too early to say, given that it is only 18 months into this new strategy, whether the new strategy will be a success.

Stakeholder perspectives include local growers of coffee beans in developing countries, UK consumers and pressure groups.

REFERENCES AND FURTHER READING

Anderson, C. 2006. *The Long Tail: Why the future of business is selling less of more*. Hyperion. New York

Ansoff, H I. 1965. *Corporate Strategy*. McGraw-Hill. New York

Braungart, M and McDonough, W. 2002. *Cradle to Cradle: Remaking the way we make things*. North Point Press. New York

Chan Kim, W and Mauborgne, R. 2005. *Blue Ocean Strategy: How to create uncontested market space and make the competition irrelevant*. Harvard Business School Publishing Corporation. Boston, MA

Dearden, C and Foster, M. 1992. *Organizational Decision Making*. Pearson Education. Harlow

Drucker, P. 1966. "How to prosper in the new economy". *Forbes Magazine*. 16 May 1998

The Economist. 2005. *Business Miscellany*. Bloomberg Press. New York

The Economist. 2007. *Business Miscellany*. Bloomberg Press. New York

Friedman, T. 2007. *The World is Flat: A brief history of the twenty-first century*. Picador. New York

Gabriel, V. 1998. *Management of Business for GCE A Level and LCC 1*, 2nd edn. Oxford University Press

Gillespie, A. 2001. *Oxford Revision Guide*. Oxford University Press

Handy, C. 1976. *Understanding Organisations*. Penguin. London

Handy, C. 1978. *Gods of Management: The changing work of organisations*. Souvenir Press. London

Handy, C. 1994. *The Empty Raincoat: Making sense of the future*. Hutchinson. London

Hashemi, S and Hashemi, B. 2003. *Anyone Can Do It: Building Coffee Republic from our kitchen table*. John Wiley & Sons. Chichester

Henderson, M, Thompson D and Henderson, S. 2006. *Leading Through Values: Linking company culture to business strategy*. Harper Collins. New Zealand

Herzberg, F. 2003. "One More Time: How do you motivate employees?" *Harvard Business Review*. Boston, MA

Marcousé, I *et al.* (2006) *The Complete A–Z Business Studies Handbook*. 5th edn. Hodder & Stoughton. London

Maynard, W. 2009. "Marketing for Non-Profit Organizations". http://www.marketingsource.com/articles/view/2101

McInnes, W. 2012. *Culture Shock: A handbook for 21st century business*. John Wiley & Sons. Chichester

Poundstone, W. 2012. *Are You Smart Enough to Work at Google?* Oneworld. Oxford

Powell, J. 1991. *Quantitative Decision-Making*. Longman. London

Reeves, R. 1960. *Reality in Advertising*. Knopf. New York

Robertson, D and Breen, B. 2013. *Brick by Brick: How LEGO rewrote the rules of innovation and conquered the global toy industry*. Crown Publishing Group, a division of Random House. New York

Rogers, E. 1962. *Diffusion of Innovations*. Free Press of Glencoe. New York

Rosenberg, K and Daly, H. 1993. *Foundations of Behavioral Research: A basic approach*. Harcourt College Publishers. Fort Worth, TX.

Russell-Walling, E. 2007. *50 Management Ideas You Really Need to Know*. Quercus. London

Shuen, A. 2008. *Web 2.0: A Strategy Guide: Business thinking and strategies behind successful Web 2.0 implementations*. O'Reilly Media. Sebastopol, Canada

Trout, J. 2001. *Big Brands, Big Trouble*: John Wiley & Sons Inc. New York

Trout, J and Rivkin, S. 2008. *Differentiate or Die: Survival in our era of killer competition*. John Wiley & Sons Inc. New York

Trout, J and Rivkin, S. 2010. *Repositioning*. McGraw-Hill. New York

Index